CYPHER 2 The War

Robert Thomas

HATCHBACK Publishing LLC
Genesee, MI 48437

Cypher 2 The War
©2017 Robert Thomas

All rights reserved. This book is protected by the copyright laws of the United States of America. This book may not be copied or reprinted for commercial gain or profit. The use of short quotations or occasional page copying for personal or group study is permitted and encouraged. Permission will be granted upon request.

HATCHBACK Publishing, LLC.
P.O. Box 494
Genesee, Michigan 48437
Since 2005
www.hatchbackpublishing.com

ISBN: 978-0-9988295-9-3
10 9 8 7 6 5 4 3 2 1
First Edition
Printed in the United States of America

For Worldwide Distribution

Dedication

This book is dedicated to every family that has suffered the loss of a family member due to senseless gang violence. We need to find a better solution on how to end gang violence. My heart goes out to every parent who has buried their child through unnecessary murders. It is time for real leaders to stand up and start making in a difference in our society and our communities. Invest in the next generation and the future of our nation will be better.

Acknowledgements

I like to thank God for the completion of this book.
All my Family members and friends who believe in me and support my work.
My wonderful Mother Martha Thomas.
My brothers Eugene, John and Matt.
My amazing nephew Zach. Z
My niece Christan Thomas.
My sister-in-law Crystal.
My best friend David Manning.
Pastor Scott Brian Sacrey and all at Encounter Church.
Racquel Reid Grandison.
Cynthia Hatcher and everyone at Hatchback Publishing LLC.
My uncle Bob and Aunt Cheryl, Kevin and Lisa.
The rest of my nephews and cousins.

Everyone who has encouraged me.
Eddie and Bertha Vikolin.
Pamela Patek.
Stacey Staimpel.
TraCee Maxine Green, it's been a pleasure serving the Lord with you.
All my friends in the U.K. Thank you for your support as well as all my wonderful friends in Jamaica and Canada.
Special thanks to my dear friends in Malaysia.
God bless you all. Thank you so much for all of your love and support.

Contents

Dedication
Acknowledgements

CHAPTER 1. And So It Begins…..8

CHAPTER 2. The Meeting…..32

CHAPTER 3. Drawing First Blood…..58

CHAPTER 4. No Turning Back…..91

CHAPTER 5. The Betrayal…..117

CHAPTER 6. Funeral For Two Brothers…..144

CHAPTER 7. Time To Regroup…..159

CHAPTER 8. Keeping The Secret…..190

CHAPTER 9. The Struggle Continues…..215

CHAPTER 10. The War Rages On…..234

CHAPTER 11. A New Man For Sara…..258

CHAPTER 12. Goodbye My Old Friend…..283

CHAPTER 13. Pressing Forward…..309

CHAPTER 14. I'm Not A Hero…..324

CHAPTER 15. And So Comes The End…..346

About the Author…..369

CHAPTER 1

AND SO IT BEGINS

It was ten o'clock in the morning and Cypher was just getting out of bed. It had been a late night and he was exhausted after getting home and seeing the group altogether back at the camp. As he sat at the edge of his bed, he couldn't help but wonder what was going to happen between him and Tonya. He still loved her so very much. After thinking about her last night, he felt maybe there wasn't any real hope of them being able to have a life together as they had planned.

Rising up from his bed, Cypher grabbed some clothes and headed for the shower to begin to get ready for his day. After which he headed down stairs to spend some time with Sara, his mother. She had been waiting all morning for him to get up. She was so relieved and happy to have him back home again.

"Good morning Johnnie" Sara said as she hugged him.

"Good morning Mom, how are you this morning?" Johnnie responded.

"I am good. I've been waiting for you to get up so we could talk. I've been so worried about you, and it's so good to have you back home again. I missed you Johnnie. I know you had the group over last night. How was your time with them? I am sure they have missed you almost as much as I have." Sara said as she couldn't help but smile.

"It was great Mom. I have missed everyone. I know you're happy to have me home, but I do need to go out today and I don't know if I will be back tonight. If not, then I will be back home in the morning."

"Why Johnnie? Where do you have to go?" Sara asked as her heart sunk within her chest. She was not ready for Johnnie to leave again so soon. She wanted time with him.

"I have to go back across town and talk to some friends, shouldn't be gone long though."

Sara was trying not to be upset but she was. "You will at least stay and let me cook you some lunch," she said with a bit of motherly authority in her voice to let Johnnie know she wasn't very happy about him leaving again so soon.

"Yes of course Mom. I won't leave till after we sit and have lunch together," Johnnie said as he smiled at her.

His response had calmed her a little. Sara cooked Johnnie's favorite meal for lunch. As they sat and ate together Sara began to ask him some questions.

"Did you get to talk to Tonya at all?"

Johnnie looked up at her. "No I didn't. She wasn't there and I wasn't alone so it will have to wait anyways. I don't want to talk to her in front of everyone." Johnnie took a bite of his chicken.

"What do you think? I mean she hasn't really talked to anyone since the incident. And I know you two haven't talked in a few weeks. I was hoping things would get back to normal between you two."

"Yes me too Mom, but it may take a little bit of time for that to happen. In the mean time I have some things to work on. So I will be in and out for a while." He wiped his mouth and took a drink of his juice.

After spending the rest of the morning and a small part of the afternoon with his Mom, he had to get going. As he put his shoes on Sara turned on the television and sat down next to him.

"I wish you didn't have to go." she said as she grabbed his hand.

"I know Mom, but I have to do this," Johnnie said as he looked at her for a minute.

Sara sat there almost in tears as he rose up and headed out the door.

***

As Johnnie was heading out to catch the bus he ran into

Steve.

"Hey Steve," he said as he stopped to talk for a minute.

"Hey Johnnie. Where are you off to?" Steve had asked.

"Back across town. I should be back first thing in the morning. I need to go back and prepare things for the guys. I will get a hold of everyone when I get back."

He seemed to be in a bit of a hurry but Steve still went on. "Can you stop by and see Tonya when you get back. I know she misses you terribly. We all miss you actually. But I know her heart aches for you. She feels just awful about how she's treated you. And it would make a world of difference to her if you would just come by to visit. She is still trying to recover from all of this and I know being with you will help her a lot. In spite of all that has happened, her feelings for you have not changed a bit," Steve explained.

"After all that happened? I didn't do anything to her. And this wasn't my fault. Does anyone remember how I got beat up and was made to watch this happen? Does anyone care about what I went through having to see what they did to her and not being able to stop it or help her at all? Everyone acts like nothing happened to me," he said very angrily.

"We do know that Johnnie. And we all understand that. We have all been worried about you and her. I am just saying, she still needs you in spite of how she was acting towards you, and her love for you remains as it was," Steve further explained.

"Okay, I have to go Steve. I will stop in when I get back," he said as he walked away.

"Be safe Johnnie," Steve yelled at him.

Cypher never even looked back. He was upset and hurt. He just kept walking.

Finally reaching the bus stop, Cypher sat down and waited on the next bus to arrive. Once the bus got there he got on and sat down. As he was staring out of the window the bus took off. He took this alone time to think about what exactly he was going to say and how he wanted to handle this whole situation. He was going back to notify the West Dragons that his group was on board for this war.

Once he got off the bus he first went to see Jason to let him know he was back in town. Jason wasn't very hard to find. Everyone knew he loved to sit at the Coffee House and drink his hot tea. Jason was surprised to see Cypher back already. Jason nodded in an inviting way for him to come and sit as he sipped his tea.

"Have a seat my friend. Wasn't expecting you to be back so soon."

Cypher had slowly walked over and sat down across from Jason. "Yeah well, I needed to let them know I had some of my own people on board as well," Cypher began to explain.

The waitress came over to see if he wanted something to drink. "I will have whatever he is having I suppose," Cypher said.

"Good choice. I find hot tea relaxes me a bit. So, how many of your own people are you bringing in?" Jason asked Cypher as they both starred at each other.

"Four. They are like brothers to me. They refused to let me do this alone and have insisted to come along."

"It's a tough road you have had to walk down. I am sorry that it is not yet over my friend," Jason said in one of the rarest moments where he actually was very sympathetic. "When are you going to go meet Ricky?"

"Well, actually as soon as I am done talking with you I suppose. I don't know anyone else around here, outside of you and them." Cypher responded.

"Unfortunately my involvement in this has to be very minimal but I will do what I can to help you as much as possible," Jason explained as he was connected to all parties involved.

He secretly had a deal with Ricky and wanted himself to see Sisko and his gang taken out. Jason always had problems with the Hells Sinners and was more than willing to do what he could to protect Cypher and help him out.

"I understand my friend. I am always thankful for what you do for me." Cypher responded as he was finishing his hot tea.

"We are brothers and I am here for you always." Cypher

smiled for the first time since returning back to Westbend.

"Yes my brother. As I am always here for you as well. I guess I should go and meet with them so I can get back home. Take care Bro, see you as soon as I can."

"Be safe Cypher. I won't be too far away," Jason responded as he watched Cypher get up and walk away.

***

There was a park down the street where The West Dragons would often hangout. Cypher took his time as he walked to see if there was anyone there trying to figure out on the way exactly what he wanted to say. He was always over thinking things and wanted to make sure he knew exactly what he wanted to say and do. When he got there he saw only a few people walking through the park so he sat down for a bit and waited to see if anyone would come. He could have went to the club house, but the park was much closer. He was hoping to save a little more time if he could get lucky and run into someone here instead. He didn't want to stay long and didn't feel good about just showing up at the club house. Hearing a voice from behind him, he stood and turned to face whoever had just said his name.

"Cypher? Are you back already?" Viper asked as he walked up to him.

"Yeah, I am back for a few hours. Was hoping to meet with someone. I am bringing with me four of my own people that will be with me." Viper nodding at Cyphers words.

"I am sure that won't be a problem. Sure wish you would join us though. I know you're one heck of a fighter. Ricky has a lot of respect for you. Normally he would not be doing this. I mean letting outsiders in. But he does trust you, and we do need the help. Your rivalry with them makes you a valuable allies."

"Yeah, well you taking their territory doesn't concern me, but nevertheless, we all have a better chance getting what we want if we work together. But when this is over, I'm done. I go my own way and so does my friends. No ties to anyone, we just go our own way," Cypher explained.

"If that's what you all want. Ricky already agreed to it, so it is as it is. I will let him know of our meeting and all you have said." Viper was eager to get this news back to Ricky.

"Thank you. I will come through every so often and keep in touch so we all know what's going on, and next time I come through I will be bringing them with me," Cypher said as he was ready to get back home.

"You really needed to talk to Ricky, but seeing he isn't available at the moment, and I am second in command. I will accept this offer on the clubs behalf and Ricky will be in touch with you later on."

As Cypher shook his hand he responded, "Very good then. I will wait to hear from him. I need to go now and catch the bus back home. I will see you soon though."

Cypher felt relieved to have at least made some progress with this whole mess. As he took the bus back home his mind drifted onto many thoughts as he played out different scenarios as to how all of this would play out. After reaching his stop, he got off the bus and began to walk down a few block. He ran into the Two Brothers.

"Hey Randy. Hey Darrell. What are you two up to?" he asked.

"Hey Johnnie! We was just up to the movie theater catching a flick. Where you coming from?" Randy asked.

"I just got back from across town. I went to meet with them to let them know we are all on board. I will be taking you with me soon to meet everyone." Cypher explained.

"Yeah alright. That sounds good. We are all ready for this," Darrell said as Randy was nodding in agreement.

"Yes we are Johnnie and Steve is itching to get a hold of them. He can barely wait for this to go down," Randy added.

"It will my brothers, it will. The day of reckoning shall come for them. They shall receive no mercy for what they have done," Cypher said with a fire in his tone.

"This time we end it Johnnie. I mean we finish them for real. I am sick of this fighting with them," Darrell said.

"Yeah me too. This has gone on for so long and its' only gotten worse. Now we must end this once and for all," Randy added.

"I agree brothers. We must finish this and end it. We don't stop until it's done for good. Let's get everyone together tomorrow at the camp and discuss it and make sure everyone is set and ready to go on this."

"Okay Johnnie. Are you heading home? If so you can walk with us," Darrell said invitingly.

"Yeah Bro walk with us. Shoot we missed you. We sure are glad to have you back home," Randy added smiling.

"Yeah sure, let's go. I need to get back home and see Mom. I don't like to leave her alone too much right now, seeing that I just got back home and all. She wasn't too happy that I had left anyways," Cypher explained as the three walked home together.

As they reached Cypher's home they paused for a minute to finish their conversation before going to their own houses. After which he went in to see how his mother was doing. He knew that she didn't like him having to keep leaving, and he really needed to spend some time with her. But he found it very hard to slow down and make time for her when he was filled with so much anger and the feeling of getting revenge was ever so present with each passing moment. Like a force driving him forward, he wanted nothing more than to get this done and put an end to all of this. For now though it was time to relax as best as he could and spend some time with his mother who had been waiting for him to get back home.

As he walked in the front door Sara was sitting on the couch watching television as if she hadn't moved the whole time he had been gone.

"Hey, Mom. I'm home. What are you doing?" he said as he went over and sat on the couch next to her. "Hey, Johnnie. Just sitting here watching some television. Is everything okay? How was your visit with your friends?"

She turned the volume down on the television so they could talk.

"It was good. I thought I would stay in tonight and spend some time with you."

"Oh Johnnie that would be great. I still feel like I'm trying to catch up on all of the lost time we have missed. He nodded in agreement.

"Yes, me too Mom. Have you talked to Tonya at all?"

"No. Not too much. You know after that happened she pulled herself away from everyone. And then you left for a while. I called her a few times and we talked for a little bit, but it hasn't been like it used to be. But I am sure all of that will change now that you're finally back. Or at least I am hoping it will," Sara said with a sense of hope in her voice that eventually everything would finally get back to normal.

"Yes. I am hoping at some point we can put everything back together and move forward. Time heals all wounds right? Maybe in time things will get better and we can rebuild what we have lost. But first I need to make things right and end this feud once and for all."

"At what cost Johnnie? Do you really think it's worth it to go after them?" She was afraid of losing Johnnie for good.

"I have been dealing with this most of my life. And they just won't stop. Now they have gone way too far and I have to make them pay for what they did to us, to Tonya. They just won't go away Mom. Some things you have to make go away. I have no choice. I have to do this. I am sorry Mom I wish there was another way, but there isn't. When this is over with, there will be no more fighting. I promise. I am going to end this once and for all."

Sara knew she could not talk Johnnie out of it. And after all they had been through, she could see that perhaps he was right. That maybe this was the only way. Maybe there was no other way to be able to move on from this but to finally go and end it. Her heart broke for her son. She knew he never deserved any of this, and could never figure out why all of this kept happening to him when he was always such a good kid. He always tried to do what was right. *Why did Mark have to die when Johnnie was so young? Why did he have to fight bullies all of the time? Why did she marry Mike?* These was the questions that Sara often asked herself.

After talking for a little while, they settled into a movie and just relaxed the rest of the night trying to forget the things that could not be settled at the moment. Johnnie hated he made his mother worry all the time. But he felt that he had no choice. He couldn't let them get away with all they had done to him and to Tonya. There was no turning back. They had to die now. All of them. He was determined to destroy The Hells Sinners Gang forever. Their blood would fill the streets from his vengeance.

***

Tonya hadn't been around much after the situation and was still feeling very much ashamed at what had been done to her. But her love for Cypher remained and she had really missed him. Even though they both still wanted to talk it wasn't like it was before. She didn't come out that much. She felt dirty and now she wasn't good for Cypher. It was hard for her to feel anyone would want her now.

For Cypher, she was still all he had ever wanted. His love for her had not changed one bit. And this fueled his hatred for The Hells Sinners, Ricco and Wayne. After all he had been through with them this was the last straw. He could never forgive them for this.

He tried to stay in close contact with Tonya as much as he could and be there for her. But going back and forth to meet with The West Dragons made it harder to stay in touch and most of the time she didn't want to talk to anyone, even him. He missed Tonya so much it hurt. He wanted to be there every minute with her, holding her and making her feel loved again. But there was business that needed to be handled, and Tonya still felt cold to people and didn't want much interaction with anyone. Even Ann felt distant from Tonya most of the time, but she also stayed in close contact with her as much as Tonya would allow.

It was going to take some time before Tonya would be healed enough to start feeling comfortable around people again. Even with those who really loved her. Sara also kept in touch with Tonya and always made her feel welcomed to come and spend time with her even when Cypher was in Juvenile Prison. Cypher knew he was going to have to really focus on Tonya and make her his main priority, but wasn't sure how to do that and put all this together at the same time. Until things get settled, he was going to have to be gone a lot. He also needed to take the group across town to meet with Ricky and the rest of the West Dragons. But for now he was home and was going to try to get some time with Tonya if she was willing.

The next day after Cypher had called Tonya and invited her over, he went out back and sat down in one of the chairs on the patio. He had gotten so used to having time to think that it became a part of his daily routine even on the outside. This was a beautiful place to sit and think. Way better than the cell he had become used to. Sara would always see him out there sitting, make him some hot tea and bring it out to him. This was something that he had picked up from Jason when they were in Juvenile Prison together.

As Sara walked out with his hot tea he looked at her and smiled. "Thank you Mom. You never forget. I am always so very thankful that you take the time to make this for me."

Sara smiled as she sat down next to Johnnie. "I am so happy to have you back home now. I am sorry for all of this Johnnie. I never meant to put you in this position to have to do this. I am so very sorry. I was supposed to protect you, and instead you had to take someone's life to protect me. I am ashamed of what I caused you. I am so sorry for the three years you lost because of me," Sara said as she sat in tears.

Johnnie got up, grabbed Sara's hand and pulled her up.

He held her as she cried. "It wasn't your fault Mom. I love you. And I don't blame you at all for any of this. I knew how much you missed my father. I really miss him too. I wanted you to be happy. I wanted you to have someone who would take care of you the way my father did. I don't blame you for anything. Mike did this to us, not you."

As Sara cried in Johnnie's arms she felt so much regret for all that had happened.

"I brought him into our lives. I should have never let him in," Sara said as Johnnie wiped her tears away from her cheeks.

"It wasn't your fault Mom. I know how lonely you were. Everything is okay Mom. I love you very much and now it is behind us. Mike is responsible for what he did. You have always been a great Mother and wife. I couldn't have done that time without your visits. You never missed one single visit Mom, not even one. You have always been there for me. It was my place to keep you safe after Dad passed away," Johnnie said as he let Sara go and they both sat back down.

"I love you too Johnnie. I love you so very much."

Sara and Johnnie sat together for several minutes enjoying the peaceful view and the quietness of being out back. Finally Tonya came. Cypher had already finished his tea and was sitting and talking to his mom when Tonya found them out back. Sara smiled at Tonya when she saw her, got up and gave her a huge hug. Looking back at Johnnie, Sara told them that she would leave them to talk and spend some time together. Picking up his tea cup she took it in the house with her. Before she opened the door she turned and asked them if they wanted anything to drink. Johnnie asked for some water while Tonya asked if there was any coffee made. Sara responding to both request, went in and got it for them before finally leaving them.

"How have you been Tonya?"

Tonya was trying to look strong before she answered. "I've been okay. Surviving I guess."

Cypher looked at her intensely. "I have missed you. I still

love you Tonya. No matter what has happened or what will ever happen. I will always love you."

"I love you too, Johnnie. I always will. But I need more time, I am not ready for anything else right now. I just need more time. I am sorry. I know this is hard for you too but I just can't do it yet."

"You blame me for all of this. I understand. I was supposed to keep you safe and I didn't."

"I don't blame you for any of this. But it's hard for me to even be here right now because I am so ashamed. I feel so dirty. And you had to watch what they did to me. I am so ashamed and was so humiliated. I had to watch you as they made you watch them raping me and having sex with me. I am embarrassed Johnnie. I am ashamed of what they did to me."

Johnnie and Tonya began to cry. He got up and held Tonya. "It's okay, Baby. This doesn't change my love for you. I still want a future with you. I want everything back to normal, back to the way it's supposed to be." Johnnie said as he held her tightly in his arms.

"I want it too, Johnnie. But I am just not ready."

Johnnie whispered to Tonya as he held her so close to him, "I will make them pay for this. They won't get away with any of it. When this is done I will come back to you and we will make a life together. Just like we had always planned, Honey."

It wasn't long after that George and Ann had also came to visit. Cypher changed the direction of the conversation. It felt good for the four of them to sit together and just talk. This had been a very emotional morning for Johnnie and he was desperately trying to make a transition now that George and Ann was there. Tonya also was trying to get her emotions under control. They had missed this George and Ann. This was the first time the four of them really got to just sit and talk together apart from the others. Johnnie had learned to slow down and experience these moments since being released from the Prison. Times like these became very important to him.

And it was very good to see George and Ann together. They had really fallen in love with each other. Both of them wanted so badly for Johnnie and Tonya to be able to get back together like they were before. It was hard to watch them struggle, especially Tonya. She still felt awkward around everyone and didn't like people to even touch her.

As they sat and talked Johnnie made sure the conversation stayed clear of the incident and his plans to right this wrong bringing an end to Ricco and Wayne. These conversations were always to be in private and away from Tonya. He never wanted this to be brought up in front of her. She had been through enough and Johnnie didn't want it to be a constant reminder. As much as he could, he was trying to make every time they had together as normal as possible in hopes to getting things back to the way they used to be.

Later on that evening the Two Brothers had come by as well to visit. Cypher was hoping things would start to feel like old times soon. But for now they weren't even close. However it was good to just sit back and relax and talk like they used to do. It wasn't long before he took the group back to the camp area for a bonfire. Cypher and George went in and got some drinks for everyone just before they all headed back to the woods to hangout. Cypher was hoping that everyone would stay like they used to do and spend the night.

Steve wasn't there and Cypher missed him. He hoped at some point he would come through and join them. He hadn't seen Steve much the past few days and began to wonder if he was okay. This whole thing had Steve so furious all he thought about was revenge and was actually getting quite frustrated with Cypher not moving faster to make this happen. Cypher wanted it also but he knew to do this right. He needed the help from The West Dragons and was trying to make sure their involvement was timely so as to not get too deeply involved in a gang war. Cypher didn't want any of them joining the gang and was trying to make sure everyone knew their involvement was temporary.

As for the West Dragons, they didn't care. They welcomed Cypher's help and any help he could bring with him. They knew he was a real good fighter. He gained a lot of respect from some of them when he was in The House. Especially from the leaders who he had done time with. Ricky knew this temporary partnership would benefit them both. And he was okay with Cypher and them going their separate ways after it was done.

That night the Two Brothers were the only ones to actually stay the night with Cypher. They stayed back at the camp when he walked Tonya home. George and Ann had already left an hour before Tonya or they all would have walked together.

Cypher was happy they got to walk alone. Even if it was just down the street. It gave them both a sense of normalcy to be able to do some things they used to do together. Even simple things like walking her home made a bit of a difference. After reaching the house Tonya kissed Cypher on the cheek and had thanked him for walking her home. He smiled at her as she walked into the house. His walk back home was much better having had a kiss form Tonya. Once he got back to the camp area, he and the Two Brothers spent the rest of the night talking about a lot of the things he missed while he was gone. And Cypher was talking about how things was in The House and the things he had to go through.

The next day when Cypher woke up, he decided to spend the day with his mother. Sara had been missing him even though he was out now. Because of all the things he was trying to do as well as get things back to normal and get caught up with the group, he hadn't had time to spend with her. So today he thought he would surprise her, just stay home and spend some time with her. Getting up early he decided to go ahead, take a quick shower and then surprise his mom by cooking breakfast. After his shower Cypher hurried down the stairs and into the kitchen only to find his mom already cooking breakfast.

"Mom, I was going to make us breakfast. I wanted to

surprise you."

"It's okay," Sara said looking back at him smiling. "You can help me. I woke up when I heard the water running from the shower. Thought I would get up and make you breakfast."

"Thank you Mom, sure I will help. And guess what my plans are for today?"

Sara looked at him intently. "Well, I'm sure you're off to somewhere to do something that you probably don't want me to know about right?"

"Well, actually Mom I thought I would stick around here and spend the day with you. I mean if you don't already have plans that is?" Johnnie said as he began to make some toast to go with the eggs and bacon Sara was cooking for them both.

"Are you serious? No I don't have any plans for today, and spending time with you sounds great. I would really love that Johnnie. I haven't had much time with you since you got home, and I have been missing you. I thought when you were finally home we would spend a lot of time together, but you have been so busy." Sara said with excitement in her voice.

She had been looking forward to spending time with Johnnie since he got home, but their time together had been very limited. Johnnie asked his mother if she wanted to go into town. He knew she hadn't got out much these days and wanted her to get some fresh air.

Sara was happy to get out of the house, especially with Johnnie. It made her excited to be able to go out, just the two of them, and do stuff together. They used to do this when he was younger, before he went to Juvenile Prison. It was something she had missed and was more than happy to get out of the house and just be in town. This might be a good time to do a little shopping while they are there also and then stop off on the way back at the Diner they used to go to. Johnnie loved the burgers there and they had the biggest ice cream deserts in the area. While Sara had him in town with her it was time to get some new clothes as well as some other things for the house they needed.

Johnnie wasn't planning it to be a clothes trip but nevertheless he knew he needed them. He put up very little argument as they went from place to place. He always hated trying on clothes. He could think of so many other things he would rather be doing.

For Sara it brought a sense of normalcy back to their relationship. Since Johnnie had returned home there was only a few times it felt like they were a real family again. Mainly because he was constantly in and out and she not seeing him nearly as much as she thought she would. But for now it felt right. After being in town for a while, Sara took Johnnie back home. He had some new clothes and shoes that he needed. He had grown a lot in the three years he was gone.

Johnnie knew he was going to have to focus on his work or he was going to lose customers. Trying to put all of this together and fight a war wasn't going to be easy while trying to maintain what had started becoming a small business. He loved having the money and wasn't about to let it all slip away from him. Wayne and Ricco had already cost him so much and he wasn't about to let them cost him this too. It was time to bust his butt for a few days and get as much done as he could.

Randy was doing the best he could with Darrell when Johnnie wasn't around, but they really needed to work just the two of them. Having Darrell helping was more money out of Johnnie's pocket. His business wasn't big enough to pay two helpers, he could really only afford Randy if he was going to keep making good money. But for the next few days he would need Darrell to help out until things got all caught up.

How was he going to take the group to meet with Ricky and still keep all of this going? He would have to take Randy and Darrell with him. This was one time he wasn't sure what he was going to do. His mind weighed heavy on his business the next few days and he couldn't seem to figure out how he was going to carry such a heavy load.

How could one fight a war and run a business at the same time? Especially when his help is also fighting in the war with him. It was something that had to be done no doubt. This war had to happen. It was just impossible to let this continue on any longer. Everything was already in the works anyways and there was no way to back out now.

Johnnie cringed at the thought of possibly risking losing his business. However, there was nothing he wouldn't do for Tonya, and retribution had to be paid. If it cost him everything, he was going to end this once and for all. Death was coming, it wouldn't be swift, but it would be fierce. Tonya would never have to feel unsafe or worry about them ever hurting her again. They would pay with their lives for this horrible act that they had performed on Tonya and the day of reckoning was upon them all. Judgment was coming. And it was coming from the hands of Johnnie Steele.

He imagined the streets filling with the blood of his enemies, and the death of every one of the Hells Sinners was to be handed out. It was all he could do to keep himself from exploding into a rage of anger as he thought about it. *Yes they all must pay the price and meet the same fate, each and every one of them.* As far as Johnnie was concerned, they all were guilty by association for being a part of the same horrid group. They ran together, they must all die together. *I will see to it.* Johnnie snapped out of the terrible thoughts he was having. It had been a long tiring day and evening had come.

It was supper time and Sara made a wonderful meal for her and Johnnie. It was a quiet dinner as they sat down together to eat. Johnnie was too tired to carry on a conversation tonight. After dinner he quietly went upstairs and took a hot shower before retiring to bed to get some much needed rest. A good night's sleep was exactly what Johnnie needed. He was physically exhausted as well as mentally drained. But tonight he was way too tired to continue on with his thoughts. As he laid down on his bed he fell fast asleep, and slept hard till morning.

The next day as Johnnie rose from his sleep he went down stairs to get some breakfast. Sara was already in the kitchen, as usually, when Johnnie came down. The aroma of fresh coffee filled the kitchen mixed with the smell of bacon cooking on the stove. Johnnie went ahead and began to make toast and set the table as was his custom. It was going to be a busy day with all the work that had piled up. It was becoming very stressful for Johnnie to keep trying to get caught back up while he was making these trips across town to get things all set for him to bring the group. He was tired and frustrated. He knew this wasn't going to be a quick ending to this war. His mind was going in every direction and it was becoming harder to focus on each task at hand. He was doing his best to concentrate on each days' details as they came. Today he needed to focus on work, which was going to be a long day of it as he had so many costumers that needed to be done. Johnnie worked late into the evening before finally returning home and retiring for the night.

In the beginning God created the Heavens and the Earth. This was the thought that ran through Johnnie's mind as he woke the next morning. *What a weird thought.* Not being real sure where that came from he almost dismissed it before thinking that maybe it was something Thomas Hilton had said. *I've been meaning to get in touch with him and just been way too busy. He has always been an encouragement to me. I just don't know about the Church stuff. However some of the things he says really does make sense. As much trouble as the Two Brothers got into all the time, one would never know they all went to Church. I respect that they have always stood their ground. Those two have always been faithful friends and have always had my back. Mr. Hilton has always been good to me also. Prayed all the time for me while I was in Juvenile Prison. Sent me letters too. In spite of all I have done, he never made the boys stop hanging out with me. They always were so understanding of what I have been through. Just real good people.*

Johnnie finally climbed out of bed. *I smell breakfast. I better get myself together and go eat with Mom. She hates eating alone. Actually I do too. I have always loved morning breakfast with her.* After coming down the stairs and walking into the kitchen, Johnnie set the table and made some toast.

During breakfast Sara was concerned about her son and the things he possibly was up to. She wanted to know what he was doing but Johnnie wasn't answering any questions.

This was the kind of stuff his mom didn't need to know about and Johnnie for sure was going to keep her in the dark as much as possible. He knew she would worry non-stop and would try to talk him out of it. He didn't need all the stress that would come from talking to her about it. He wasn't turning back now and there was no need for the argument that would follow this conversation.

After breakfast he got himself together and went to see how Tonya was doing. It had been a while since he had been to see her after the situation and he was hoping she would come out and sit with him on the porch like she used to. The last time he had come, she would not see him. Since then they have talked and she has come to visit him. So now he was hoping to take another step in the right direction. Things had still been a bit edgy but it was getting better. Johnnie was being very hopeful that it would continue to go that way.

Showing up unannounced was risky but he wanted to see how it would go if he just showed up without any kind of warning or preparation. He was very nervous about this, but he needed to see how she would handle him just showing up. Upon his arrival, to his surprise, Tonya came out immediately and sat with him. She had missed him terribly and the time they had been together had been much better then she had hoped for. They still had a long ways to go, but she was starting to warm up a bit.

As they sat and talked, things began to become more hopeful for Johnnie. They had a nice conversation before he had to go and meet up with George to discuss a few things. Once Johnnie got back home he immediately called George to let him know he was home. After a brief conversation George was on his way to discuss a few things in preparation to going across town.

George and Johnnie had always been best friends and trusted each other completely. Once George arrived he and Johnnie took a walk back to the camp area. After reaching the area, the two friends sat together and began to discuss what Cypher had on his mind.

"Sit with me for a bit Bro. I want to talk real briefly before the others get here," Johnnie said as they both sat down on the logs next to each other.

"What's going on Bro?"

Johnnie looked a bit serious as he began to speak. "When we get there stay close to me. I want you to be with me at all times. And if anything happens to me I want you to get the rest of the group back home."

George not fully understanding the situation began to take it too lightly. "Ain't nothing going to happen to us Bro. We always clown these fools. Ever since the first fight with Wayne we have been winning this war. Besides, we're going to go there and mess them up and be back home before you know it."

Johnnie began to shake his head as he sat there hearing all George had to say about this situation. "I don't think you get how serious this is George. People are going to die on both ends. This is for real Bro and you need to take it extremely serious. Maybe I need to make this clear to the whole group. None of you need to be thinking that this is going to be a walk in the park. This is going to be a very nasty war like none we've ever been involved in before. And you need to take it as such."

As George sat listening to what Cypher was telling him, he began to realize the severity of the situation. "Yeah maybe I am taking it too lightly. It's just that we haven't lost to these clowns yet and I just figured it would be like it always is. No worries though, I got your back all the way to the end Bro."

Johnnie breathed in a long sigh as he knew George was telling the truth. He would go all the way with him for sure, no matter what.

"Yeah I know Bro, and I really appreciate that. Anyways, the rest will be here in a few minutes and then we can go over everything and make sure we are all on the same page."

After sitting and talking for a while the rest of the group began to show up. The time was getting closer to making this trip and things needed to be discussed. Once everyone was there, Johnnie stood up in the middle of everyone and began to speak.

"I know you all are eager to get this over with. But I am afraid to tell you that this will not be a swift battle. This war will take some time. I need to know for sure that you all are ready for this. You also need to understand that people on both sides are going to die in this war. I'm not saying you specifically will die, but it very well could happen. So having said that if anyone wants to get out, now is the time to do it. No one will look down at you. This isn't an easy thing and we all know it. We are not gangsters, nor are we ruthless killers. So if anyone wants to leave, I will completely understand."

Johnnie paused and gave a few minutes for anyone to leave if they wanted to. After his pause he looked around at everyone. No one had left and all had remained with him.

"So be it. Then we will move forward with this conversation. We need to go there for a week. What I have proposed is this. We all say that we are going camping together, and that I am paying for it. This way we are not taking money from our parents for this trip. It wouldn't seem right to do so. I will cover all that we need. Plus it will give us the time we need to get acquainted with them."

George who was always by Johnnie's side spoke up.

"When are we leaving to go there?"

"We will go this weekend and stay until the following weekend. After that I assume we will know exactly what our role will be and what we will be doing as far as our involvement in this war. Only advice I feel that I need to give you is this, watch how you handle yourselves while we are there. We don't need any problems or issues. Remember these are our allies. We need their help if we are going to end this once and for all. Pack as if we are going camping. Bring clothes, pillows, blankets, and etcetera. Everything you will need for a week. Other than that, get mentally prepared for what is coming. Make sure you are ready for this. It will not be easy, but you must search your hearts in this matter and make sure this is something you can not only handle but also live with."

"Johnnie, what was it like when you had to kill your step dad? I mean I know it was something you had to do, but was it hard to pull the trigger?" Randy asked as they all looked on. Many was wondering the same thing and was very glad that Randy had asked that question.

"I knew I had been thinking about it for some time, but when it was time to do it, I guess I didn't really think about it. I just did it. I felt that I had no choice. So I just did it. It wasn't easy making that decision, but I felt there was no other way out so I had to do it. I killed another when I was in prison. I had to. He was going to kill me so I threw him over the rail to his death before he could stab me. So in all fairness both times it was for survival not revenge. So in all honesty this will be different. This time it's for revenge. Plus I also went on a hit when I was there with The West Dragons as a test to see if I would actually do it. Having done it they agreed to allow us to join them in this war." Johnnie explained in hopes they would understand this would not be the same as what he had done.

"Do you regret any of it?" Steve asked.

"Yes I do. I regret not only having to take someone's life, but I also regret that it was the only way to end what was going on. I regret that I had no other choice."

After Johnnie was done with the meeting they all sat around and talked for a few before breaking up and going home.

The next day Johnnie felt better about this knowing he

had given them all a chance to get out if they wanted or needed to. Knowing they all stayed with him was comforting to him in a sense. But he had also hoped they would have all walked away from this. However no one did.

    This was a very trying time for Johnnie. His love for his friends made the situation even the more difficult. There was no way to guarantee anyone's safety. Risking their lives was not the answer he was seeking but none the less they were all determined to go either way. They had all pretty much been a part of this from the beginning and none of them were about to turn back now. Things had escalated to new heights and they all felt it was time to end this once and for all. The price would be very costly to Johnnie if anything bad was to happen to any of them. Even though it was by their choice they had joined in this great fight that was about to take place. They had always stuck together and wasn't about to stop now. Especially Steve. Not after what they had done to his sister. He was all in no matter what anyone else decided. It was time to pay the piper and Wayne was at the top of the list. They all felt no matter who got hurt or died in this war, Wayne was for sure going to be gone. It all started with him and he was the root cause to everything that had transpired. Surely it was him who was going to pay the greatest price for what had happened.

    After finishing up a good work week, Johnnie had collected from all of his clients. He took the weekend and the next week off to go across town for a week with the group to meet up with the West Dragons. He also had a personal meeting with Jason that no one knew about. There were things that still needed to be done and things he still needed to be secure for the group before things were ready to jump off. This was a very intense and trying time for Johnnie. He constantly battled the sense of fear that continued to grip him. He was always thinking and rethinking if this was something he should have just kept to himself. But they had always fought the Hells Sinners together and it didn't seem right to not give them a chance to decide for themselves. Nevertheless there was no guarantees any of them would make it out of this alive. Either way this war was going to finally settle this feud once and for all. And even if it took his last breath to do so, Wayne was going to get what he deserved.

After everything was ready and everyone had got their things all packed to go on what was supposedly a camping trip, it was time to meet up to go across town. Johnnie had got everything all set while waiting on the group to assemble at his place. Once everyone got there Johnnie did a brief meeting before heading out to meet up with The West Dragon's. As they all sat around together Johnnie began to speak.

"I don't have much to say really before we go. We have all been preparing for this. But if by some chance things go wrong, you all get back home. No matter what you stay together and get back home. Okay. One last time before we go. Does anyone want to back out?"

No one said anything. No one was about to back out now. It was time to do it and everyone was ready to go as far as it took to end this war once and for all. As Johnnie looked around and saw no one was going to back out, he grabbed his stuff.

"Then let's go."

Everyone picked up their stuff and they all headed out together to go meet up with destiny. The war that had to happen was now close at hand. Steve was finally feeling relieved that now they were on the move and he was ready to get some revenge on his enemies. The rest of the group was feeling scared but Steve was way too mad to feel anything other than anger, at least for now. Fear would set in later once things began to happen.

CHAPTER 2

THE MEETING

    This was it. It was finally time to go across town and meet everyone. This was a very nervous time for the whole group, especially Johnnie. His worrying for the group at times was overwhelming. For the rest of the group the only thing that was comforting was they all knew each other, so at least they had a few people they were already comfortable with.
    The bus ride was extremely quiet. No one really knew what to talk about. They all sat with their own thoughts. This wasn't how they were. None of them had ever killed anyone a part from Johnnie. They all felt as if they were pushed into something they were never supposed to be a part of. Wayne had pushed them into it. They had taken things too far and had to answer for it. This war had been going on almost ever since they started going to school. Wayne had always been a problem. And then he had brought in some of his friends to even the odds and created such a huge mess there was no way out of it now but through death. It was never going to stop until they were all gone. It was as if Wayne wanted this war to happen. He had to know they would come after them for this.
    The bus ride across town seemed to feel longer than ever as they all sat thinking on how this situation had developed and perhaps how it would end. The only two who talking were Johnnie and George who said a few brief things.
    As everyone was in their own thought suddenly Darrell stood up and began to speak. "You know what? It's about time we do this. For the first time since we met Wayne, we are finally on the offensive side of this fight. I am sick and tired of always having to defend us and myself. This time

we are taking the fight to them and I am happy we are finally doing this. Maybe we should have initiated more. We were always trying to be the good guys, and for once we are on the attack. This is our time now and The Hells Sinners are going to wish they had never met us."

Darrell had pumped every one up and the mood began to change. They felt he was right. Finally they were on the attack instead of the defense. Johnnie knew what was awaiting them, but for their sakes he let Darrell pump them up. He knew they needed it. They were all scared but Darrell's speech got everyone hyped up and ready for battle. That was exactly what they needed coming into this.

Once they arrived, they met with Viper who was in the park waiting for them. They all went to the club house to get settled in, to meet everyone and get acquainted with the gang. After a short walk through the park they arrived at the club house where Ricky Mack was waiting for them with the main core of the gang which were the leaders.

"Welcome to our club house. I am Ricky, and the leader of this gang. These are my other leaders. Each one has a special function within this gang. You will get to know them and will respect them. But first we eat and have some fun while we get you all settled in."

Everyone sat down after getting a plate of food that was already prepared for them. They all talked amongst themselves and ate as they were trying to get to know each other. This was a good ice breaker for the group to get settled in and talk with the other members that was there. Afterwards, before Ricky got up to start talking, Cypher spoke up.

"I have to go meet with a friend. I will be back shortly."

"Do you need a ride?" Auto asked.

"Yes, actually I do. Can I use a phone real quick?" Cypher asked before heading out.

"Sure, Cypher. You can use the one behind the bar," Ricky said before he started to speak to the newcomers.

Cypher slipped behind the bar and made his phone call.

"Hey, I am in town. Can we meet? I need to talk to you right away."

"Yes of course my brother. I will meet you at my spot. You know where to find me," the voice on the other end of the phone said before he hung up.

"Okay, I am ready Auto. I will see you guys in a little while." No one knew what Cypher was up to but no one asked either.

As they pulled up to the Coffee House, Cypher told Auto to wait for him as he got out of the car and went inside. Auto watched as Cypher went over and sat down at a table where Jason was sitting.
"It's good to see you my friend."

Smiling, Jason responded, "It's good to see you as well. I wish it was on better circumstances. I am assuming this meeting is more towards business?"

Nodding Cypher responded, "I need some guns. Five to be exact. And I need them as soon as possible." "Guns is no problem. I can have them for you in the morning. So you here now to help get this war started?"

"Well, we are meeting up with the West Dragons to go after the Hells Sinners. I have the whole group here with me this time."

"Yes, Ricky told me it was about time for this war to start. I had no idea you would be here so soon though."

"Yeah, well, after what they did we have to end this once and for all. The group is ready, or as ready as they can be."

"Yes I agree. Are you guys sure you're all up for this?"

"Jason, my brother, there is no other way. We have to end this."

"Okay, Cypher. Meet me in the park tomorrow morning say around eight. I will have your guns. I can give you a fair deal. Three hundred bucks for all five with some bullets included."

"That sounds like a pretty good deal."

"Yeah it is, because you're my brother."
Jason knew he could have gotten a little more on the street for these guns, but he had to help Cypher.

"I will see you in the morning my friend," Cypher said.

"Okay, my brother. Take care and be safe. I won't be far if you need me."

"Thank you Jason for all your help. I really appreciate this."

"It's no problem Cypher. You know I will always have your back."

They shook hands as Cypher got up and walked out of the Coffee House. He got in the car and headed back to the club house. After they returned, Cypher sat in on the rest of the meeting. This was a good time to sit back and observe his group and examine their reaction to what was being said. Cypher new Ricky would give it to them straight and he needed to see their facial expressions to what was being told to them. This would give him a better feel as to who was going to be able to stick it out with him. Not that he didn't trust his friends, but this wasn't what they was accustomed to. This war was going to take things to a whole new level.

Once the meeting was finally over, they all unpacked and began to get settled in to what would be their home for the next seven days. The rest of that day was spent sitting back and getting themselves acclimated to their new environment. They also talked about the situation and other things. Cypher grabbed George and had Auto take them to get some food and supplies they would need while being there for the next week.

In the meantime, Ricky was getting his gang ready to set things off. He was tired of waiting and wanted to make his move to take this territory that he had been trying to get for a very long time. He needed more time to try to figure out exactly how Cypher and his group would fit in but he was tired of waiting to start this war. This was a different kind of situation for any gang to use outsiders, but Ricky clearly understood that having Cypher and his group with him would make things a little bit easier.

After shopping, Cypher and George came back, put things away, rejoined the rest of the group and chilled the rest of the night. Everyone seemed relax at the moment, however, they were curious as to where Cypher had went off to during the meeting, Darrell especially.

"Where did you run off to earlier Johnnie?"

"I had to meet someone and take care of some business," Johnnie responded as him and Darrell sat next to each other and talked. "I will explain everything tomorrow when I get back."

"When you get back? Where are you going?" Steve inquired as he was curious to where Johnnie had to keep running off to.

"I have to go meet a friend, get a few things from him and then I will be back. No big deal, just need to get a few things that we will need is all."

It was weird having Johnnie run off on his own while everyone was trying to get settled in. But as of yet he did not want to get them all excited about what he was doing until he got what they needed. He had played it off to Ricky that they had guns already, but the truth was Johnnie hadn't actually talked to Jason about it until that day. He didn't want to deal with anyone but Jason with this situation. Cypher and Ricky had become pretty good friends in The House while he was locked up. But when it came to stuff like this, he knew beyond a shadow of a doubt he could one hundred percent trust Jason and knew also he would come through for him.

As it began to get late, they were finally starting to wind down and get tired from the long day they had experienced. Cypher and a few of the others laid down to try to get some sleep. It was a bit exciting for Darrell and Steve but they were on edge. For Cypher, this whole ordeal just never fully sat right. He still kept thinking if there was another way to handle this, but there wasn't if they really wanted this to end for good. That still didn't keep him from rethinking things. He knew it was a great possibility some of them would not make it out of this war alive. That was something he wasn't sure if he could live with.

Nevertheless it was a reality he had to face. Even though

they were all here on their own. They had made this decision on their own and that's how it needed to be. No one was here because they felt guilty or pushed into it. They wanted revenge. They wanted this to end, and no matter what, they were in no matter where it took them.

The next day Cypher arose earlier and began to cook breakfast. The smell of eggs and bacon filled the air as it awakened the rest of the group that had still been sleeping. Fresh coffee was made and George began to make some toast as Steve set the table while the Two Brothers picked up from the night before. Once the food was done everyone sat down at the table and ate together. In a sense it felt like being back at home when they stayed at Johnnie's back at the camp and Sara would cook for them all.

Once everyone was finished with breakfast they all pitched in and cleaned everything up to keep the club house presentable. After which Cypher took off to go meet Jason in the park as they had planned the day before. When he arrived he was surprised to see Jason already there waiting for him. Cypher was early himself and had expected to have to wait a few before Jason arrived.

Jason had put together a nice package of guns for Cypher from the dead bodies of the victims he had killed. Jason always took their guns for resale as a way to make a few extra dollars. Three hundred dollars free money was a great pay day when you come from an orphanage. Although Jason didn't stay there anymore he still knew the value of free money.

For Cypher this was a good deal. Some of these guns would play a key role in diverting the evidence away from them since the guns they was using was taken off known thugs. Some of which had not yet been found and later would be assumed to have been killed in this war.

"Here you go Cypher. Five guns just like you asked. All nine millimeters. Each gun has one full clip, but I am sure Ricky can help you obtain more bullets. I wish I could stay and talk my brother, but I have to get my business done as well."

"Yeah I understand Jason. Thank you very much for your help. I really appreciate this," Cypher said as he handed Jason the three hundred dollars and took the bag of guns from him.

"Let me know if you need anything else. You know how to reach me," Jason said as he shook Cypher's hand.

"Thanks Jason. You're always a big help to me. I owe you my friend."

"You don't owe me nothing Cypher. Anything you need, just let me know. I mean anything Cypher."

"I will Jason. Thanks again."

"No problem Bro, I will see you soon," Jason said as he turned and walked off to meet with Pauli to see what he had lined up for him today.

Once Cypher returned back to the club house he got everyone together in the TV room and handed out guns to each of them. Everyone was a bit excited about getting their own gun.

"Wow, Johnnie where did you get these from?" Randy asked.

"Yeah Johnnie, how did you get these?" Steve added.

"From a friend. That's all I can tell you." Cypher responded as he sat down. "Listen. These are not toys and you need to be very careful with them," he explained sitting nervously and on edge about this whole thing.

No one else had ever killed anyone before from this group and it concerned him because he knew what it felt like to have to take someone's life. It wasn't easy to live with. He tried to express that to the group a few times but they seemed to be sure this is what they all wanted to do. Johnnie was sure also when he did it before, when he shot and killed his abusive step-dad. But the things that followed was very difficult and this was weighing heavily on his mind. Time would tell if any of them could even really pull the trigger, but unfortunately that was something they wouldn't find out until they were in that moment.

The morning had passed by as if in a moment and the afternoon was filled with visitors from other gang members they had not met until today. Soon it was late evening and everyone was heading out. It had been an interesting day and now it was getting late and they were finally getting tired. Everyone went to their own area where they had set up their bedding. Cypher slipped out to get some fresh air and clear his mind before he tried to go lay down and get some sleep. While sitting on the porch alone thinking and trying to get his mind set right, Randy came out to join him.

"Hey Johnnie. Are you okay?"

"Huh? Oh yeah man. I am okay. Just trying to get some fresh air before I lay down for the night. How are you feeling about all of this Randy?"

"Hey man I know we aren't killers. But this has to stop Bro and I am tired of fighting them. This has been going on for so long. After this is done you know we can live our lives without the constant problems and fighting with them."

"Yeah, well, when you take someone's life, I mean you have to live with that Bro. You can't never take it back or go and say you're sorry. Once it's done it's done."

"I know Johnnie. We have all thought about that and have even talked about it when you wasn't around. But we all have come to the same conclusion, it's time to end this once and for all."

"Yeah I guess in that we are all on the same page."

"We sure are Johnnie. You get out of life what you put into it. They have hurt people, murdering and raping. Now its come back on them and they are about to reap what they have sown. They created all of this. Not us. This was their doing. The way I see it, we are just carrying out what they deserve."

"Yeah maybe. Either way we are all in this now. I just hope everyone is mentally prepared for this."

"We will all be relieved Johnnie when this is over with. But for now, it is what it is. We know the risk. We know some of us or even all of us might not make it out of this alive. But we all agreed that it's what we have to do. One of us has to go, either us or them and if this is the only way to make that happen, then so be it."

"Yeah I suppose so Randy. I suppose so."

"Let's get some sleep Johnnie."

Johnnie took a deep breath and followed Randy into the club house to try and get some rest. As Johnnie laid down it took him a bit before he was finally able to fall asleep He thought about some of the things Randy had said to him out on the porch. It did make sense to him. He had the same kind of thoughts as well. He just wished there was a better way. After a while of lying there going over the conversation and being extremely exhausted, he finally fell asleep and was able to sleep all night.

The next morning as they all arose and sat down for breakfast, they ate together as Cypher began to talk to them about daily duties they needed to do to keep this place kept up. Each person was given a specific task so everyone knew what they needed to do each day. Shortly after clean up, Ricky came in and sat with the group talking about what the plans were for the Hells Sinners. No one knew exactly when things were going to pop off except for Ricky. The only thing they knew was it wasn't going to be while they were staying in the club house. Ricky didn't want anyone staying there when this happened because he knew this would be the first place that would get hit when the Hells Sinners would retaliate. He also liked the idea of another group coming in from another place to hit the Hells Sinners. He felt this would cause great confusion for them if they didn't know where the other hits were coming from. After the meeting and getting to know the group a little more, Ricky got up to leave.

"Hey um, Johnnie, come take a walk with me for a minute."

"Yeah sure Ricky," Johnnie responded as they both talked outside together.

"What's on your mind Ricky?"

"Well I wanted to discuss with you about how exactly do you want to split this group up? I mean there are five of you, only need three on a run. You understand right?"

"Yeah, sure, I understand. Well George and Steve will be with me, and you can take the Two Brothers with you."

"Okay, yeah, that sounds good to me. Um one more thing, you seem to be a little comfortable with pulling the strings. Let's not forget who runs this gang."

"Well, seems to me as if you been pulling the strings all along Ricky. I mean after all, you never needed me to go on a hit with your men to prove myself. You used me to do some of your personal problems that had nothing to do with me. Sure I let you use me, just to show you that I am serious, but none the less, you used me just the same.

"Wait a minute Cypher. What makes you think I used you huh? My men needed to know they could trust you. That's all."

"Your men know. I was in The House with some of you. You all knew I was there for murder and even saw me kill once while I was in there. Let alone you all saw me fight like there was no tomorrow to defend myself. Now let us also not forget that we are only working together to help each other. You don't own me and I don't own you. We agree? And when this is over, we go our separate ways."

"Yeah I agree. But when you're here under my place, you do as I say. I don't care what you do when you're back at home, that's your business."

"I can agree to that to a certain point, just don't forget who I am."

"Ain't no one forgetting, now let's not let this become a problem," Ricky said.

"There isn't any problem, just want mutual respect is all."

"So do I."

After their brief talk Johnnie went back inside to talk to the group. "Well. It seems as if we will be breaking up into two groups. Steve and George will stay with me and Darryl and Randy will be going with someone from the gang." Johnnie got up and went into the other room to make a phone call while the rest of the group talked amongst themselves.

"Hey Bro can you get a car for a few hours?"

"I can get anything you want. You need to go somewhere?"

"Yes Bro I do, won't take long. How soon can you come pick me up?"

"I can be there in less than thirty minutes."

"Sounds good Bro. I will be waiting."

As Johnnie walked back into the room to sit with the rest of the group he noticed everyone was calmer then he had expected.

"Is everyone alright?" Johnnie asked as he sat down.

"Yeah Bro we are all good. Just chillin' before we go light it up you know?" Darryl said as they were all looking at each other.

It wasn't much longer Johnny's ride showed up. "Okay guys, I need to take off for a few hours but I will be back before time for us to go."

"Where you off to Johnnie?" George asked.

"Just need to go with a friend for a few hours is all. I will be back."

The group was starting to wonder about Johnnie and him leaving a lot to go off and do stuff on his own. That wasn't like him to keep things a secret from them like that and it really started to bother them. George was looking out the window as he watched Johnnie pull off with his friend before returning back to his seat.

"So what's up Bro? Is everything okay?"

"Yeah everything fine man, just something I feel I need to do."

"So where are we heading to?"

"I will tell you how to get there, but for now please, just drive my friend."

"Yeah, okay Bro."

Johnnie took a deep breath as he looked out the window while riding.

"I wish this was all over with already."

"Yeah I hear you Bro. You have a good heart man. You have a killer's heart now, but you still have a good heart. Not like me you know. I just have a killer's heart, nothing good in there at all. Just death."

"I don't know Bro. I don't feel like there is much good left," Johnnie said while he looked over at Jason.

"Don't sale yourself out short Bro. You have a lot of good in your heart. You're always there for me whenever I need you."

"Yeah I guess so. Maybe I am okay for an orphan and all," Jason commented as he laughed.

"Pull in here Bro."

"A cemetery Bro? Why are we here?"

"Just something I need to do. Follow that path to the left Bro."

"How far down?"

"Stop here. Wait here Bro, I will be back."

Johnnie opened the door and slowly got out as he walked down a row of tombstones until he came to the place where his father was laid. He stood there for a moment before kneeling down at his father's grave to weep.

"Father, I am so sorry about how I turned out. I tried so hard to be like you. Life just wouldn't let it happen. They wouldn't let it go, and now I have to bury them. They have left me with no choice. All I wanted was to be like you, Father. I just couldn't make it."

Johnnie sat there for a minute as he gathered himself together before returning to the car where Jason was waiting. After he was finished he slowly walked back to the car and sat there in silence as Jason drove them back out of the cemetery.

"Are you okay Johnnie?"

"Yeah, I'm okay. I just need some time to think before we get back there if you don't mind."

"No I don't mind at all Bro."

The rest of the ride was very quiet as Jason drove Johnnie back to the club house. Jason pulled slowly into the driveway.

"Are you sure you're okay Bro?" Jason asked again.

"Yes I'm okay Jason. Thank you for taking time to take me over there. That means a lot to me."

"No worries Bro, don't even think of it. Call me if you need anything else. I will be around."

"Okay. Thanks Jason, I will see you later."

When Johnnie walked into the house everyone was sitting at the kitchen table playing cards while waiting to go out on the run.

"Hey welcome back Johnnie," George said as he walked in.

"Thanks George. How are things going here?"

"Everything is good Johnnie," Darryl responded.

"Everything okay Johnnie?" Randy asked.

"Yes everything is fine. Just waiting now."

"Join us if you want. We are just playing some cards while waiting also," said Steve as he was trying to relax and stay calm.

"Yeah sure, maybe a few games anyways," Johnnie said as he sat down with the group and played some cards with them. Even though he hadn't felt up to it, he needed to spend time with them.

"We will be going home soon. They don't want us staying here during our attack because of the possible retaliation that will more than likely follow. Once we head out to do this we won't come back here. Afterwards we will go straight back to the camp for the night."

"I'm ready. This sitting around waiting isn't getting it for me. It's time to get this started. I hate waiting," Steve said to Cypher as the rest agreed.

***

Tonya had no idea what was going on, but for the first time she felt as if the group had moved on without her and she was left behind. But no one wanted her to know what they were doing. She would have felt as if they were doing this for her and she would have been right. This was something none of the group was willing to let go. Tonya would have tried to stop them if she knew what they were doing and they knew it. Steve hadn't had any contact with his family since they left. He was concerned about Tonya and was itching to get back home to make sure his sister was doing okay.

Cypher also missing Tonya was getting anxious to get back home and see her as well. It was hard enough to not include her in this but to be away from her for days after finally getting her to start spending time with him again was very hard. His love for Tonya hadn't faded one bit and his heart was heavy concerning her all the time. He knew she still needed time to heal but he was very optimistic that in time they would be able to reestablish their relationship.

***

As the group was away, Christina Hilton had invited Tonya to go out to lunch with her so they could talk. Christina had taken her to a nice place out of the way where they could just talk quietly with no interruptions or distractions. There was a nice place where they could eat outside off by themselves where they would have a bit of privacy. As they talked, Christina began to ask her how she was doing and inquire about her and Johnnie.

"I know it's been a while since we talked. We haven't had a chance to get to see you. How are things going with you and how are things with you and Johnnie?" Christina asked.

"It's been hard to be honest. I feel so dirty and I feel like everything I could have given Johnnie has been ripped away from us now. I feel depressed all the time. I feel worthless and dirty. I don't know what will come of Johnnie and I after what happened. I know he still loves me but what I was saving for him has been taken from us."

Tonya was struggling to even talk about this but it was good to at least be able to get these things off of her chest and finally say some things she had buried and wasn't talking about.

"Johnnie loves you very much. From the time he met you until now, you have been in his heart. I remember when you moved in. Randy came home and talked about how pretty you were and how it looked as if Johnnie had taken to you. Seems as if Johnnie never looked back. He will always love you Tonya."

"I know he will. But I feel so ashamed. He saw what they did to me. They made him watch. I was so humiliated in front of him. What they did to me was horrible and for Johnnie to have to watch was even worse. His very enemies having sex with me as they raped me while he watched was more than I could handle. It seemed like it went on forever. There was so many of them and they all made sure they took a turn on me while Johnnie helplessly watched. I know it killed him, I just know it did. How can I now be anything to him? We had plans to get married and build a life together and now everything is undone. How can he love me anymore after this? How can he even still want to be with me after what he had to watch? I am dirty and unclean. All was taken from me. I was saving myself for Johnnie and he was saving himself for me. He wanted us to get married first and then build a family together like his father did and now it's all been destroyed."

This was the first time Tonya had been able to say these things to anyone. In a sense it brought her relief to finally be able to talk about it. Tonya had always felt a special connection with Christina which helped her to say what she needed to say.

"Johnnie won't just let you go because of this. I know he still wants to marry you and have a family. His love for you is very deep Tonya. You're not dirty or unclean. There is healing from this. Your life isn't over. Your life with Johnnie isn't over with. Thomas and I are both praying for you. God can heal you and restore you from all that was done to you. He can heal you both, you and Johnnie."

Christina had always been a comfort to Tonya because of her faith in God. This was something Tonya never understood, but she did admire that Christina was always a positive role model. Christina had that ability to make people feel welcome when they would come visit her. With all that had happened, it was refreshing to have someone in her life that accepted her no matter what, and right now Tonya needed to be accepted.

"I don't know much about God and all that stuff. I only know that all my life I have felt a sense of something much greater than me was always there. Well, until this happened anyways. Now I don't feel anything to be honest. I just feel numb as if no one could ever love me now." Tonya began to tear up as she talked. It was very hard to keep her emotions under control as she tried to talk.

"Well you're not worthless and God does love you. Your life isn't over with. God still has a plan for your life. You still have a purpose. I know Johnnie isn't giving up on you either. He loves you very much."

Both sat picking at their food as they talked. This was a very emotional time for them and it became difficult to sit and eat.

"I know Johnnie does, but I struggle just being around him. I love him so much. He was everything to me. Had he not seen what they did to me I would have probably never even told him. I know it would have killed him. I know it eats at him every day. I am afraid that at some point he will go after them if he isn't already." Tonya began to sob as tears ran down her cheeks.

She lowered her head as she wept bitterly until she felt Christina pulling her up and embracing her as she cried. Christina held her as she wept comforting her and reminding her there was still hope for a future and this hadn't destroyed her or Johnnie.

"Everything will be okay in time. I know it looks like everything is destroyed but it's not. You and Johnnie will get through this and in time you two will be able to move on from this."

Continuing to cry as Christina was hugging her Tonya was gasping for words to say. "I know Johnnie still wants to be with me, but I can't even understand why. I feel so filthy and I try so hard to wash it off and can't. I try to be what he needs and wants but how can I do that now? How can he still want to have a future with me after all of this has happened? Johnnie is the only boy I had ever loved and been with. I never dated anyone but him. He was my one and only and now before I could give myself to him, it was taken by so many men at one time. I was a virgin and it was taken from me in front of the one who I was saving it for. What can I give him now that is special that's just for him? What special gift is left for me to give Johnnie?"

Christina completely understood the importance of what Tonya was saying. "You can still give him your love. Your heart and your love is something they could never take away from you. That is what is most important. That is what you can still give to Johnnie. I know him. That is what he still wants from you."

After their time together Christina took Tonya back home perceiving this was a lot for her to handle and she needed to get some rest. As she pulled into the driveway to drop Tonya off, Christina had asked if she could pray with her. Not wanting to offend her she consented because Christian had shown her much kindness.

"God of Heaven and Earth. You have created all things and by Your wonderful hands many good works have been done. Now I ask Lord, that in Your great mercy and compassion with which You have loved us with, that You reach down now and bring healing to Tonya. Shower her with Your wonderful love in Jesus' Name, Amen."

As Christina finished praying for Tonya they both sat for a minute as tears ran down Tonya's face. Leaning over, Christina embraced her as they hugged one another.

"Thank you so much Christina. I didn't know until now how much I needed that. I don't know much about this kind of stuff, but I do know that I felt something that I needed." From this day forward Christina and Tonya would have a strong bond together as their friendship would grow.

***

Johnnie awoke early in the morning feeling troubled and uneasy. His conscious was troubling him as he sat alone thinking of all that had been done and what was about to take place. Always wanting to do right, he had given it some thought to just go back home. But every time he thought about it his heart was filled with such great anger. He felt responsible for his friends being here and was afraid for them. He did not want any more harm to come to them. He thought very hard on even sending them back home and going on with this alone.

 As the rest of the group began to wake up, Johnnie pulled himself together not wanting his friends to see him in a moment of weakness. It was important to him to always remain in control and to appear as a strong leader at all times so the rest of the group would not lose confidence in him. As of yet he was still unsure of how he wanted to handle things. He was torn between the war and not wanting to lose any one else. For at this time in his life he was still unsure if he would ever fully regain Tonya back as what they once was. Much fear and conflict gripped Johnnie with great uncertainty. The group had to make up their own minds for he could not bear losing anyone of them just because they followed him into this war. Having thought much about it, he once again asked everyone if they were sure this was what they wanted to do. No one pausing, they all said at the same time this was what had to be done, and no one was wanting to go back home. This was their war also. Especially Steve who was very much going to see this all the way to the end after what they had done to his sister. There was no way he was about to let this go.

 During the day as they sat and talked some of the members came by to visit and get to know them better. They had a huge back yard at the club house. This was one of the main reasons they picked this place to be their club house. Having been a nice day out, many of the members brought their girlfriends by and lots of food. They wanted to have a cook out.

 The ladies worked in the kitchen preparing the food while the guys all sat around talking and playing card games with each other. Viper and Snake brought the food for the ladies to prepare while Venom brought the charcoal for the grills. Venom was good at grilling and had three grills set up out back he would use at the same time. This worked because there were many members and girls who would always come.

When Killswitch and Trailblazer showed up everyone got hype, for they always brought the beer for the parties and cookouts. Finally after some time, the rest showed up and Ricky Mack was ready to do some serious drinking. Joe the Pimp had brought some of his ladies for the new guys to enjoy as a gift. This was common for him to do with all the members, but today it was for Johnnie and his group. It didn't matter who all had them once the group was finished with them. Joe always considered them club property anyways and didn't care what the boys did to them just as long as they all had fun.

Most of the time the ladies felt safe but there were times when things would get out of control and certain women would get abused terribly, even to the point of death. Especially if HK was in a foul mood. He would often abuse one of them as before, during, and after sex. Joe never said anything about it, not only because he was afraid of HK, but also because he would often make good on it with a considerable amount of money.

Smooth J usually spent his time behind the booth deejaying and spinning tunes for the parties. That was his passion. He loved music and took great pride in his massive music collection. Everyone went out back to chill and hangout. Some of the guys helped Smooth J setup his equipment out back so he could spin outside and provide music for them. The group was enjoying the female company as they all sat around with them talking and laughing. The ladies were hanging all over them and the group was enjoying it very much as they kissed and felt on each other.

Johnnie refused to be comforted by any female other than Tonya. His heart was still with her and she was all he ever wanted. Even to the point of denying himself pleasure for the night. His thoughts was on her always. It wasn't easy to decline such great pleasure however, but for loves sake he denied himself. However, the rest of the group indulged in all that was offered to them. Enjoying every bit of pleasure that they was given. As for Johnnie he did not. He never drank and didn't want to start after all he had been through with Mike and how he would act while being drunk and how abusive he would get. Plus he wanted to keep his head clear and his wits about him.

It bothered Johnnie at the whole scene of his friends enjoying the moment, but deep down inside he knew they needed it. This was a scary and trying time for the group. They were all on edge and needed this distraction. Johnnie didn't want to seem distant from the rest but it was very hard for him to relax and enjoy the moment. He just couldn't find it in himself to be here for fun when he knew what was about to take place and how it would be life changing for himself and the group.

They weren't killers and neither was he. All he had done up until the time he came here was all for self-defense and protection. He hated what he had done and now they were all about to kill for revenge. Possibly for protection as well he thought to himself. He didn't think they would ever stop and neither did the rest of the group, and after what they had done, there was no way they were going to risk any further harm from these animals who only knew how to hurt people. They were evil and they had to be stopped. There was no telling who else they had done this to. How many other women had they raped and hurt? How many other people had they senselessly victimized? No, they just couldn't be allowed to continue on, they must be stopped.

***

As Tonya laid on her bed alone in her room she couldn't help but think about Johnnie. Up until this point she had only focused on her pain and what had happened to her.

Closing off her love for Johnnie and shutting everyone out until today, she hadn't even understood why she agreed to go with Christina. But one thing was certain, something happened today. Something had changed. Something that Tonya didn't understand. She missed Johnnie, she missed how he loved her, and how he would look at her with such great love in his eye. She missed how he would hold her and touch her. She wondered at how things would work out with her and Johnnie, if things could ever be the same after this. *How could he desire her after what he saw them do to her? She was dirty and tainted by his very enemies. How could he ever look at her the same or hold her as he did before? How could he even want to touch her like he once did? If there was a God, could He fix this? Could He really make things new again? Christina had mentioned about healing and restoration, but how? How could God fix what has already been done?*

***

While she pondered on these things she had no idea of the sacrifice Johnnie was making for her by not allowing himself to indulge in all that was being offered to him by these women that Joe had brought for him to enjoy and to use as he saw fit. But all Johnnie could think about was Tonya, and it didn't seem right to him to have another woman when the very reason why they were here was because of what had been done to her. It just didn't seem right to dishonor her while trying to honor her. This caused Johnnie to struggle to find his place at the party. He wanted so badly to go off on his own and be alone while the rest enjoyed all that was offered to them. But he knew he had to stay. He participated the best he could by engaging in conversations sitting just a little off from the group but trying to appear to be closer than he really was. The truth was his heart was far from this fun but he faked smiles when needed to mask the fact he wanted to go be alone and think about Tonya.

Those who knew Cypher from The House was eager to spend time with him and talk. He gained so much respect from them when they had done time together. They knew him as a strong, tough kid who would handle his business and do what he needed to do to survive. The rest of the group saw how the gang looked at Cypher, and how they respected him the same way they had as well.

"It's so good to have you here with us Bro, I missed you after you got out. Wasn't sure if I would ever see you again. You know people still talk about you? Man you was a beast in The House," Viper said to Cypher as they sat and talked.

"Yeah? I hated that place, but I am sure we all did. I learned a lot in there though. I was hoping to get on with my life once I got out you know. I was doing pretty good at it with building my own business and all. However, Wayne and Sisko just couldn't let me be. They had to keep on. I am so sick of these losers. Their death is the only thing that will finally end this feud once and for all. I won't stop until every last one of them is wiped away from the face of the Earth."

Cypher's emotions began to surface quickly during this conversation. That was something he always tried to hide from others. Viper knew how he felt, for he himself hated Wayne and Sisko as well.

"We will get them Bro. No worries there. I want to see their end come also. I have been fighting them a long time too and I would love to see them no longer exist. The whole gang is nothing but bullies who love to inflict pain on others. They love to humiliate people and torture them. They have no mercy. They are all full of evil and need to be purged from this Earth. That's something me and you both agree on Cypher. They need to die. They are the reason I joined this gang. It was my only protection from them and now I get to finally inflict my revenge on them. I also have a reason to see the end of them, my brother. They raped my sister and my mother. Made them both watch as they were both being raped. Taunting them as they all took turns, switching back and forth. My sister never recovered. She all the time struggles with trying to commit suicide. All the time wanting to kill herself. She was so pretty Cypher, now she has scares all over her body from cutting herself. My sister was a good student, got good grades, now she is hooked on drugs trying to kill the pain they inflicted on her."

For a moment Cypher starred at Viper before he spoke, "What about your Mother? Did she recover?" Cypher asked as he was trying to find some kind of hope for him and Tonya. He was looking for something to encourage him that at some point they would be able to make it through this and start over.

"Yeah. She did. She had to. She has to take care of my sister. Her life is such a mess now."

The anger in them was being greatly aroused as they sat and talked. "We will get our revenge my friend. Trust me, we will get our revenge," Cypher said.

They got up to go get some food that was now finally ready as the aroma filled the air. It had seemed like a long morning as it slipped into the early afternoon. The food was good, and everyone enjoyed it as they ate their fair share. Food, beer, and women were all they could ask for to indulge in and it was there as much as they wanted. But for Johnnie the food was enough for him. Everyone else made sure they got their share though.

None of them had ever been with women like this before. George had a girlfriend but they never did anything. Ann was a good girl, and she loved George very much. This also weighed heavy on Cypher as he was surprised at how fast George could play with another woman while Ann was back at home waiting for him. He knew George loved her, but he couldn't imagine he would ever do this kind of thing. As he sat and finished his food he caught eyes with George and motioned for him to come over to where he was.

"Excuse me honey, it would appear that our fearless leader needs me for a minute."

"Mmmm hurry back lover boy."

George gave her a small kiss as he got up and went over

to see what Johnnie wanted him for.

"Have a seat George. I would like to talk to you for a few minutes."

"Yeah sure Bro, what's up? Isn't this party great? And man look at the women. They sure do know how to put on a good barbeque don't they Bro?" George said assuming everything was okay.

"Yeah they sure do Bro. Actually that's kind of what I wanted to talk to you about. Seems like you have forgotten about Ann while sitting over there with Little Miss Thing. Man what's going on with you? You know Ann loves you," Johnnie said in a disgusted voice.

George sat surprised at Johnnie's tone. "Hey, relax Bro. I'm not doing anything wrong, just a little kissing is all, no big deal."

Johnnie shook his head as he looked at George. "And just where did you plan on taking this to? How far are you planning on going with this? You looked a little too comfortable over there with her."

"Come on Johnnie, relax huh. There is enough to go around. And besides, no one needs to know anything. These women are ready for some action just like we are. Maybe you should join in instead of sitting it out huh? There are a few who keep looking at you. Why not grab one and have a little fun with her Bro?"

Johnnie's anger started to rise at the response George gave him. "Really George? You told Ann that you loved her, and this is what you do the first time some cheap girl throws herself at you? As for me, I'm not indulging in the hoeville challenge because I do love Tonya. I love her very much, and my heart is with her. I am not so easily swayed as you are, my brother. I don't care what anyone offers me. I love Tonya and I won't jeopardize that love for no cheap thrill by some girl I never even met before. I am surprised at you George. I thought you was a better man this this."

George became ashamed at the words Johnnie spoke to him as he was cut to the heart by the truth.

"Yeah okay. I get that Johnnie. Maybe you're a better

man then me. It's just that I never been able to have a girl that would go all the way with me. Ann and I have never gone beyond kissing and this was a chance for me to finally be able to go all the way, you know. But I do get what you're saying, and you're right. I need to be faithful to Ann. I'm sorry Bro. I should have never even touched her."

Johnnie was relieved George understood where he was coming from. "It's okay Bro. No harm was done right? Just don't forget about your girl. Keep Ann in focus so you don't go too far. I'm your friend George, I don't want to see you do something that you will regret. I know you and Ann both love each other so just be careful. I don't want to see anyone get hurt unnecessarily. Especially not any one that we love."

"I feel the same way. Sorry Johnnie. I just got a little too excited about what I could finally have. But you're right. I do love Ann very much and she is worth waiting for."

Johnnie shook his hand as George got up and went back over to sit back down where he was before. As the girl went to sit back down with him, George stopped and dismissed her.

"I can't honey. I have a wonderful girl back at home that I love very much."

Looking sadly at George she responded, "Well isn't that too bad. I was really liking you. We could have had some real fun."

George almost grabbed her and pulled her back down on his lap but he let her walk off instead. *Yeah, we sure could have had some fun. So everyone gets laid but me and Johnnie. Ann better appreciate me that's for sure.*

Johnnie knew George was going to have enough regrets from this trip when it was over with and he didn't want him to have to go back home with this hanging over his head as well. There was going to be bloodshed and pain inflicted by their hands and neither of them wanted to go back home having also cheated on the women that they loved. Even though Johnnie didn't know whether or not him and Tonya would ever be anything again, he still loved her and was going to remain faithful to her until she absolutely made it one hundred percent clear that they would never be together as a couple again. His heart would not let him betray her.

    Later that night Steve and the Two Brothers were very drunk and in the bedroom with the three girls they had been playing with all day. Johnnie went out on the front porch to sit and think while everyone was busy with the women. George, however, who had drank way too much decided to join Johnnie on the front porch.

    Being a little too drunk he tried to talk with Johnnie, who was enduring this conversation that was irritating him. George was trying to express his love and gratitude to Johnnie for the years of friendship they had. Johnnie wanted to get up and leave but he knew George was just trying to show how much he cared about him. Every part of the conversation was jumbled together with other things because George couldn't stay focused on what he was trying to say. Whatever thought entered into his mind seemed to come out of his mouth. Even if it was unrelated to what he was talking about. Johnnie hoped soon the alcohol would force George to pass out and go to sleep. Which it did after some time. Johnnie had to help George back into the house once he realized he was starting to nod off. The boys were in the bedroom having fun with the girls so he laid George on the couch and let him sleep there for the night.

CHAPTER 3

DRAWING FIRST BLOOD

The week had finally come to an end, and it was time to go back home. The day was spent gathering their stuff together and cleaning the Club House. Johnnie knew what this day was going to bring. But no one said much about it as the nervousness began to grow more intense. He wanted the group to just stay relaxed but the tension was in the air.

Johnnie made some coffee for everyone. He began to cook breakfast for the group and the girls who stayed the night with Steve and the Two Brothers. By the time they all started to wake up, breakfast was just about done and Johnnie had just finished toasting all the bread. The bacon was sitting on paper towels as the grease was being absorbed from it. Scrambled eggs was just about done as they all sat down together at the table. The girls were impressed with Johnnie's ability to cook. They had never had anyone cook for them like this. Usually they were forced to do all the cooking and cleaning. It was nice to wake up and be able to sit and relax while someone else took care of them.

As the eggs were finished Johnnie motioned to the group to get up and serve their guest. It was the least they could do for them. After all, they had just used them to satisfy their own lust and pleasure. These girls, even though they were used for sex still needed to be treated decently. Johnnie hated all forms of abuse and these girls needed to feel as if they was like every other woman. He knew deep down inside they were hurting and this wasn't the life they hoped for. Whatever reason they were living this life style was none of his business but they were still women and deserved to be treated as such. Perhaps this was the only time someone would treat them as something other than a sex object or a piece of meat. Johnnie sat down and began to talk with the girls to make them feel as if they was a part of the group. They appreciated the way Johnnie made them feel at home even though he never touched any of them. It was nice to be treated like a lady by someone who didn't want sex from them. After breakfast they all took showers and the girls wanted to help out with cleaning the place up but Johnnie wouldn't let them. He felt they had done enough by pleasuring his friends. After the group had spent the rest of the morning together talking, Joe the Pimp finally rolled up around eleven to collect his girls. They had hoped he wouldn't show up for a while. They were enjoying the company of the group who made them feel like anything but hookers.

After they left, Johnnie began to talk to the group letting them know they would spend the rest of the day here and leave tonight to go back home. Nobody knew Johnnie had stayed in constant contact with his friend Jason while he was there. Jason knew everything that was going on and was helping Johnnie to work through the anxieties he was feeling, while encouraging him the best he could. Jason knew Johnnie had to go through with this, and there was no turning back now.

Every time Johnnie was able to sneak off for a few minutes, he and Jason would text. Jason was constantly telling Johnnie to hang in there and not show any signs of fear. He had to remain as a confident leader so his group could feel secure in his leadership. He knew Jason couldn't get directly involved but at the same time he knew his friend would be there for him. Being able to have Jason available to him did calm him a bit and gave him a little more assurance in this situation.

Jason had also talked with Ricky Mack about the group being there and he made it clear he wanted them to be taken care of. He was not about to let Ricky use Johnnie or his friends. He also made it clear things better be on the up and up. He felt Johnnie was his responsibility even though this was not his fight nor was it his war. But nevertheless,

Johnnie was his brother and he wasn't about to let anyone use him with wrong intentions.

Later that night two cars pulled up at the club house. Everyone had their bags packed and was ready to go. Auto and Killswitch came into the house to collect the group.

"Are you all ready to go?" Auto asked the group.

"Yeah we're ready" Cypher responded.

"Good, because its time."

They looked at each other for a moment as the situation became very real.

"Time to get this going finally," Steve said as he tried to get the rest of the group hyped.

"It's time for our first hit on The Hells Sinners," Killswitch responded.

"Let's do it then!" Darryl said.

He was ready to get this thing started as well. He had so much hate for The Hells Sinners, namely Wayne and Ricco.

"Bring all your stuff. You're not going to be coming back here. We do this hit and take you straight home," Auto explained as everyone grabbed their belongings.

"Sounds good to me, Steve added as he took up his bag of clothes and sleeping bag.

Killswitch took Steve and the Two Brothers with him in his car, while Cypher and George rode with Auto. This was just as Cypher and Ricky Mac had planned with the exception that Steve went with the Two Brothers instead. Darryl and Randy rode in the back seat with Steve up front in the passenger seat next to Killswitch as he drove. In the other car Cypher rode up front with Auto and George was in the back by himself.

This was it. The moment of truth, the moment when it all came down to whether or not they could really do it. Cypher knew he was ready, but he wasn't sure of the others. They never done anything like this before. They never killed anyone and he wasn't too sure they could. *How would they handle the moment? How would they handle it afterward? Would they freeze up or pull the trigger?* A sigh came from Cypher as he took in a deep breath.

They were getting closer and the tension was thick in each car. Everyone was nervous. *It's hard to control fear in a moment like this.* George was scared but didn't want to show it. They all were scared for that matter. The waiting was over. The talk was over.

Now it was time as both cars crept up the street with their headlights off. The windows were rolled down. Every gun was cocked and loaded. Steve was ready to inflict revenge on them for what they did to his sister.

Randy on the other hand felt sick to his stomach with fear as he struggled to keep his hand straight from shaking. He was shaking so bad he was afraid he might not even hit anyone. *That might not be a bad idea anyways. How did I get myself into this? Man, I am not a killer!*

As they slowly rolled up by the house Cypher and George let off the first shots followed by shots from Steve in the second car.

Randy's gun jammed on him as he tried to shoot. "My gun's jammed! My gun's jammed!" he yelled as he was looking around for someone to help him.

Darryl pulled him down into the seat and put his gun out the window and aimed it back at the house firing off three shots as they had just passed. Both cars sped off and headed for the expressway to go to Southbend Heights. Everyone was hyped up and scared at the same time. Cypher breathed a sigh of relief that the first time was finally over with for the group. Now they were on their way back to Cypher's where he would talk with them and see how they all were after this.

Finally being dropped off, the group went back to the camp area where they would be spending the night. Everybody needed time to calm down and get their heads right before going home. This was an intense time for the group and they needed to be able to talk about what had just happened. Cypher never got that chance to be reassured or comforted, so he wanted to make sure the group had time to express their feelings whether good or bad. Certainly there was some fears that needed to be discussed.

Cypher was confident no one would suspect them. This was a gang related hit on another gang and no one would know it was them who carried out the assault. Once they got settled in, Cypher built a fire and they set up their bedding and sat by the warm fire trying to gather their thoughts and process what had transpired.

Randy really struggled with it much more than the rest of the group while George felt more at ease now that it was over. At the time he felt sick and thought he might even puke, but now his nerves had calmed a bit, he started to feel much better. Randy on the other hand was having a hard time coming down from the excitement and the anxiety that came with it. His gun jamming on him freaked him out and he was now terrified to even try again.

"Johnnie do you think we will get caught?" Randy asked. The rest was also wondering the same thing.

"No we won't. We are doing it this way to cover us, so no one will suspect us. This is gang violence and we are not a part of any gang. They will be looking at all the rival gangs and not us. We ride under the cover of this gang and we shouldn't ever be looked at as suspects," he responded.

He was trying to ease everyone's mind. However, for the most part he was right. The way this was done, why would anyone suspect them?

"Yeah I agree, this was a smart move Johnnie. No one will ever think that it was us," Steve added, who was happy to finally inflict real damage to The Hells Sinners. Finally getting revenge for what they did to his sister felt pretty good and he was far from done.

"So what do we do now?" Darryl asked.

"We wait," said Johnnie.

"Wait for what?" George inquired.

"For the next hit. They will let us know when we go out again. Then we will split it up. The next hit will be their men, and not by us. We will keep switching it up," Cypher explained to the group.

"When will we know?" Randy asked.

"Well, they will get with me the night before and I will

have you all come over and we will go over the plan and get everything set," he furthered explained.

It took most of the night for the group to settle down enough before they were finally able to fall asleep. The sun came up and the morning was passing before the group finally woke up. It had been a long night and everyone was tired. The whole ordeal had left them exhausted. Each one gathered their stuff together and went home.

After everyone was gone, Cypher cleaned up the camp area and went inside to see his mother who had missed him and was waiting for him to return.

"Well hello there, Johnnie. How was your camping trip?" his mom asked as she hugged him. "I missed you. So happy you're home. I hope you plan on staying for a while. You seem to always be going somewhere."

Johnnie smiled at his mother before responding back to her. He knew he needed to chill for a bit so staying home sounded like a good idea.

"Yes Mother, I have no plans today, so we can spend some time together if you want. I don't feel like going anywhere today so I was thinking we could just talk. I know you miss me, and to be honest, I miss you too."

Johnnie made some toast to hold him over until lunch time. Sara was very happy her and Johnnie was going to be able to catch up. She felt as if she hadn't seen him in months. He had been so busy with his work and then being gone for a solid week made it seem like forever.

After Johnnie checked his messages, he made several phone calls to set everything up with his customers. He had a lot of extra jobs waiting for him on top of the usual jobs he needed to get back on. Everyone needed their lawns mowed and some needed their bushes trimmed again. It would be good for him, Randy and Darryl to get back to work and make some money as well as being able to focus on something else for a bit. There were plenty of jobs to keep the three busy for a while. There were quite a few maintenance jobs that needed to get done as well.

After returning all the calls and getting everything set for them to go back to work, Cypher called the Two Brothers to let them know they would be going back to work the following day. They were happy to have the day off to relax but at the same time, they were eager to get back to work and make some money.

They both loved doing lawn care which was great for Cypher. That allowed him to focus a little more on repairs and maintenance when those jobs came up. He knew he could trust the Two Brothers to do a good job and get things done even if he wasn't there to help them. They were very good at what they did, and they respected Cypher and never wanted to let him down. He was a good boss towards them and they appreciated that about him.

As the day went on, Johnnie and his mother Sara enjoyed watching old movies together. Some of these movies Johnnie hadn't seen since he was a kid. It all brought back some great memories for the both of them. Johnnie didn't remember much now about Mark, his father. Just some of the things he had taught him and the times they would all three sit together and watch a movie on a Friday night when Mark didn't have to work the next day.

As Johnnie got older he found it was getting harder to remember things about his Father. Mark had worked long, hard hours and wasn't there as much as he had wanted to be. Nevertheless, Johnnie stilled missed him. His father was his hero when he was growing up, right up until he died. One thing he would never forget was the words his father spoke to him and the times he taught him how to handle things. Johnnie could still hear his voice as they sat and talked. Some of the ways Johnnie had grown was from a direct result of the wisdom that his father had shared.

Lunch was nice. Everything had tasted so delicious and Johnnie enjoyed not having to be the one to cook. Later that evening, Johnnie helped his mom cook dinner. Fried chicken with mashed potatoes and corn was a favorite.

During dinner Johnnie thought about a truck he spotted he wanted to purchase when they were on their way home the day before. After having dinner with his mother, he stepped out for a few to go have a look at this truck. He had been saving up to get something for the business. He needed to be able to pick his guys up and drop them off. Plus it was time to start carrying his own tools if he ever planned on his business growing. After going and looking at the truck, Johnnie decided to go ahead and purchase it so he could pick up the Two Brothers in the morning.

***

Steve had gotten in late morning and took a shower after getting in. He had skipped breakfast and waited for lunch which wasn't far off. Tonya wasn't accustomed to the group doing things without her, and she had a lot of questions about their trip. Steve hated to lie to her but he knew he couldn't tell her what they had done. She had thought they had went on a camping trip. No one wanted her to know they went seeking revenge for what happened to her.

She was mostly interested in how Johnnie was doing. She missed him terribly. After her talk with Christina she was more open to start spending time with him and the group again. Since moving into the neighborhood this was the longest they had been away from each other. It was time to start trying to talk to him again. They had started too, but then she backed off and so he focused on his business.

Steve tried to direct the conversation as to keep from having to say too much about where they went or what they did. He began to instead keep Johnnie as the focus in hopes that would keep Tonya from asking more questions about the trip. As they sat and talked, Steve began to remind Tonya just how much Johnnie loved and missed her. He was sick without her and Steve knew it.

"You know he won't even talk to another girl? All he thinks about is you. You're still his everything Tonya. He feels lost without you. I watch him and I see how much he hurts."

Tonya began to cry as they sat together talking. "I know. But you just don't know how hard it is to see him after what has happened. We were so in love and was going to spend the rest of our lives together. He had to watch what they did to me Steve. I feel like every time he sees me, it's a constant memory of what happened. Don't you think that is more painful for him?"

"No, Tonya," Steve said shaking his head at her question. "Because he never forgets anyways. The only thing is, not only does he have that memory, but now he doesn't have you as well. That is even more painful for him. Not being able to have the woman he loves is the worst pain for him Tonya. He needs you. He loves you. You two can still have something beautiful. You still can have a great life together. If you would just try."

Tonya got up to walk away with tears streaming down her face. She turned back to Steve. "You don't understand. I love Johnnie more than anything. But right now I just can't. I hurt too. I miss him all the time. I miss what we had, what we once was. How could it ever be the same now?"

Steve got up and walked over to Tonya hugging her as she wept bitterly. "Listen to me, Tonya. Nothing in this world will ever take away the love that Johnnie has for you. You have no idea what he is willing to do for you. That boy will give his life for you, Tonya. Don't let them win. Don't let them take this away from you two. Don't let them destroy your love for each other. Just give it a chance. Let your love live again."

Drying her eyes she knew Steve was right but it was so hard. Tonya felt like no one understood the shame and humiliation she was put through. The pain of being raped by men she hated. She had to live with the fact they used her to hurt Johnnie in the worst way while taking from her the only gift she could have given to him. It was pure torture having the men she despised use her like a worthless piece of meat as they found pleasure in having sex with her. Knowing her enemies used her for their own pleasure was almost more then she could bare. There were times when she thought about committing suicide. It haunted her seeing their faces as they all took turns on her and seeing Johnnie struggle to get free to help her until he had no strength left. So many times she sat alone in her room and thought about killing herself. They took everything from her and she hated every single one of them. She had spent days trying to wash away the dirt she felt from them yet never feeling clean even after every shower. She still felt dirty and worthless. They had destroyed her life and it was all she could do most days to just stay alive. The thoughts of suicide was constant some days. There was no peace from the pain she constantly felt.

Steve saw it. He saw the change in her, the pain in her eyes. The hopelessness that had replaced what was once full of fun and excitement. She was now a girl who had been reduced to a helpless victim. Steve couldn't help but want revenge as much as Johnnie did. They were going to pay alright. It was their mission to kill every single one of them. There was no way Johnnie and Steve was going to stop till there was none of them left. Not a single one.

***

The next day it was time to get back to work for Johnnie. After picking up the Two Brothers in the new company truck, Johnnie dropped them off and went downtown to get insurance and plates for his truck. He put them on a big job so he would have time to get everything done before they finished. He had been saving up for a while, but this would greatly deplete what he had saved. He had inherited his father's tools, so at least that was something he didn't have to worry about. His father had every tool Johnnie needed to handle any job that would come up. Next on the list was a few good lawn mowers and a few weed whackers. Once he secured those items, his business would be self-sufficient and he would no longer have to use client's equipment any longer. Johnnie was excited about his new purchase and now felt more like he had a legitimate business.

It took Johnnie all morning to get everything squared away with his new vehicle. By the time he got finished with everything it was close to lunch time. *The Two Brothers should almost be done by now*. On his way back he decided to grab some lunch for everyone to save some time. When he returned back to the job-site the Two Brothers had just finished cleaning up the yard and the equipment they were using. They were waiting for him. Johnnie did a quick walk through to make sure they didn't leave any mess behind. For now, they were using a broom to clean off all the sidewalks and driveways but Johnnie was looking at getting a few blowers also. When Johnnie arrived he saw how great everything looked and knew Darryl and Randy had worked very hard. They always did such a great job. The grass was cut right, the bushes was trimmed properly, everything was cleaned up and looking very neat. It was having good workers like this that made Johnnie's business even better. He knew he could rely on them to get it done right every time, which took a lot of stress off when it came to the business.

Darryl and Randy was happy to see Johnnie when he pulled up. They were ready to go and was extremely happy he brought them lunch. They were hungry and ready to eat. It was a good morning for them all. They were able to get the biggest job of the day done and out of the way. Johnnie drove while they ate so they could get to the next job faster. He already ate his lunch on his way back to pick up the Two Brothers.

The next few jobs Johnnie had some small repairs to do while the Two Brothers would work on the lawn care. The back porch railing was very lose and needed to be fixed at old Mr. Richard's place. He was a good customer and always had nice cold water ready for the boys to drink when they got thirsty. It was an old place and Johnnie was doing repairs on something almost every week. The back yard was massive so he had time to fix things while Darryl and Randy worked on getting the lawn done. Randy was more detailed with his mowing and had an eye for detail so he always took the front yard. It was smaller so when he was finished he would go to the back and help his brother.

By the time they were done with the back, Johnnie had fixed the railings, swept off all the walkways and the driveway. Everything looked good as always and all the brothers had to do was clean off the mowers that belonged to Mr. Richards. While the Two Brothers were getting that done, Johnnie was talking to Mr.

Richard about his mowers. "Mr. Richards, may I ask you a question?"

"Sure Johnnie what is it?" Mr. Richards replied.

"Well, I was curious if you had ever considered selling those two mowers?"

"Well, I guess I never really have Johnnie. Are you interested in purchasing them?" Mr. Richards responded.

Johnnie looked back at the two mowers. "Well, Mr. Richards, I could use a few mowers of my own and these are in great shape. I would pay you a very good price if you would consider selling them to me." "Hmm. Yes it could be possible I suppose. What would you offer?"

"Well let's see. I haven't really thought about it until just now to be honest. How does five hundred a piece sound? I know they are quite expensive when you buy them new. These are very good mowers and have been taken care of." Johnnie said.

"Yes, well they haven't had much use on them to be honest. So you would offer a thousand dollars for the pair?"

"Yes sir, I would."

"Well, how soon would you want to buy them?"

"I need to buy a trailer first. How about next month?"

"Yes, okay Johnnie. You have yourself a deal."

"Great Mr. Richards! Thank you very much." Johnnie said as he shook his hand.

"You're welcome Johnnie. You boys have a good day and make sure you all grab a bottle of water to take with you. I sat them on the front porch for you."

They thanked Mr. Richards for the ice cold bottles of water and headed out to the next job. Having the two biggest jobs done, Johnnie wanted to knock off a few of the smaller ones before calling it a day. He had one more repair that needed to get done so that job was next on the list. He needed to replace a few boards on the privacy fence and replace one of the stones on the walkway in the back yard that was leading up to the back door patio area. The Two Brothers had a lot of bushes to trim so they would be busy for a bit while he did the repairs. Darryl worked on trimming the bushes and hedges while Randy did all the mowing. Every place they went to was so beautiful. The landscaping was breath taking at these homes. After Johnnie fixed the fence he started on digging up the broken stone from the walkway and replaced it. About the time Johnnie was done, the Two Brothers had everything finished and was ready to go to the last job for the day. It was an easy mow job with just a little bit of trimming. This time Randy did the trimming and let Darryl do the mowing. While they were working on the yard Johnnie was going over all the invoices from the day. Everything looked good and he was very well pleased with today's accomplishments. As soon as the boys were done they could go home for the day. Johnnie went behind them and got all the clean-up done so when they were finished, they could just go home.

   After dropping Darryl and Randy off at their house, Johnnie was ready for a nice cool shower and some dinner. So much was accomplished today he finally had something to feel good about. Plus it was nice to be back to work and get his mind off of the war they were in.

   He could tell Randy was really struggling with this. He was waiting to see if Randy was going to come to him and talk about it, but if he didn't soon, Johnnie was going to go to him. It was important that Johnnie knew where everyone was at about this war. He needed to know if Randy could handle this or if he needed to back out. One thing Johnnie knew for sure, they couldn't have anyone out there who wasn't all the way in and wasn't sure about this. Keeping everyone close was going to be hard. He knew there would be struggles. Of course they would have doubts or regrets. They weren't murders. They were just young men trying to end a life-long feud they never wanted nor asked for. Earlier the next morning, Johnnie got up, had breakfast then was off to work after picking up the Two Brothers.

***

While everyone was busy, Tonya went to be alone at the water back behind the camp. She had a lot to think about concerning her and Johnnie. She never stopped loving him and to be away from him was killing her. Every day she was hurting to be with him. She was tired of being apart from the man she loved. Everyone had been telling her just how much Johnnie loved her and was missing her. She felt depressed and alone as she sat by the water trying to figure out what she should do. She wanted revenge for what they had done to them and what they had done to their relationship. She hated them. So much anger was swelling up inside her. The hurt and the pain was constant. How she longed for Johnnie to come and put his arms around her and comfort her.

Tears fell from her eyes as she sat by the edge of the water crying. *I have pushed him away. How am I ever going to fix this?* It was so quiet. Only the sound of the running water could be heard as she sat remembering all the times they spent back here swimming, playing, and chasing each other around. She hadn't been with the group in a while and missed everyone. She felt alone and afraid wondering if her and Johnnie could ever get passed this. She wasn't even sure if she could but she was starting to want to try.

After wiping the tears from her eyes, she got up and walked back through the woods. She took her time as she remembered all the things they used to do back here and what she has missed doing. Finally reaching the edge of the woods, she sat for a minute and just relaxed where she and Johnnie used to sit together taking a deep breath as she took in the beauty of everything that was around her. This place was so breathtaking. It was such a beautiful and peaceful place to sit and think while relaxing. It had been a while since she was here. It was good to be back even if she was alone. After sitting for some time, Tonya finally gathered herself and walked back home. Walking up to the house Tonya found Steve sitting on the porch.

"Are you okay, Sis?" Steve asked being surprised to see her out walking around.

"Yeah I'm fine. Just was out at the camp back by the water sitting and thinking is all."

"What was you thinking about? Johnnie? You know this is hard for him too, Tonya," Steve said in hopes she would understand he was also carrying this burden.

"Yes, Steve, I know. I think about him all the time. I do still love him. I wish so badly to get revenge on them. I am surprised Johnnie didn't go after them. Even though I know it would be suicide to do so."

"Well actually Sis, he is." Steve responded.

"What do you mean he is? Tell me what is going on," Tonya said as she raised her voice a bit.

"Shh. Relax Sis and keep your voice down," Steve said as he looked around to make sure no one heard her before continuing.

"Okay listen. When Johnnie was in Juvenile Prison you know Wayne and some of them was in there too."

"Yes," Tonya answered.

"Okay. Well, Johnnie made some friends with a rival gang of the Hells Sinners. Anyways, when he took off for a while and no one knew where he went, he was with them working on building an alliance with them and us to go to war with the Hells Sinners," Steve explained as he tried to keep their voices down so no one would hear them.

"Steve, you can't be serious? Don't tell me Johnnie is actually going to do this?" Tonya asked.

"Keep your voice down. Yes he is and already has. There was no way he was going to let them get away with this. He won't stop now until they are all dead. You don't understand what this has done to him."

"Are you saying he has already gone after them?"

"Yes, Sis and us with him." Tonya looked intently at Steve with a shocked look on her face.

"You mean to tell me that you went with him?" Tonya asked very nervously.

"Yes I did and I will continue to go until this is done. I wanted revenge on them too Sis for what they did to you. Did you think we were going to let them get away with this? We are all involved. All of us George, Randy and Darryl too," Steve told her as she sat there in tears not knowing what to think.

"Are you guy's crazy? You could all get killed!" Tonya said as she pleaded with him to stop.

"It's too late now Sis. We have already hit them and we will continue to hit them until there is none of them left. No more defending ourselves against them. This time we are going after them. This time it's about revenge. We can't turn back now."

"Listen to me, Steve. You all can't keep on with this. People are going to die!"

"You don't understand Tonya, people are already dead."

"Steve, please talk to Johnnie. Make him stop!"

"No Sis. He won't stop! Not until they have paid for what they did to you."

"Then I will go and talk to him."

"Don't bother, Sis. You don't know how much hurt and pain is driving Johnnie. How much anger and rage is inside him now. I promise you Sis, he won't stop until they are wiped off the face of the Earth."

Tonya was scared for her brother and Johnnie as well as the rest of the group. But there was a sense of honor she felt from being avenged by the man she loved. A part of her couldn't help feeling the love Johnnie had for her. He was still her hero, her knight in shining armor who had rose up to defend her. How could she not love him knowing he was risking his life to make sure they would never hurt her again? Since this happened she finally saw the evidence that Johnnie's love for her would never fade. He truly loved her and she knew it. This was going to be harder for her now because she still wasn't ready for her and Johnnie to be back together yet. But she knew in her heart she wanted to try.

Somehow just knowing what Johnnie was doing changed some things. But she was far from being able to be with any one at this point. There was a lot of healing that needed to take place in hers and Johnnie's life before they could try to be together again.

***

It had been another long day for Johnnie and his crew. Work had piled up but they were getting a lot of work done. Randy and Darryl where now doing most of the mowing so Johnnie could get repairs done and focus on trimming trees and hedges. The mowers Johnnie had purchased were going to make things so much easier for them.

After dropping off the Two Brothers Johnnie went home and got cleaned up before checking his messages. Tonya had left a message asking if they could get together and talk for a bit. This always excited Johnnie even though he constantly tried not to get his hopes up. Nevertheless, he could not wait to see her. Once he finished his late dinner he gave her a call to see when she wanted to get together. He was happy when she said she was ready now if he was free to sit and talk. Happily agreeing he went back to the camp area to wait for her and to get a small fire going while he waited. Johnnie couldn't help but to smile big as he saw Tonya coming across the backyard lawn as she walked towards where he was sitting.

Before speaking, Tonya took a deep breath as she sat down next to him. "Johnnie," she said as she felt his hand taking hers, "Steve told me about you all joining up with some gang to go after Wayne and them."

Surprised at her words Johnnie looked at her very intently. He responded with a sigh of frustration, "He told you huh? I didn't want you to know."

"Yes I know Johnnie, but he is my brother. Listen to me

Johnnie, I don't want you or anyone else to get hurt."

Gripping her hand as they talked, Johnnie answered, "It's too late for that now. We can't turn back. This war has already started and has to be finished."

Tonya being very grieved at Johnnie's answer began to try to talk some sense into him. "They will do whatever you do. If you go then they will go. If you stop, then they will stop. But they will follow you Johnnie no matter what you decide to do. I know you and Steve want to finish this, but George, Randy and Darryl don't need to be involved in this. If you tell them to stay out of it, they will."

"Tonya, they made their own decisions to go through with this. I kept giving them a way out and none of them would take it. They want to finish this once and for all." Johnnie lovingly looking into her eyes as he spoke to her. "You knew I wasn't going to let this go. You knew I would go after them for doing this to us. I won't stop Tonya until they all pay with their lives. I want blood for what they have done to us. And I will get it. They will pay for this, every last one of them."

"Johnnie please listen. I don't want you to get hurt or even die. Or what if you go to prison for the rest of your life? Then what Johnnie?"

"I thought about all of this. The police will never suspect us anyways. This is a gang war. No one even knows we are involved in this. Besides, with the help of my friends we can take them out for good and never have to worry about them again."

Tonya feeling so sad about all of this wiped the tears from her eyes as she continued to try to convince Johnnie to let it be. "I hate them too Johnnie, but it isn't worth all of the killing and all of the risk you are taking."

"I will not turn back Tonya. This has got to finally end. They went too far with what they did to us and now I have no choice but to take it further and finish them all off."

"Please Johnnie, just let it go. I am begging you. Don't go on with this."

"I have to. They saw to it that I would have to do this.

They knew I would come after them for what they did and now it's time to get even with them." Johnnie pulled Tonya to her feet and held her. "When this is all over with then things will be different, I promise. I love you so much Tonya but I have to do this. I just have to. I love you too much to let it go."

"Okay Johnnie. I do understand and I love you too. But please Honey, please be careful. I want to try to slowly start seeing you again but I have to be honest, I still need a lot of time. I'm just not ready yet but I know I love you."

Johnnie was holding her tight in his arms. He held her so close to him they could feel each other's breath. "Take all the time you need. I will wait for you. I love you Tonya."

She pulled away from him. She knew he was tired and in need of rest. "I better go Johnnie." She kissed his cheek and went to walk off. Johnnie pulled her back to him and kissed her soft lips for the first time in what seemed like forever.

"I love you, too, Tonya. Stay in touch please. I need you."

She shook her head yes as they kissed again. "Yes, Darling, I will. I need you too. Just be patient. I need time. But I really do still love you."

Johnnie gave her one last hug before letting her go as he walked her home. He held her hand all the way to her house, then kissed her one more time before she went inside.

"Goodnight, Johnnie."

"Goodnight, Tonya," he responded as he watched her disappear into her house.

***

The next day as Johnnie awoke, he was feeling uneasy about Steve telling Tonya about the war. He understood it but it just didn't make him feel good. After getting his clothes together he jumped in the shower as he tried to shake that feeling off. *Things have to be settled. I wish there was another way but there isn't.* Johnnie stood under the water as it was running over him while he was trying to clear his mind and get ready for his day. *Things always turn out this way. Every time I try to get somewhere in my life I have to deal with people who just won't go away unless I make them go away. My father was a great man, he became the best construction worker in this city. He was so well respected and loved by everyone. He was always helping people. That's all I ever wanted to do is be like him. But these people keep pressing me. They make me have to do this. I didn't ask for any of this. But like always I have to end it.*

   Feeling frustrated with his thoughts as he got out of the shower Johnnie got dressed and went down to cook some breakfast for him and his mother who was still sleeping. That isn't like her, I better go check on her before I get breakfast going. Johnnie slowly opened the door and quietly walked in to check on his mother who was still sound asleep. Being concerned, he walked over to her bed that she was laying on with the sheet only halfway pulled up. Johnnie gently shook her a bit as he sat down on the bed next to her.

   "Mom it's past your usual time to wake up. Are you okay?" Johnnie asked her as she slowly opened her eyes trying to focus on what he was saying.

   "What time is it Johnnie?"

   "It's seven Mom. Are you feeling okay?"

   Sara sat up and wiped the sleep from her eyes while trying to gather herself together.

   "Yes, I am okay Son. Just really tired this morning."

   "Okay, Mom. Well, I am going to fix some breakfast. Do you want me to make you something or do you want to sleep some more?"

   "No, I am getting up. I feel hungry this morning."

   "Okay, well, I'll make us some breakfast. Just come down when you're ready."

   "Johnnie are you working today?"

   "Yes Mom. I have to pick up Randy and Darryl at eight. I don't know when we will be home, we have a lot to do today."

"Okay. I will be down in a few."

"See you when you come down."

Johnnie got up and walked out of the room to head downstairs. He began to wonder if maybe he should just stay home as he was making some coffee. *It's going to be one of those days, I can feel it.* By the time Sara finally came down, Johnnie had everything already done and waiting for her. She sat down at the table and took a drink of her coffee.

"Mom, are you sure you're okay?" Johnnie asked as he was finishing his breakfast."

"Yes, I'm okay, Johnnie. This tastes really good Son. Thank you for making breakfast this morning."

"Do you want me to stay home today?"

"As much as I would love that Johnnie I know you have lots to do today."

"Okay, well, I need to finish getting ready then so I can go pick them two up and get this day started. Do you want me to clean this up before I go?"

"No, Johnnie. I will take care of that. You have enough to do today. It was really nice of you to cook breakfast for us. Be safe today and make sure you have enough water with you."

"I will Mom, and you try and take it easy today. You look rough this morning."

"I will be fine Johnnie."

"Well, I will have my cell on if you need me."

"Okay, thank you."

"I will see you later, Mom. I love you."

"I love you too, Johnnie. See you when you get home."

Randy and Darryl were outside waiting for him when he pulled up. They were ready to go as they hopped into the truck. Everyone was geared up for the day. It was the half way mark of the week and they were all itching for the weekend to hurry up and get here.

Although it was a big distraction from the war they were fighting, they felt like they needed some down time. The group new this was going to be the hardest thing they had ever done in their lives but they had no idea how much it was going to put a strain on them mentally. They felt scared about getting caught even though Johnnie assured them that was not going to happen. They we're not a part of the gang war as far as anyone was concerned and the police didn't even know who they were. Johnnie was a bit afraid as well but he had to always look confident in front of the group. He had to remain positive about things to keep them from being too overwhelmed. He could tell Randy was really struggling with everything that had transpired and as soon as he could get alone with him and talk, the better. But for now it was time to put in some work and get things done.

   It was a nice day out as they were working hard to get as much done as they could throughout the day. The houses they went to had smaller lawns and didn't take as long so they were able to get more jobs done. Johnnie was happy they did the bigger jobs first so the rest of the week would be much easier. Only a few more small repairs on the list so he could help out more with the lawn care.

   Johnnie kept a close eye on Randy as they worked together. He could see the struggle within him but they all had that struggle, only Randy's was more evident. Darryl seemed to be holding it together pretty good but he was always the tougher one out of the two. Randy, however, was a bit milder in his personality and things bothered him much more easily. He knew he would have to find some time to get alone with Randy and see how he really was doing. He needed to know if he could handle this. It could be disastrous if any of them cracked. He needed to get with George as well. They hadn't really talked either since they made their first hit. Johnnie was so busy with work he hadn't had much time to talk to anyone except for Tonya and the Two Brothers but he worked with them and saw them every day.

   The next few jobs were easy that they could blow right through. Miss Langly had a nice yard with no trees or bushes. Mr. Stevens had a small front yard but a big back yard but very little things to mow around. After finishing the next two jobs, Johnnie took them and stopped at the park on the way home so he could have a talk.

"Why are we stopping here Johnnie?" Darryl asked as Johnnie parked the truck.

"We need to talk," Johnnie responded as he was trying to figure out the best way to approach this.

"What's up Johnnie?" asked Randy.

"I need to know how you two are doing after this. I want you both to speak openly and just be honest with me."

"I'm okay, Johnnie. I mean yeah, it does bother me but they had it coming right? I mean it's not like we killed innocent people you know. These people spend their lives hurting other people," Darryl said as Randy remained quiet.

"What about you Randy?"

Randy took a long drawn out sigh before responding to Johnnie's question. "To be honest, I don't think I can do it again. I can't get it out of my mind, Johnnie. I think about it all the time. Especially when I try to go to sleep. I'm scared. I am afraid we are going to get caught and go to jail. I see things when I close my eyes Johnnie. I see people getting shot. I see them falling. I see them dying. I see them laying there in pools of blood. I keep thinking about my gun jamming and wonder what if it happens again and I get shot while trying to fix it."

Johnnie knew there was issues stemming from this with Randy.

"I get that brother. I knew this was messing with you. I understand. You have to pull yourself together. You can't let this break you."

"I know Johnnie but I can't. I keep trying and trying but I can't. I just need to get out of this."

"Okay, Randy. You're done. From here on out you stay back at the camp and wait for us. I can't have you out there like this. It's too hard for you. I know you tried and that means a lot to me. But this isn't easy for any of us and it's not even who we are. If you need to back out then I understand. I wish I didn't have to do this either my brother, but they have left me no choice. Everything will be okay Randy. Just take it easy and try not to think about it anymore."

Feeling bad for Randy, Johnnie knew he couldn't take him with them on the next run.

"What about you Darryl? Are you still in or do you need out also?"

"Man forget that. I am sick and tired of these punks, the crap they keep doing to us and putting us through. I don't care anymore to be honest. I am in till the end. If you want to stay behind Randy then that's fine, but you keep your mouth shut about it. I'm going Johnnie."

"Okay then. At least I know where we all stand. I can handle that. I knew not all of us would be able to handle it. To be honest, I don't even know where George is at either. I still need to talk to him as well."

"As much as George hates Wayne, I doubt he is losing any sleep over this," Darryl said as Johnnie drove off to take them home.

Johnnie felt relieved he finally had the talk with Randy. Now maybe Randy could relax a bit knowing he isn't going with them anymore. He also felt a little more relaxed knowing Randy wasn't going with them. He really hoped Darryl would have said the same thing, but Darryl had a more heated temper and liked to fight. George was next on the list and he was going to contact him when he got home. Of course, they were all scared. They understood what would happen if they all got caught. The risk was great. Every time they go out they risked getting caught or even killed.

After getting home from dropping the Two Brothers off, Johnnie hurried and got a quick shower. By the time he was done getting cleaned up Sara had dinner on the table. She was happy Johnnie was home early enough for them to sit and have dinner together. She hated always eating alone and was extremely happy Johnnie would be home for dinner tonight. Johnnie was surprised when he came downstairs and saw dinner on the table and his mom waiting.

"Wow, Mom. Thank you. It's nice not to have to get home and rush to get cleaned up and then reheat leftovers." Johnnie said as he sat down and ate.

Afterwards as Sara cleaned up the dishes Johnnie called George to see if he could come by for a few minutes. George was glad Johnnie called. He felt they needed to talk as well. George hadn't heard from anyone but Steve. Steve told him he hadn't heard anything from anyone else either. Once George arrived they went out back to talk where Sara couldn't hear them.

"I'm happy you were able to come over George. I feel like we need to talk about what happened and I need to know how you feel about it."

"Well, I mean, I feel alright I guess. I am a little scared about getting caught, and to be honest I will be very happy when this is all over with. How is everyone else taking it?"

"Well, Randy won't be going out with us again. It's just too hard for him. You know Darryl, there is no quit in him once he gets started. What I need to know is whether or not you can handle this or do you need to back out as well?"

"I hate doing this, but I won't back out. I can handle it. I just hate killing people Johnnie but I am with you on this. We have to end this and I don't see any other way."

"I don't either. I struggle with it also George. But one thing we all agree on is that we are tired of this. We all say the same thing and believe the same thing. I will be happy when this is all over."

After their talk George and Johnnie felt better. It was good to know where they all were at and how they felt. Johnnie would touch basis with Steve the following day, but for now he was going to relax and try to enjoy the rest of the night.

Early the next morning it was back to the grind as the week was starting to wind down. Just a few more days and the weekend would be here. It was a nice sunny day out and looked as if it was going to be extremely hot. Johnnie got himself together and headed out a bit early so he could stop and get some ice and water for the cooler. It was so nice having his own truck now.

While at the gas station getting water and ice he grabbed some donuts for breakfast and a hot coffee. Sara didn't get a chance to see Johnnie this morning. She was a bit worried as he never left without having breakfast and saying goodbye to her. But Johnnie was in a mood today to get as much work done as he could so they could get off early on Friday. Saturday he was going to go look at some trailers to haul his lawnmowers on. If it hadn't been for all the tools his father left him he wouldn't be able to purchase these other things that he needed.

As Johnnie was pulling up to pick up the Two Brothers he received a text from Ricky Mac. Johnnie pretty much knew what that meant. He checked it and responded while he was waiting for Randy and Darryl to come out. All Ricky said was for Johnnie to call him on Saturday. Johnnie replied *OK*.

After his response to Ricky he began to go over the work orders for today's work load. There was a lot of small jobs but some driving was involved. They had a few jobs that weren't close so Johnnie wanted to get them in before lunch and have all close jobs for the rest of the day.

Finally the Two Brothers came out and got into the truck. Johnnie was happy to be off, going on down the road to get these far away jobs done, which gave him some extra time to finish his coffee. He didn't much care for these long drives first thing in the morning. It made it a lot harder to get motivated.

Driving always made him feel a bit lazy. But these where new jobs he was able to pick up now that he had a truck. This was their first time out there to these two places. Once they were done though, then they could get lunch in and breeze through the rest of the day.

It was really heating up as they were working hard to get these two jobs done. The first was now finished and the second wasn't far from it, and they were definitely getting hungry. Johnnie noticed a small Deli on the way out there they could hit on the way back. After finishing up, they got everything cleaned up and put back then was off to get some food. It was a bit of a drive before they came back across the Deli. They had never ate here but as hungry as they were, they didn't really care where they stopped to eat.

    Johnnie was reminded of the restaurant his mother used to take him to as he walked inside and sat down at one of the tables with Randy and Darryl. The menu looked pretty good. Breakfast was served any time, and that was very appealing to Randy who had his eyes set on pancakes and sausage. Johnnie got the usual cheeseburger with a side order of fries while Darryl ordered chicken strips basket with barbeque sauce and fries. The service was pretty good and the food came out fast and hot. The waitress kept up on their drinks so Johnnie was going to make sure she got a real good tip.

    After lunch they headed back into town to finish up the smaller jobs. They were all in the same area so they could run through these quickly and hopefully be home before five. They were halfway through the day and looking forward to getting tomorrow done as well. If they got all of these done today then all they would have for tomorrow is one big job and two small ones, so they was all pushing to get these jobs done. Getting out early on Friday was the goal they wanted to reach.

    The cold water Johnnie brought came in handy as the sky was a nice clear blue with no clouds at all in sight. But that meant the sun was beating down on them as they were working hard to try and get everything done. By the end of the work day they were all beat and wore out. The hot sun had taken its toll on them and they were ready to go home.

    It was late evening before Johnnie dropped them off before getting home himself. He was happy they did get everything done like they wanted to. It took a little longer than he had hoped but at least it was done. After finally getting home and taking a quick shower he heated up some food his mom had left. Barely even wanting to talk he sat and ate his food before going off to bed. Sara hated it when

Johnnie was too tired to talk. She had spent a lot of her days alone and always looked forward to his company.

After a hard nights' sleep, Johnnie was up and ready to go at it again. He loved Fridays. He always made sure they had an easy work day and could get off early. After getting himself together, he was on his way downstairs to the kitchen to cook. Sara was starting to get used to Johnnie making breakfast in the mornings. She remembered when he was younger and would make the toast and set the table, now he was making breakfast too. Most mornings all she had to do was sit down and eat.

Johnnie loved to cook though and breakfast was his specialty. It was the only meals he ever really cooked. The rest of the day he was gone working. He would stop somewhere, grab some food and his mother always made extra for dinner. He would just heat up leftovers when he got home.

After breakfast Johnnie finished getting ready. He was on his way to grab the Two Brothers and get this day started. They were ready to go when he got there. They piled in the truck and headed off to get it all done. It was going to be another hot day so Johnnie stopped off and grabbed some more ice and waters for them.

"Easy day today," he said to them as they were all hyped up about the weekend.

"Yeah I like the sound of that Boss," Darryl said as they rode to the first job.

"This first job is going to take a while though, but only a few small jobs after lunch, then we are done," Johnnie explained as they came to the first job.

The Two Brothers were happy to know this was most of the work for today and once they got this job done then the rest was all downhill. Lunch came fast and the first job was finally done. They were ready to eat, sit down and relax for a minute.

Johnnie didn't say anything about the text he got from Ricky the other day. He wanted to see what he had to say first. After lunch they went and finished the last two small jobs and was done for the day. Wasting no time, Johnnie got them all home as quickly as he could so they could get cleaned up and meet afterwards with the rest of the group. Before he was going to make any plans, he was going to sit with his mother for a bit and spend some time with her.

After a little while he contacted everyone to come on down but he made sure Steve got there before the others so they could talk for a minute before the rest showed up. Once Steve got there, him and Johnnie headed back to the camp area, sat on the logs and discussed the situation. Johnnie had made Steve aware of the situation with Randy and how it was effecting him and that he wasn't going to be coming along any more. Steve understood that. It was hard for all of them. He also discussed with Steve about the conversation he had had with his sister about the war. Steve explained everything to Johnnie who was very understanding. He just didn't want Tonya to be mad at any of them for going to war. Steve reassured Johnnie she wasn't. She was just scared something bad would happen to them and Johnnie understood that. Shortly after they finished their talk, the rest of the group showed up and was talking about various things throughout the rest of the night.

Tonya had remained home. She still wasn't ready to reinsert herself into the group. With the exception of Johnnie, she was like a sister to all of them. They all loved her and missed her very much. It was sad not having her there as they felt her absence. It just didn't seem right with her not being there, especially with Ann coming with George. Ann tried to get Tonya to come but she just wasn't ready to do so. Things didn't feel the same for the group. Things felt a bit eerie for them and it was hard for them to shake it off. Johnnie did his best to keep things as fun as he could, but it had little effect on the group as the night came to a close.

It was Saturday morning and Johnnie was barely out of bed when his phone rang. It was Ricky calling him. Johnnie knew it had to be serious for him to be calling this early.

"Hello Ricky, what's up?" Johnnie said as he answered the phone.

"I need your group Monday night for a hit. It will be fast you know, since you all know what do to now. Will you guys be there?"

"Yeah man, we will be there. Well, all but Randy. He won't be coming with us anymore. It was too hard for him. I'd rather leave him behind if it's going to be a struggle for him."

"Yeah that's not good. Situations like that you need to handle."

"I did handle it. He stays back." Ricky wasn't very happy about this at all.

"Yeah, whatever. Meet us at the club house with whoever you're bringing."

"I will be there."

Ricky was not in a good mood by the end of the conversation and didn't even say bye when he hung up. *This isn't how I wanted to start my day.* After the phone call he went to take a quick shower and get some breakfast before he dealt with anyone else. *For now, everything else can just wait.*

After getting all cleaned up and having breakfast with his mom, Johnnie went out back to do some thinking before contacting the rest of the group. Rather than get right into it he decided to take the morning for himself and get with everyone after lunch. It was such a nice morning and this time to relax was just what he needed. It was a good time to just sit, breath and gather all of his thoughts together.

There was plenty to think about and now Ricky was also on his mind over the Randy situation. This was an aggravation he didn't need right now with everything else going on. Work was always a priority as well as Tonya. The war was always a pressing issue he often thought about and the group as well. Trying to keep everything together was becoming much harder for Johnnie. He knew all of this wasn't going to be easy but the stress was finally starting to get to him. He often wondered if bringing this whole thing up to the group was even a good idea at all. But he knew if they had found out they would have been very angry with him for not bringing them in. *Nevertheless it is what it is and I can't change anything now, all I can do is walk through each step of this.*

At least things with Tonya are starting to look promising and work is going pretty good. But I can't help but keep feeling like I need a vacation. All of this is really wearing me down mentally. I am starting to feel tired but there is no way I can take off right now. In fact, it's going to be a long time before I am going to be able to get away again. Johnnie laid his head back and just took in the fresh air as he was breathing. The outdoors sounds of the birds and other small animals scurrying about was somewhat soothing as he just laid back and listened with his eyes closed while relaxing.

As the morning slipped away and noon approached, Sara was busy in the kitchen making lunch while Johnnie was out back relaxing. She could always tell when he was stressed and she knew he needed to be left alone for a bit. It was hard watching her son go through everything he had to deal with. She wanted to protect him and keep him secure but that was never the case. Johnnie handled his own problems and rarely asked for any help. She knew he had to work things out for himself so she just gave him the space she knew he needed.

After everything was ready, Sara made them a plate of food and brought it out to Johnnie as she sat outside and ate with him. It was so nice outside and Johnnie was already out there so it was a good time to just sit and enjoy their food together.

"Thank you Mom. I must have dozed off for a bit."

"It's okay Son, I know you're tired."

"Everything looks so good Mom. You're always such a great cook."

"Thank you, Johnnie," Sara said smiling as big as she could.

After they finished, Sara was cleaning up and Johnnie went

inside to make some phone calls to get the group assembled together back at the camp. He walked back and waited for them to show up while making a fire. George came right over but the rest was a bit longer before they all started trickling through. George and Johnnie hadn't talked much these days. It was good he came over before everyone else. Johnnie was working most of the time and George was with Ann as much as he could be which didn't leave much time for them to just hangout like they used to. It was good to sit back and just talk while they waited.

When everyone came, Johnnie told them about Monday and made sure everyone was ready and that no one else wanted out before he made any further plans to go forward with this as a group. Johnnie was very well prepared to go alone if need be. But everyone else was also ready to go as well, all except Randy who was going to stay back at the camp and wait.

Johnnie didn't tell them Ricky wasn't happy about Randy not coming along. He felt it was better to keep that to himself. He didn't want any more problems and was hoping Ricky would just let it go and keep his mouth shut about it when they went on Monday to join up with them. But that was Monday's problem. Right now he needed to concentrate on his group and not worry about Ricky and his attitude problem. He had given thought about calling Jason and talking to him about it, but he didn't want to make the issue any bigger then what it was. Jason had a way of taking up for Johnnie and he didn't want to make any more waves then necessary.

The rest of the afternoon they talked about random stuff and had fun laughing and telling jokes. As evening approached they went home and Johnnie went in to help his mom cook dinner and relax for the rest of the night.

Sunday came and went with very little of anything happening outside of the usually routine. It was just a chill day for everyone. Sunday was usually a recharge day where everyone just kind of chilled and relaxed while getting some much needed rest. The only real highlight to this day for Johnnie was Tonya had called him and they talked on the phone for a bit. This made Johnnie feel very good as it continued to give him hope things would continue to go in the right direction. It was always nice to hear her sweet, soothing voice. Nothing made Johnnie feel better than being able to spend time with Tonya even if it was just a phone call. At least he got to talk to her and for now, that was good enough. He knew this was going to take a very long time but as long as she was making efforts, he could handle it. His heart still ached for her and hearing her voice calmed his heart as they talked. He still needed her and wasn't about to give up the one thing that kept him going, his love for her. Nothing hurt more than having to be away from her, which continued to fuel his hatred for Wayne and The Hells Sinners every time he thought about it.

   After a quiet evening, Johnnie went to bed and laid there for a bit thinking about his conversation with Tonya. He replayed her voice in his head before finally falling asleep. Tomorrow it was back to the grind with work and war. It was good to have one day with nothing to worry about and some time with Tonya before having to get back at all the other stuff that was awaiting him on Monday. But for now, it was time to sleep.

CHAPTER 4

NO TURNING BACK

    It was early Monday morning when Johnnie's alarm went off. It was time to get up and get ready for work. Another week had passed and a new week was beginning. He knew he was going to have to work hard today to get out early enough to get dinner, get cleaned up and then meet up with The West Dragons. *Hopefully, this will put me a little closer to ending this war.*

    The schedule was pretty heavy but everything was real close together so maybe they could catch a break and get it all done a little early. Johnnie hated crunching things in. Everything seemed to be so stressful all the time. *For once why can't things just run smooth and work out the way they are supposed to? They pick my hardest day of the week to want to do a hit.*

    Johnnie stacked Mondays so the rest of the week would be easier. He was at a point where things were going to really start frustrating him. His whole life Wayne had been a problem and he still was, and Johnnie couldn't wait to catch him. He didn't want to hit Wayne on a drive-by. Johnnie wanted to get him alone and fight to the death. He wanted Wayne to die by his bare hands. It all started with him. He was the reason for all of this. It would be so poetic to get Wayne last and make him pay after watching all of his friends die. That would be exactly what he would deserve. *I wish I could make that happen.*

    Johnnie started making breakfast. Time will tell how this is going to play out, but there was other factors involved as well that no one knew about. After breakfast he was well on his way to pick up the crew. Trying to stay focused on work today seemed to be a struggle for all of them. He had considered just ending the day and taking them home but things needed to get done and they needed to refocus and get it done.

    Johnnie rarely had to push these guys but today was different and he sure understood. The sun was beating down on them all day which was making it even worse. It felt as if it was the hottest day of the year. It wasn't so bad on the mowers but once you got off it was another story. They were all hot and irritated with this day as it went on. All they wanted to do was get it done, go home and handle their business with the Hells Sinners or soon to be dead bodies. There was no real set limit to the day's work load. Mondays was just go as far as they could before it got too dark to work but obviously that wasn't the case for this Monday. Johnnie knew when to shut it down. Just a few more jobs off the list and he was taking them home. It was definitely time to put an end to this hot, miserable day, go home and relax. They had to get mentally prepared to go out later on to make their hit.

    After getting home Johnnie got a nice cool shower to help bring his body temperature down and then dinner. After that, it was about time to get everyone assembled together. He made the call and they came. Randy came as well but he wasn't going to go out with them. He was just going to wait back at the camp by himself.

    It wasn't long after when two cars pulled up and picked them up. Johnnie was unusually irritated this evening. This time things would be a little different, no going to the club house, just straight to The Hells Sinners and then right back home. They were hoping for a clean sweep without anyone being able to follow them. This was the third hit. Johnnie and his group wasn't involved in the second hit and was happy not to be. That was the deal. They would alternate for now. But at some point they were going to send the whole gang for a huge all out gun fight. Ricky was putting it together. But Johnnie was not good with that and would later decline the idea altogether. In the mean time they would keep doing drive-bys every week on different days. It was so random that no one could predict when it was coming.

Randy was back at the camp feeling guilty about not being with them for this hit. He knew he should have been there and was feeling ashamed for staying behind. For the first time in his life, he was embarrassed at his lack of participation.

Everyone was quiet as they rode across town to go into Westbend. Auto was making small talk but the rest of the group was only talking when spoken to. They weren't in the mood for chit chat. Mentally they were focused on just making this hit and getting out of there as fast as they could. As of yet, The Hells Sinners hadn't even retaliated. The way things were going, no one really knew for sure where the hits were coming from and nobody was talking about who it was. Everyone was keeping it all on the down low and just acting as if they didn't know anything.

Auto slowed down just before they reached the corner and cut the lights, then slowly turned onto the block where The Hells Sinners were partying. Both cars crept around the corner from different directions so they could do a double hit. One car approached from the left while the other came from the right. The timing was set perfectly with the big white club house being closer to the right end of the block which made it perfect to pull this off. As the first car hit the gas and sped up to fly by the house, Darryl fired off four shots and hit both men who was sitting outside keeping watch. After they flew by the other car, Auto drove fast by the house as Johnnie and Steve fired off all their shots. They hit some of The Hells Sinners as they came running out of the house and met the gun fire head on. Dropping a few more of them as they were hit by the gun fire, Auto took off fast and drove straight to the expressway to get out of there. Several lifeless bodies laid outside in pools of blood. Some of The Hells Sinners jumped into a car and tried to run them down but could not find them anywhere.

This is what was making it so hard for The Hells Sinners to catch who was doing the hits. They would hit the expressway so fast and disappear that no one knew where they had went. Every gang always went back to their club house after a hit but no club house was open as The Hells Sinners went looking for the shooters. No one suspected anyone from Southbend to be doing hits on them so they never got on the expressway to chase. They always went the other way to head towards the other gangs' club houses.

This confused The Hells Sinners while keeping Johnnie and the group in the clear. They wondered how long they could keep this up before getting caught, but at least for now they were able to keep picking off gang members without suffering any loses themselves. As far as they were concerned, they were winning this war as long as they could continue to do these hits and disappear fast.

The ride was quiet once again as no one said anything all the way home but they were all thinking the same thing. Tonight was another success and a step closer to ending this war. No one knew who all had been shot. They would have to wait and hear it on the news later on the next morning. They all watched for the names of the ones they knew but their names had not came up as of yet. Every hit they would look to see if Wayne, Sisko or Ricco was mentioned. But once again they were not. Paco had been killed while in juvenile prison by Jason who was in there because of Paco snitching on him. When Jason found out he snitched on him to lighten his own sentence he killed him.

After they were all dropped off they went back to the camp area and met with Randy. He was sitting on a log, by the fire with his head down not wanting to look up at any of them.

"Hey Randy. What's wrong man?" Johnnie asked him as he saw the way he was sitting.

"I should have went with you guys," Randy responded with shame.

"What's going on Bro?" Darryl asked as he went over and sat next to his brother.

"It's just that not going was worse for me than going was. I just can't stay back anymore. I have to go with you guys."

"We will talk about it later Randy," Johnnie said.

After sitting with him for a while and talking about all that happened, they departed for their own homes. As Johnnie laid down for the night his thoughts were on Randy. He was wondering how he was going to try to work this one out with Ricky. He knew Ricky was mad and probably didn't want Randy involved any more. But as far as Johnnie was concerned, if Randy wanted back in, then he was in. Even though he was partially relieved Randy had stepped out, he also understood Randy had a right to be there also. This was their war too and Randy was a part of the group. He had always been there through all of the fights and Johnnie wasn't about to tell him no.

There were two wars going on and Ricky needed to understand that. The West Dragons had their feud but Johnnie and his group had a different feud. Even though they were helping each other the reason for their feuds were very different. Johnnie understood that but he knew Ricky didn't. For Ricky it was all about his fight and he was happy to have some extra help but he wasn't respecting Johnnie and the others for their reasons for being involved in this.

Ricky honestly didn't care about Cypher's friends. He only cared about winning the war. To him, having Cypher with them was a big deal but he didn't care about their reasons for being there. It just gave him more options and extra fire power. The Hells Sinners was the largest gang in town and having a few extra men was always welcomed when taking on a gang of this size. Either way, it was Cypher's problem and he was going to have to deal with it.

Early the next morning as the boys went to work with Johnnie, Christina called and made arrangements to take Tonya out for the morning. It had been a bit since the last time they had talked and she wanted to check up on her. Christina had some extra money she had set aside so they could go do some shopping and have lunch together. She was very concerned about Tonya, and she also over heard the boys talking about her a few times. She knew she had still been withdrawn from the group.

Christina knew isolation was not a good thing for anyone who was struggling from a major traumatic event such as what Tonya had been through. The fear alone that most rape victims suffer after something like this is bad enough, but the feeling of loneliness and depression can be very dangerous. It was important for Christina to keep getting Tonya back out in public and having time to speak into her life to encourage her. She needed to feel loved. She needed to know people cared about her and she wasn't alone.

Tonya needed Christina in her life, she needed mentorship from Christina to pump new life into her and to encourage Tonya to keep going when she felt like giving up on life. Tonya was thankful Christina was taking the time to spend with her and was making efforts to be there for her and to help her when she needed it. It was making way more of a difference than Christina had known. She always loved Tonya and she knew how much she and Johnnie was in love with each other. She knew Tonya was good for him and he needed her. It was a rough time for everyone.

Sara and Christina were starting to spend more time together as well. They used to be very close before Mike entered the picture. Now that Sara had finally recovered from that mess and Johnnie was back home, she was finally starting to reach back out to her friends. Sara was missed by everyone but she needed to be alone and heal from everything that transpired. It was great for Sara to be back out again with Monica and Christina.

It was a nice day out as Christina went to pick up Tonya. Neither had ate breakfast so they stopped off at a small bakery for some pastries and coffee. It was nice sitting by the window and watching the birds swoop down while they enjoyed a nice conversation. It was refreshing for Tonya to be able to spend the morning out.

She was beginning to enjoy Christina's company the more they were together. Christina was so loving and kind towards her and very understanding of her situation. It made Tonya feel at ease and more comfortable as they talked and shared things with each other. She had always loved Christina. Being the only girl in the group until Ann had come along, Tonya needed Christina to talk with a little about everything. While the Two Brothers had pool parties and cookouts, Christina had always made sure she made time to talk to Tonya. She wasn't pushy either. She knew how to take her time and just let the conversations develop as they talked. If Tonya wasn't ready to talk about something, she would change the subject and come back to it at another time.

After finishing breakfast, the two went outside, walked around for a bit and talked some more before finally going into some shops to look at clothes. There was a lot of nice dresses for sale and they both were trying on quite a few of them. They picked out a few they really liked and Christina bought them. While they were looking at the dresses, Christina was talking to Tonya about her and Johnnie coming on a date with her and Thomas. Tonya and Johnnie had never been on a date with them before. It felt kind of weird to her but nevertheless she agreed to go out with them. Now all Christina had to do was get Johnnie to go as well, which would probably not be hard since he was missing Tonya so much.

Thomas always liked to talk with Johnnie anyways so it would be a nice outing for the four of them. Thomas often talked about wanting to do things with Johnnie after the passing of his father but then Mike came into the picture and Johnnie went away for three years. Once he got out, Johnnie became so busy with work and the war, he never had time to go sit with Thomas even though he had invited him several times to do so. Thomas knew Johnnie needed a spiritual father to help guide him and be there for him as a friend and a mentor. Perhaps this outing together can be the start of something for them.

Christina was always optimistic and believed in the end things would always work out for the good. After leaving the clothing store, Christina and Tonya stopped into a shoe store to buy some shoes to go with the new dresses they purchased. After spending some time browsing, they tried on a few pairs that they liked. It was a good day for shopping. There was a sale on a lot of things and they had a buy one and get the second pair for half off sale. Both picked out two pairs each that went with their dresses and headed out to do some more shopping or at least window shop now that they already got some things.

 There was a food court in the middle of the shopping area where they had planned to stop for lunch. They were enjoying this morning out together and there was plenty of stores to look through. With the Two Brothers out working for Johnnie they had no time limit, they could spend all morning together and even into the late afternoon if they wanted to. It was a stress free day for them with no rush. They could take their time and do whatever they wanted to do.

 There was a unique candy shop there as well that sold candy made fresh. They had all kinds of candies and most where only sold there and not in any of the local stores. This made it a huge success for candy lovers and they did get a ton of customers who loved the candy. Every time Christina shopped there, she always had to pick up a few items for the boys who absolutely loved the candy. They would complain for days if they knew she had went there and didn't buy them anything. They picked out a few things they liked before Christina grabbed a few of the boys favorites. Before they left, Christina let Tonya pick out something she thought Johnnie would like. She had a great idea to have her give it to Johnnie and then ask him to go out on a double date with them. To her, it was the perfect plan. How could Johnnie say no while Tonya was giving him a gift? Plus this also secured it so Tonya would definitely go out with them also. In fact, it was working because Tonya started to get excited about it now that she had something to give to Johnnie. The more Christina talked about it, the more Tonya was wanting to do it.

 After a nice morning of shopping, they were getting hungry and stopped off at the food court to grab some lunch and relax their feet for a bit. They were in the mood for Chinese food. They grabbed a booth since they both had a lot of bags with them. Tonya had felt good all morning and was so happy to be out with Christina, she just clicked with Tonya and knew how to make her feel better. As they talked, Christina began to inquire of how Tonya was feeling and how things were going for her since their last time out. She had been praying for Tonya ever since she heard of her terrible situation. She made a lot of small talk before asking her any serious questions so Tonya would be comfortable and more relaxed.

"Have you had any real contact with Johnnie?" she questioned as they ate their food.

"Yes I have, but not that much. We did sit outside and talk one evening for a while but that was it. I thought he might have called me but I guess with work and such he has been pretty busy."

"Yes the boys have been getting home late evening most nights. Johnnie has a lot of jobs lined up every week and it sure keeps the boys busy and out of trouble. Working with Johnnie has been real good for them."

Of course Christina had no idea about the war the boys were in. It was hard for Tonya to not come clean about it but she just couldn't. She knew if she had, everyone would be mad at her and she was already feeling so alone, she just couldn't risk completely losing everyone, especially Johnnie. Even though she knew he would probably be understanding about it, she just couldn't risk it. Plus she didn't want to get any of them in trouble.

"Yes Johnnie's business is doing very good and I am extremely proud of him. After all he has been through it amazes me how he just keeps on going and continues to try and build a future for himself. Most people by now would have given up and became a slave to the system."

"Yes, but Johnnie just isn't that way. He has too much of his father in him."

"You knew Johnnie's father? I never met him. He passed away before we moved into the neighborhood."

"Oh yes, Mark and Sara where very good friends of ours

and we would get together as much as Mark's job allowed for it. He worked so hard just like Johnnie does. He was a great provider for Sara and Johnnie. He was the best at what he did and was very well known and respected in the community."

"Johnnie doesn't talk about him much but when he does his whole face lights up with the most wonderful smile."

"Yes Mark and Johnnie were very close. Mark was a good father and a wonderful husband. Sara was deeply in love with him and mourned for a few years after his unfortunate death. I thought she would never get over her grieving from Mark's death."

"How much is Johnnie like Mark?" Tonya asked in curiosity.

"A great deal to be honest. Mark was a handsome man just like Johnnie is. In fact, Johnnie gets his strong build and his work ethic from his father. Mark was so smart. He had a lot of wisdom and was well known for giving advice to people who needed it. Johnnie too has a great deal of wisdom. That is probably what helps him to keep going no matter what he has faced. Both of them were tough characters and strong men. Mark was a great leader and I see a lot of that same leadership quality in Johnnie as well."

"Yes, Johnnie is a great leader. He cares about all of us so very much and will do anything he can to help us."

"That's the Mark in him. His father was a giver also. Mark would help anyone and give to anyone who was needy. I wasn't surprised when Johnnie started working in the community, his father did the same."

"I wish I would have been able to meet him," Tonya said with a sadness to her tone.

"He would have loved you."

"You think so? You really think Mark would have liked me?" Tonya asked with hope in her voice.

"Oh yes, Mark would of absolutely adored you. He would have been so proud of Johnnie for picking such a wonderful woman to be with. Sara always talks so highly of you as well. She loves you like if you're her own daughter and often talks about how she hopes you and Johnnie would get married someday."

Tonya was smiling so huge at the words Christina had spoken to her.

"I love Sara. She has always been so good to me and treated me like family from the time I met her. She was so welcoming towards me and Steve when we moved in. She was just so loving and caring towards us. It was just so fantastic."

"So how have you been doing? I know last time we talked you were in a real struggle."

"It's still hard for me to be with the group. I miss them terribly but it's just so hard to face everyone. I feel so ashamed especial with everyone knowing what they did to me. Johnnie has been great. He always makes time for me when I want to talk no matter what's going on at the moment. But I don't know, it just hurts so much when I see him. Sometimes he just sits there and looks at me and I don't know what is going on in his mind. His eyes used to sparkle when he saw me and now it's just a stare."

"That night about killed Johnnie and nobody knew why he disappeared, but we were all afraid we would never see him again and even worse, when he stayed away for that long. The boys say that he is lost without you. I hear them talk when they are in their room as I pass by. Do you want to be back with Johnnie?" Christina asked hoping that Tonya would say yes.

"Yes, in time I do. I love him very much, but I feel like I can't be the woman he'd fallen in love with now. I feel like I'm damaged and so dirty now."

"Oh Tonya, you are not damaged or dirty. I know Johnnie doesn't think like that either. You just need to let God heal you from this and restore your relationship with Johnnie."

"Can God do that? How can He fix this? How can He heal me from what has happened to me and to Johnnie also?"

"That's the beauty of God. He can do anything. He created everything and by His hands all things was formed and made. This is part of the great sacrifice that Jesus made for us in His sufferings that by His stripes we are healed."

"I don't know what that means."

"Well, Jesus was beaten severely so we could receive healing from God. But he also heals the broken hearted and restores our lives. Jesus did more than just die for our salvation. He came to set us free and give us a new life. He does more than just heal our bodies but He gives to us inner healings from those deep wounds caused by others. No matter what you have done or what has been done to you, God still loves you and wants to fix it, if you will allow Him to do so. It's a process but He will slowly work in your life and take His time to fix everything and give you a second chance at life."

"That's what I need. All of it. I need all of it. How do I get it? What must I do to get Him to help me?"

"All you have to do is just ask Him. Reach out to Him and invite Him to come into your life and be a part of your life."

"Can you show me how?"

"Yes, Tonya just pray this prayer with me. Father, I know I don't know You but I want to get to know You. I am asking You, God to come into my heart and be a part of my life and fix everything in me that is broken. Heal every part of me that needs healing and restore my life. Forgive me for my sins and save me Lord."

There was a sense of peace that came over Tonya as she prayed this prayer with Christina. She hadn't felt anything like this in so long. It was as if a cool breeze on a hot summer day had swept across her, relieving her and making her feel refreshed again. They sat there and cried together as Tonya accepted Jesus while forgetting they were in the food court. It was as if everything else in the background had faded out and it was just the two of them. After several minutes they both gathered their things and got ready to head back home. Tonya hadn't felt good in so long it was overwhelming and she even had a bit of excitement back in her voice again. She had been so down and depressed that the feelings she was having in this moment was so extreme for her. She could barely keep herself from crying some more.

Later that night as Tonya was lying in bed, all she could think about was Johnnie. It hurt so bad not seeing him, always wondering what he was doing and how he was doing. Everything hurt but missing him hurt the most. Without him in her life was like a huge hole in her heart. She wondered if she was losing him and how long he would actually wait for her. *What if he had met someone else before she was ready? What if he fell in love with someone else before she was able to get herself back to him?* She didn't want to rush things but there was this fear of losing him that was starting to set in. The more she thought about what Christina had offered about her and Johnnie going out with them, the more it started to sound like a good idea. If nothing else, at least it would give her and Johnnie a chance to see where they were with each other.

The night seemed to drag on without any sleep as she just laid there thinking about Johnnie until she finally starting crying. Missing him and loving him so much just hurt so bad she felt like her hands was tied and there was nothing she could do but possibly just watch her love slip away as she tried to get herself together. *He said he would wait for me.* She laid there crying but she hadn't heard from him. *Has he given up on us? Has he changed his mind?* Finally Tonya cried herself out as she fell asleep.

In the meantime, Johnnie was sitting back at the camp area by himself thinking about Tonya. The sky was pitch black with no stars shining through the thick of the night. Everything seemed very still and quiet. Things at times seemed to him like it was starting to go in the right direction and then she would pull back again. There was times he had hope then he would feel hopeless again in this situation. This continuously fueled his hatred and anger for revenge. He knew how Tonya felt about this war but how could he ever let it go? He felt as if they had ripped their love from each other's hearts. As they bleed out, he was determined to watch them bleed out as well as he delivered punishment on them for what they had done. If it meant his own life just to kill them he was willing to do it. He was dying everyday because of them.

    Johnnie hadn't felt this much pain since the death of his father and the abuse of his mother. They had crossed a line they would live to regret. This time it was going to cost them their lives. There wasn't enough of their blood that would satisfy his hate for them. Death was all they had to look forward to now. As he sat alone he couldn't help but think about whether or not she still loved him like she used to. Maybe she blamed him for all of this. Maybe she couldn't ever love him like she used to. All the time Tonya had stayed away filled Johnnie's heart with loneliness. He decided before he finally gave up on them, he would give it all he had to try to keep them together. If it didn't work at least he knew he had tried and given it his all. Maybe it was his fault. Maybe he had pushed too much instead of letting some things go. *Maybe I shouldn't have gave her this much space. I know she wanted it but maybe I should have fought harder for us. Every day without her has made it feel like we are just too far apart now. Maybe we will never get this worked out. Maybe we will never be together again. I will kill every last one of them for this. None of them deserve any mercy what so ever.* Tears fell from his watering eyes as he sat on one of the huge rocks that was off to the side of where he usually sat.

    I can't go back now. It's either them or me. I'm tired of always suffering loss at the hands of others. This time it ends even if it's me who dies. I don't care anymore! I've done the best that I can with this life but things just never work out for me. I have done all I can to try to live a good life and do right. Seems like someone else is always pulling the strings and taken everything that is important away from me. How could Tonya still love me? Even I hate what I have become. What they made me become. I was never supposed to be like this. I was never supposed to be a killer.

All I ever wanted was to be the kind of person that my father could be proud of. All I ever do is fail him. Why couldn't I just have a normal life and be like my father? If I live through this, I don't think I will stay here. Maybe I can go somewhere where no one knows me and start all over. Just disappear and never come back again. Sell the house and take mom with me and just put all of this behind us and move on. If it takes my last breath Wayne dies. I failed everyone. I led this whole group into a bloody war. Why did they have to follow me into this? I will burn everything down before I will ever let them win.

As the tiredness of the long day began to sweep over him, Johnnie headed in for the night to try and get some much needed rest. He was exhausted. Work was long and the war was always looming over his mind. His heart constantly ached for Tonya. It was all becoming way too much to handle. There was no break in anything. There was no down time to recover and try to gather his thoughts together. Everything was in a constant motion pushing him forward, forcing him to try to endure all of these things. This war was far from over and he was feeling wore out from it already. The stress from all of this was getting to be too much to handle as Johnnie felt himself coming to a breaking point.

Finally climbing into bed he tried desperately to quiet his mind so he could get some much needed rest from all of this chaos. It had been a hard time for everyone. This war was effecting the whole group. George and Johnnie barely saw each other anymore. He was always with Ann and Johnnie was always working. When the weekend comes they used to all get together but lately Johnnie and the Two Brothers had been exhausted. Johnnie needed downtime and time to himself, as he was running himself into the ground. The weight on his shoulders was getting heavier. The stress was getting worse. Keeping everything together was getting harder.

Ann had been trying for several days to get Tonya to come out with her and George but she just didn't feel like being with them on her own. Had Johnnie been there she would have went but he was wrapped up in all of his other things that for now he just didn't have time for it. Tonya barely saw anyone at all as it was but she was starting to try to make efforts to come out of her shell a little more after spending time with Christina. She began to feel as if things could start to get better. The more time she spent with Christina the better she began to feel and the more she wanted to see Johnnie.

In the meantime there was a problem brewing for Randy that no one knew about. Ricky had really taken a disliking to him after he bailed out and then wanted to come back in. That was not how Ricky did things and he wasn't happy that Cypher was okay with it. Cypher was starting to not care if Ricky liked things or not. He had way too much going on to worry about what upset Ricky. As far as Cypher was concerned, that was the least of his problems. Maintaining his business was his first priority. He was making good money now and business was growing. His name was getting out there as being extremely reliable and people trusted him. Many knew his father and had loved him and was willing to give Johnnie jobs because of it.

When Mark died the company had given Johnnie a trust fund for when he turned eighteen which he had never touched. He had always left that money there in case his mom ever needed it. He didn't ever want to see his mother have to go get a job to try and pay the bills. Now that his business was pulling in good money, he knew he could take some of it and grow his business as he expanded.

There was a great deal he had come across that would solve a few problems for him. He had come across a truck with a trailer that was for sale. They weren't in new condition but they were good for what he needed them for. The price was good so he bought them. He had previously made a deal with one of his customers on a few mowers and now it was time to cash in on that. Having two trucks now, he was able to hire another worker and split up to cover more ground. The Two Brothers would be able to just mow and keep moving forward. Johnnie and his new worker, that he was going to hire, would be able to come behind them and do a fast clean up job after they were done with their repairs. He tried to keep them all as close as possible as he could scheduling things in the same area as to where Two Brothers would be. That wasn't always the case but it helped when he was able to do so.

   They had worked hard all week to get caught back up but Johnnie had taken the morning off to get this truck and trailer he needed. After which he went and bought the two mowers. After he was done with all of that it was getting towards lunch time. He wanted to go and talk to Steve before doing anything else. A quick call and he was on his way to go pick him up. But first he needed to take Darryl to pick up his new truck and trailer that he had spent the morning getting legal. With Darryl only living a few houses down, this was perfect. The Two Brothers could come and grab the truck with the invoices and just go to work.

   After getting the truck, he met with Steve and took him to lunch while Darryl and Randy went to pick up the mowers. He decided to give them the day off so the Two Brothers could get the truck ready for the next day, making sure they had all their equipment. He sent them out to grab a few new weed whackers and a new blower to keep the walkways and sidewalks cleaned off. While with Steve he talked about bringing him in and teaching him how to fix things as they would be doing several odd jobs every day. Johnnie had picked up a few parks to mow and was now starting to pick up some painting jobs as well. He knew Steve helped out a friend with some painting before and liked it.

   Steve was excited to have a full-time job and work for Johnnie. He knew this would be a great opportunity to learn how to do more things. He loved to work with his hands. After lunch, Johnnie took Steve with him to go pick up painting supplies and get him his own tool belt and tools. After which he bought a tool box for his truck to go across the back of the bed so they could store all their tools. It was a costly day, but it was a good day.

Johnnie was very happy to have Steve as an employee and part of the team. This however didn't sit well with George who thought he would have been Johnnie's first choice. But Steve had been doing odd jobs already and had more experience then George. George had been caught up with Ann all the time while Steve was always trying to hustle up some work to make money and Johnnie knew that. It had seemed more reasonable to get Steve going who had some experience and then bring George in later.

But for George, he saw things a little differently. He felt being Johnnie's best friend should have made him the first choice. George was starting to feel pushed away a bit by Johnnie who had always put George first before everyone else. But this was business and Johnnie didn't need this drama either with all of the other things that he had to deal with. George had never expressed any interest in his business until he had hired Steve. He made the choice that he felt was right for his business and didn't really care about George's complaining about it. But for the sake of their friendship, he calmed the situation and promised George the next spot on the team. After getting everything settled Johnnie had taken the rest of the day off.

After Steve got back home he had told Tonya about Johnnie hiring him to work for him. She was excited for Steve and wanted to know how Johnnie was doing. As they talked Steve mentioned how Johnnie had taken the rest of the day off. She knew this would be a good opportunity to get with him and give him the gift and talk to him about going out with Thomas and Christina Hilton on a double date. After her and Steve finished their talk, she had called Johnnie about her coming down to see him. This made him extremely happy that he was going to be able to spend some time with her.

When Tonya had come down to see Johnnie, she found him waiting out back on the patio for her. He was so happy to see her and it was very noticeable by the smile on his face that he couldn't hide. As soon as she came to where he stood he hugged her. They held each other for several minutes before sitting down together.

"I miss you so much, Tonya," Johnnie said to her as he held her hand.

"I miss you too, Johnnie."

She looked as beautiful as ever and Johnnie fought trying to keep his composure as he desperately wanted to kiss her.

"Christina has been taking me out and spending time with me."

"That's good. Christina is a good woman. Very smart lady who knows how to help people who are struggling. She spent a lot of time with my mom while I was gone away to juvenile prison. I always appreciate that about her. Thomas and Christina always prayed for me while I was in there and that meant a lot to me. It was a great comfort knowing I had people praying for me. They always made sure my mom was taken care of," Johnnie explained as they sat and talked.

"Well, when we were out I got you something," Tonya said as she gave Johnnie his gift.

"Oh thank you. I see you two were at the candy shop. I haven't been there in a long time. Not since I got out of The House. Mom took me there when I first got back home after my release."

"Yeah, I like it there. They have so much candy there it's crazy. So much to choose from," Tonya responded as Sara had come out for a second to see if Johnnie wanted anything.

Finding Tonya there she offered her something to drink. She was so happy to see Tonya and Johnnie together. She gave Johnnie a smile when she noticed him holding Tonya's hand. After a small chat with Tonya she went in and got them some tea and then left.

"Johnnie, I want to ask you something. As I was with Christina, she mentioned about maybe you and me going out with her and Thomas."

Johnnie looking puzzled for a second. "You mean like on a double date?"

"Yes, Johnnie. Just the four of us. Wouldn't it be great to

go out with them?" Tonya asked with great excitement in her voice. She really wanted them to do this and was hoping Johnnie would say yes.

"Yeah, okay. I would love to take you out with them. It's been a long while since we've been out on a date anyways."

Johnnie couldn't believe Tonya had just asked him to go on a date. This was amazing and there was no way he was about to pass this up. He had started to lose hope in them ever getting back together and now here is Tonya asking him out on a date. So much excitement arose up within him he kissed her without even thinking about it.

"Oh, Johnnie you still love me?" she asked after he kissed her.

Johnnie took her hand in his as he looked into her eyes. He gave her another kiss before responding.

"I never stopped loving you Tonya. And I never will. You are everything to me and that will never change. You are all I have ever wanted. You're my dream, my passion, all I have ever wanted was for us to be together. I have waited for you all of this time hoping at some point we could get back together and rebuild."

"I still struggle Johnnie but I do love you and have always loved you. I want to start taking small steps to being with you again."

"Really?" Johnnie asked as his whole being felt like it was about to explode with such great excitement as joy rose up within him.

"I have waited for this moment Tonya. I was starting to think it wasn't ever going to happen," he said as he held her in his arms and kissed her.

"Small steps, Johnnie. I still need a lot of time but I don't want to lose you and at least this is a start."

"Yes Honey, whatever it takes. You're all I ever wanted and needed. Nothing will ever change that. Nothing. I just need you with me. I hate us being apart. It's the worst feeling ever. This has been an amazing day. I got everything I needed for my business and now this. Finally things are beginning to turn around. I needed a day like this. You have blessed me Tonya way more then you will ever know."

Johnnie could barely contain himself with all of this excitement he was experiencing from the day. Having Tonya back was a dream come true for him. He felt as if a huge weight had been lifted off him. Tonya had curled up with him as they spent the rest of the evening cuddling together. Sara had ordered some food for all of them. When she had returned with the food, she brought theirs out and then went back in to let them have their alone time together. Sara was almost as excited about seeing them together like that as Johnnie was. She loved Tonya and always had hoped one day she would be her daughter-in-law.

They stayed together late into the night until Johnnie was so tired he could hardly keep his eyes open. He hated for this night to end. But as the night had drew to a close, he knew he needed to get some sleep before work. After a wonderful evening Johnnie walked Tonya home to make sure she got there safely. After seeing her home he gave her a good night kiss and returned home to try and get some sleep which didn't come easy with all the excitement from the day. He was struggling hard to get some rest before work but his mind wouldn't let him. He laid there thinking about Tonya until finally falling asleep just a few hours before he had to get back up.

It felt as if he had just fell asleep when the alarm had went off. *Ugh! It can't be time to get up already. I just fell asleep.* He grudgingly got back up. *I hope this day goes by fast.* He was happy to see the Two Brothers there early to grab the truck. Johnnie invited them in as he cooked everyone breakfast. Sara was happy to see Darryl and Randy. It had been a long time since she had them here for breakfast.

Johnnie hadn't even got there paper work copied for them yet. After breakfast he wrote it all out for them so they knew exactly what to do for the day, then they were off to get the day started.

Johnnie was so tired. He thought it best to let Steve drive as he was struggling to focus. Steve knew he was up late when he looked at his clock after he heard Tonya come home.

Darryl and Randy were excited to be off on their own. It was their first step towards independence in this company. Johnnie was really showing how much he trusted them to go get jobs done on their own. They had always worked hard for Johnnie and deserved this opportunity. This was going to be good for them as they continued to grow in the business. Johnnie had hoped to be able to come behind them and do the clean-up but that just wasn't going to be possible. He and Steve were getting so many jobs to do, the Two Brothers were going to have to do it all on their own, but they were ready for it. They loved the work and took great pride in making sure everything they did was perfect. Clean-up wasn't a big deal anyways. It only took a few minutes to blow everything off and make it all look neat.

This was an exciting time for Johnnie who seriously needed these things to happen at this time to keep him motivated and encouraged. So many negative things was happening all around him and it was dragging him down. So many times he found it very difficult to stay focused on positive things with all he had to deal with. This was a time for refocusing and getting his business going in the direction he wanted it to go in. Now that things were looking good for him and Tonya, he needed to also refocus on her and put all he had into making this work out. He finally felt that now maybe they could make some real progress which was very encouraging. Previously they would spend a little bit of time together and then it would fade back out and that was frustrating him to no end. But now with an actual date being set up, he felt more at ease they could start moving in the right direction as well. Even if it was slowly, it was better than not at all. There was so much going on but good things was happening.

Johnnie was very proud of the Two Brothers who had stepped up to the challenge to go out on their own without him and make it happen. He trusted they would get it done as they always had before when he was there with them. He knew they could handle it on their own. He believed in the Two Brothers and was blessed to have them as a part of his team.

   Steve was eager to get in and become a part of this team as well. He needed the work and knew Johnnie would treat him good and take care of him. Johnnie knew his father would have kept pushing until he made it and that was exactly what he was going to do. No one was going to stop him from becoming successful. He was determined now more than ever to make it all come together. He had a fresh vision about his life with Tonya and it was motivating him to not let anything or anyone destroy his future. One way or another, he was going to build a future with her and nothing was going to get in the way of that. There was a fresh excitement in him now and even though he was tired he was feeling great about how everything was coming together.

   As they day went on the fatigue started to really hit Johnnie. He was exhausted and really needed this day to end. Steve had done a great job and was easy to teach. He was a quick learner and worked hard. Johnnie liked that about him. Even though George had gotten upset he wasn't asked before Steve, he knew he had made the right choice.

   The Two Brothers had spent the entire day off on their own, done everything on the list and was very proud of their accomplishments. They worked hard all week to get as many jobs done as they could to get caught up before Friday so they could get off early as they had been behind from not working that much on Monday. Not forgetting also about having yesterday off as well. The days were long but they made it. They hustled to get it all done.

   Johnnie and Steve had done a small paint job, fixed a few fences for a customer and then picked up a window for Mr. Tomlinson and installed it for him. Johnnie began to grow as a carpenter. The rest of the day, they did some landscaping jobs before Johnnie finally gave in and called it a day. He went as far as he could go but he was too tired to keep going. It was late afternoon but Johnnie was ready to go home and get some rest. The Two Brothers worked into the late evening and didn't quit until the light from the day began to fade. They had no choice but to finish up the last job they were working on. Johnnie had given them a list that was quite extensive because he knew they weren't going to want to work late on Friday. He wished for himself he could have gotten a bit farther. Steve was good with his hands and he worked hard. Johnnie was already thinking about once he got Steve to where he could go on his own, he would buy another truck and send him out on his own and then hire George to work with him as well.

When Johnnie made it home there was a message that Tonya had called and wanted him to call her back. Christina had set everything up for the date and Thomas had agreed to go along with it. It had been a bit since they had been out on a date and he loved Johnnie and Tonya. He was happy to see them making efforts to be together. He always felt they belonged together.

After Johnnie talked to her, he got cleaned up and then laid down for a bit to get some rest before their date that night. It wasn't long and Johnnie was fast asleep. Sara woke him up so he wouldn't miss his date with Tonya. He thought he set his alarm but he forgotten and now was in a hurry to get himself together. Sara wasn't about to let him be late. She knew how important this was for them. After she helped Johnnie pick out a nice outfit to wear, he was soon off to pick up Tonya. Feeling a bit more refreshed from his nap and a cup of coffee, he was ready for a good night out with the woman he loved and a couple that always been so good to him.

After picking up Tonya, he drove back down to the Hiltons so he could follow them. Tonya looked so beautiful in the sexy red dress she was wearing. Johnnie put on a nice black suit with a red tie that was perfect to match the dress Tonya was wearing. The Hiltons also dressed up and Thomas was looking sharp in his suit as Christina was stunning in her black dress. Thomas had set up reservations for them at a fancy Jazz Lounge. It was expensive but the food was amazing and the Jazz band was really good. It was a favorite spot for Thomas and Christina when they wanted a romantic night out. It was one of the classiest restaurants in Southbend Heights.

  Tonya was excited about going to a fancy restaurant with Johnnie. He had taken her out to eat before but this was different. This was one of the most romantic places you could go. The conversation was mostly about getting caught up with each other. The food was terrific, and for the price of the meals, it should have been. The lights were dim and the stage was lit up as the band played in the background while they ate. The room was dark with candles and flowers arranged just right to lighten each table perfectly. The lights on the walls were turned down to a soft illumination. The lit up stage gave off just enough light to set the mood as they played. The romantic ambiance of the whole scene was beautiful with the way the lighting glowed ever so softly.

  After they had enjoyed a nice dinner, Johnnie and Thomas took the hands of the beautiful ladies and lead them to the dance floor for some slow dancing. As they swayed together to the soft sound of the music that was playing, everything was perfect. The room was filled with love as couples were eating and dancing while the band played on, setting the perfect tone for lovers to enjoy such a deep night of romance.

  Tonya was loving being back in Johnnie's arms as he held her close to him. She laid her head on his shoulder as he held her tight in his arms while loving her. He was slowing turning her in circles as they swayed together to the music. The dance floor was lit up by a huge ball of light that put out different colors that kept changing as it turned while highlighting the dance floor with beautiful bright colors.

  The whole evening was wonderful. Johnnie and Tonya had such a great time with Thomas and Christina. They laughed so much as Johnnie and Thomas were talking about things they had experienced. Every conversation was refreshing and joyful. The evening couldn't have went any better than it had gone. After a few hours of dancing and socializing, the evening was getting late and it was time to head out. Johnnie and Tonya went back to his house and spent the rest of the night together. They held each other under the bright shimmering stars that filled the dark night sky. The stars lit it up as a smile from a long awaited loved one who had returned home from a long journey. Johnnie held her all night. He embraced her with such great love. She laid back against him as he wrapped his loving arms around her while they cuddled together until the dark night began to fade into the morning.

    They we're extremely tired as Johnnie kissed her and took her home so they could get some rest. As there date came to a close, they knew no matter what happened, they were meant to be together. Their love remained and the fire of their love was being set again as their hearts began to burn together for each other. It was real, true love that could never be quenched by any circumstance or situation. They were truly in love.

CHAPTER 5

THE BETRAYAL

It had been a little while since Johnnie and the group had heard from Ricky. It was time for them to make another hit. Johnnie's heart had been so lifted up and encouraged by the things that had been happening for him as of late. It felt great spending that time with Tonya and he wasn't ready for the phone call he had coming with Ricky. As his phone began to ring he contemplated on not answering it. He knew if Ricky was calling then it was time again. He was starting to wonder how long this was going to drag out. He wished it would have been over already but it seemed little progress was being made.

"Hello Ricky, what can I do for you?" Johnnie asked as he reluctantly answered the phone just before Ricky hung up.

"Hey Cypher. We need you and your group to come with us on a hit. We have information that this coming Tuesday, The Hells Sinners will be at an outdoor event and we will be able to get a lot of them at one time."

"What kind of event are we talking about?"

"It's one of the biggest flea market events of the year."

"You mean this is a public event where innocent people will be at as well."

"Sometimes you have to strike when the opportunity arises."

"Listen Ricky, I want to end this war just as badly as you do, but open firing into a public crowd is not what we do. Shooting up their club house is one thing but a public event? No man, we can't do that. That is not us."

"You're saying that you're not coming along with us on

this hit?"

"I am saying that this is something that we won't do Ricky. We don't shoot up public places where there are innocent people. We are not killers man! I can't believe you are even asking us to do this, let alone that you are even planning it knowing innocent people will be there and in the line of fire."

"There are always casualties in war Cypher."

"This war is between us and them, not innocent by standers. Their casualty is unnecessary and we can't do it. I cannot ask them to go along with this Ricky."

"Okay Cypher. Suit yourself."

Johnnie knew Ricky was angered by him turning down helping them out but this was wrong and he wasn't about to have this hanging over his head or the groups for that matter.

After Ricky hung up he had a private meeting with Venom and Cobra concerning Cypher and another member of his group.

"It appears that Cypher needs a little motivation. I am sending you two out to make an example out of Randy. Make it look like The Hells Sinners were the ones who did it."

"Okay. Does it matter if he is alone or not?"

"Yes, make sure he is alone then tag him with The Hells Sinners patch logo so Cypher thinks it was them."

"We can do that," Venom responded although he didn't agree with it. But there was little he could do to keep it from happening. He had to do what Ricky ordered him to do whether he liked it or not.

"We will keep an eye out for when he is alone and then hit him."

"Perfect. I don't care how long it takes. Just get it done."

"We're on it," Cobra said. They went to get things prepared for a quick run through the neighborhood to see if they could get lucky and find him.

In the meantime, Johnnie was calling the group to discuss the issue he was having with Ricky. He wanted to get their feedback and see how they felt about this whole mess they were finding themselves in. He wasn't happy with Ricky at all and was beginning to see this was a huge mistake getting tied in with him and the West Dragons. It seemed like a good idea at the time but things were getting out of control. They were not about to become like The Hells Sinners and hurt innocent people for no reason. This is what they were fighting against to end and there was no way they were willing to do the same thing. They were here to fight with The Hells Sinners, not cause innocent people to become senseless victims. He couldn't even understand how these people had no real value for human life to just kill whoever was in the way just to get at their enemies. This was for sure not how they operated. The very thought of shooting into an open crowd angered him to no end.

Maybe it was time to have a talk with an old friend. He needed some advice on how to handle these issues with Ricky and he knew just who to talk to about it. It was time to go see Jason and have a one on one meeting about all of this. If anyone could help him with this it was Jason. But that would have to wait until he talked to the group later on in the day to get their input as well as how they wanted to handle this situation. It could be they would all want to pull out. Nevertheless, they needed to know what was going on so that they could make their own decision if they wanted to continue on with them or back out.

It was Johnnie's responsibility to the group to present all and every situation to them so they could make the right decision concerning themselves according to how they felt about it. He was really beginning to regret joining up with them. Even though he had built a good friendship with Ricky when they did time together, but all of this was now starting to put a strain on that friendship or what he thought was a friendship.

Johnnie spent part of his day hanging around the house trying to relax a bit. He had made several phone calls to the group about getting together early evening for a bit, but for now he just wanted some down time to relax and try to regroup. He was beginning to spend more time on the back patio where he found it to be relaxing and a place of solace. It was beautiful back there. His mother, in her time of grief, had taken up gardening and planted many bushes and flowers. Johnnie maintained the lawn care but she had become so used to keeping up with the shrubs, plants and flowers that she didn't want anyone else to do it for her. Keeping up with the house was easy enough with only her there most of the time, so taking care of the yard work for her became a way of keeping herself busy and helped put her mind at ease.

    Sara loved being a house wife and a mother so for her to be alone most of the time got a bit lonely but she had this to keep her motivated and preoccupied so she didn't become lazy. Monica would often come by and spend time with Sara. Christina came for morning coffee three to four times a week when the boys were off working with Johnnie and Thomas was gone to work as well. Tonya's mother, Tammy would come down once in a while but she called Sara a few times a week to keep in touch and to talk about Tonya and Johnnie.

    Tony and Tammy loved Johnnie. It was hard for them to watch what had been going on with him and Tonya. They wanted Johnnie to eventually become part of the family but things had become so difficult for them for a while they thought it would probably never happen. Sara always inquired of Tonya when she and Tammy would talk though. It was hard for all the parents to watch this fall apart when they knew how much these two loved each other and everyone was so close. It just seemed natural for Johnnie and Tonya to be together.

    Sara was very proud of Johnnie. Every time he took on a new job she felt as if he was becoming more and more like his father. Johnnie had become a loyal customer at Mr. Smith's Hardware store. Since Mr. Smith had helped him to get his start. He built up his first clients through Mr. Smith so he felt it was necessary to be loyal to him.

***

Later on early that evening they got together to discuss the situation of Ricky wanting them to do a public hit. It was clear some things were going to have to change if they were going to keep working together as a team. They obviously wasn't on the same page as far as things they were willing to do and things they weren't willing to do. The group had never even considered doing anything like this and it didn't sit well with any of them. George was extremely upset they would even ask them to do that. Randy, who was about to get back involved was now once again rethinking the whole situation. He didn't want to step back into this and then step back out over having to do something he knew he wasn't going to be able to live with. He hated not being able to be committed to the group but things wasn't going as they had expected and this was too much for him. He thought maybe he would wait and see how things would develop. This didn't make Johnnie happy at all because he had already told Ricky that Randy was coming back in with them. Darryl and Steve also didn't feel good about this but they understood this was how gangs operated, but it just wasn't for them. One thing they agreed on was they were not ever going to put innocent people in harms' way over their personal feud with The Hells Sinners. They knew it wasn't right and they were not about to do that. No matter how Ricky felt about it.

Once they got that all settled, Johnnie needed to talk to Randy to get him to either commit or step all the way out. He needed to know exactly where he stood with them. He couldn't have him in and out all the time, either he was with them all the way or he wasn't going to be able to be in it at all. This war was very serious and everyone needed to either be committed or left out, but there was no half way for any of them. The only thing they wasn't going to commit to was killing innocent people just to get at The Hells Sinners. There had to be a clear line they wouldn't cross and that was it.

Johnnie was begging to wonder if he would eventually have to deal with Ricky. He wasn't real sure on how he was going to approach this situation but one thing he knew for sure, he was going to have to have a clear answer from Randy before the next time him and Ricky talked. If he was to come back to Ricky with Randy deciding not to rejoin, then that was going to have to be final. Johnnie understood Randy's struggles but decisions had to made and they had to be final at this point. There could be no more going back and forth for anyone now. They were too deep into this and everyone involved had to be one hundred percent committed.

As the weekend ended and the group had decided not to participate, Johnnie wondered just how much this was going to affect things. He had even considered pulling out altogether, but he felt he needed to make sure Wayne and the rest got what they deserved. For him, as long as they lived this would never be over with.

After putting in a long day and returning back home, he made a call to his friend Jason who he felt could give him some advice or at least some insight on how to handle this. Jason knew any time Johnnie asked for a meeting with him that it wasn't going to be good. Jason had been watching and following what all was going on and knew they were making progress against their rivals while the Hells Sinners was still in a state of confusion as to what was going on. They had come to realize it had to be the West Dragons but they wasn't sure as to why they could never find them. After every hit it was as if they all just disappeared into thin air, nothing led back to their club house.

After talking to Jason, Johnnie decided to have a short work day the next day so he could go sit with Jason for a while and try to get things somewhat under control. He definitely needed some advice from someone who had inside information into all of this and who also had experience in dealing with gangs. All of this was new to him and the group and he needed some guidance from someone he could trust. After a quick shower and a light dinner, he was soon off to get some sleep.

The next day as Johnnie arose feeling refreshed after a good nights' sleep. He was eager to get things going today so he could shoot over to meet up with Jason. As it would be, Steve and the rest of the group was ready to get going as well. Randy and Darryl came for the truck and trailer and was soon off after a short meeting with Johnnie. Once they were off, Johnnie drove down to pick up Steve. When he pulled up he found Tonya sitting on the porch waiting for him. Normally he just waited in the truck but with Tonya being outside, he got out, went and sat with her while he waited for Steve to come out.

"You're up early. Is everything okay?" Johnnie asked. He never seen Tonya before work and was curious if anything was troubling her that morning.

"Everything is fine, Johnnie. I was just awake and knew you would be coming to pick up my brother. I thought it might be nice to get a good morning kiss from you."

Her words perked Johnnie up quite a bit as he leaned in and kissed her. He loved the feel of her soft, sweet lips against his as he held her hand and their lips pushed tight. Steve came out the door to find them kissing as he jumped off of the side of the porch.

"I am ready to go Bro whenever you two love birds are done kissing."

Johnnie smiled at Steve as he went to get up before leaning down and kissing Tonya again.

"Maybe I will see you after work," Johnnie whispered in her ear as he was pulling away from their last kiss before he left.

Steve couldn't help but notice a bit more excitement in Johnnie this morning.

"Must have been some kiss," he said with a slight chuckle that seemed to have caught Johnnie of guard and embarrassed him a bit.

"Best kiss ever," he responded with a laugh as he was trying to hide being embarrassed.

"Look at this morning, Steve. Bright, clear, blue sky. Not

too hot and not too cool. A soft wind blowing through the trees as it makes the grass dance back and forth. The flowers swaying in the wind as if all of nature was dancing before the Lord."

His comment had thrown Steve off a bit. "Are you getting religious on me Johnnie? You know Tonya has been talking a little bit about God as well. Where is all of this coming from?"

"I don't know to be honest. It just kind of came out. Weird isn't it? I never really ever had a thought like that before."

"Maybe being out with the Hiltons has rubbed off a little on you."

"Maybe. Either way I have to admit it was a nice thought. I don't know Steve, I just feel good this morning."

"Perhaps that kiss has affected you Brother."

"Ha, ha yeah. Her kisses always affect me," Johnnie responded with a laugh. "Today is going to be a good day Steve. I do have to leave early. When its time I will give you the option to go home or I can drop you off with Randy and Darryl."

"Okay, Bro. No problem. I guess it will depend on what time you leave. If it's too early I will go help them out but if it's later afternoon I might just go to the house."

"Sounds good to me Bro. Whatever you want to do is fine with me," Johnnie said.

Finally reaching the first job it was time to get busy as Johnnie and Steve got everything together and started work on a broken fence that needed mending. A few bricks from the walk way needed to be replaced as well.

As the morning went on, they got a lot of small jobs done and it was soon after lunch when Johnnie decided to call it a day. Steve opted to go meet up with the Two Brothers and get some extra hours in instead of going home. After dropping Steve off with them, he headed home to get cleaned up so he could go meet up with Jason who was already heading to the Coffee House to wait for him. Johnnie was very disturbed with the way things were going with Ricky and needed to find a way to deal with this without it getting out of hand. After getting himself cleaned up from the work day he was off to go meet with Jason and try to find a quick way to resolve this issue before it became bigger.

As Johnnie pulled up to the Coffee House he wasn't surprised to see Jason already inside waiting for him as he sat at his table drinking some hot tea. Johnnie walked in and immediately went over and sat with him. As they began to talk a waitress came right over and took Johnnie's order. He also got some hot tea. These two hadn't sat drinking tea together that much since their time together at The House.

"So what can I do for you Brother?"

"Well to be honest Jason, I am having some problems with Ricky," Johnnie began to explain.

"What kind of problems are you having?"

"Well, for one, they wanted us to go on a hit and shoot at The Hells Sinners in a public crowded place and I refused to do that."

"Yeah, he should have known better than to ask that of you. That is one problem I do have with these gangs. They see an opportunity to get at each other and they don't think about the innocent lives that are affected by it. All they see is opportunity," Jason replied.

"Right. And there is another problem I am having with him also. You met Randy once before. He is with me and a few others that you know about. Well, Randy is struggling with all of this and backed out of going on any more hits, which of course made Ricky mad but it is what it is. So now Randy wants back in. When I mentioned this to Ricky he got even madder."

"The thing you have to remind Ricky about is that you guys are not members. You're outsiders helping out. You're not bound by the rules of the gang because you are not gang members and Ricky has to allow for that. It seems to me he is trying to get you to adhere to his rules when you are not bound by them. What you have to do is get Ricky to see your point of view and remind him that you have a temporary partnership. I know Ricky always wants things done his way, but you have to remain true to yourselves Johnnie. You can't allow no one to change you or make you live by their own standards. You have to always live by your own standards. People will always try to own you or manipulate you. You have always done good at standing up for what you believe in. This is no different. Stand your ground like you always have and make sure he doesn't try to change who you are."

"Yeah, you're right Jason. I knew you would help me to figure this out. You don't know how much I appreciate you Jason. You have always been there for me, no matter what it is."

"We have always been there for each other my Brother. If things get too far out of control then come to me and I will step in and work your way out of this. But for now, be careful how you deal with Ricky and make sure that once this is all over with that you find your way out of it all together. I knew this was going to be hard for you guys and Ricky should have known that also. I will continue to be watching everything that is going on."

"You been watching?" Johnnie asked.

"Yes, of course I have. I am the one who made it possible for this war to happen. In fact some of the guns I gave you came from Hells Sinners members that I killed. Kind of ironic huh? The Hells Sinners being shot at by their own guns. I found that to be very poetic."

"Wow are you serious?"

"Yes I am," Jason said as he began to laugh.

"That is kind of funny. What is your reason for involvement in all of this?"

"To be honest, I never liked them. This war between them and the West Dragons has been brewing for a while. After what they did to your girl, I made a way for it to happen. I didn't expect you to be involved in it but Ricky has wanted this war for a long time. For them it's all about territory. For you, it's about revenge. That's part of the problem you are facing with Ricky, you're both fighting together against The Hells Sinners but for different reasons. They only want the territory because it's more money for them. Your fight is to avenge the love of your life and fulfill that pain they have cause you all. Which is way more noble than killing for money, even if I have to say so myself. I have never killed for love Bro, even for me, it has always been for money. In a way I admire your purpose for killing. Perhaps someday, I may find myself in a similar situation where I may kill for love instead of money. What a romantic idea isn't it? Avenging the woman you love. Killing for her honor and making the ones who hurt her pay with their dear lives. What a hero you must be to her? Her knight in shining armor who risks his own life to make her safe once again. She truly is a lucky woman to have you Johnnie. To think that you're willing to go after the biggest gang in the state and put yourself in harm's way just to keep your girl safe from any more harm. I admire that about you. Even though it is completely crazy, I do admire it. Heck, I would even say it's probably the craziest thing I have ever seen in my life Bro. You got some guts my Brother, I give you that much. You have a fighter's heart. I love that about you."

"Yeah, well, sometimes it gets me into places that I don't want to be in. This war is weighing tremendously on me. I really want it all to just be over with to be honest."

"Yeah, I can imagine. This is a huge undertaking that I was surprised to find you involved in. I felt you were getting in over your head, but I understood why you was doing it. I would of too, to be honest with you. It's a hard road Brother and there is no quick fix here. If you want to see this to the end, it's going to take a lot of courage and a lot of strength. From all of you too, not just you. I will never be too far away though. No matter what, I got you Bro."

"Thanks Jason. You have always been there for me. You have always let me fight out my own battles but I always knew that if I was losing you would only let it go so far."

"You know it Brother. Okay. Well, I need to get back on the grind Bro. Call me if you need me."

"I will Jason, and thanks again for your help."

"Any time Johnnie, stay safe and be careful."

"We will, talk soon."

After the meeting was over, Johnnie felt he had a better grip on how he was going to deal with Ricky. For now though, since he had the rest of the day off, he decided to go by and see if Tonya wanted to go out for a while. He had never surprised her with a date before and thought today was a good time to do it. He had her on his mind all day. Perhaps Steve was right about that kiss because he couldn't wait to get back to her. Tonya was surprised when Johnnie showed up at her house without Steve. Nevertheless she was very happy to see him and the smile on her face made it hard to hide that.

"Where's Steve?"

"I dropped him off with Darryl and Randy. I had to cut out early and go to a meeting and he decided to pick up some extra hours instead of coming home."

"Oh I see. And what brings you here then? Missed me?" Tonya asked as she was hoping for the right response.

"Of course I missed you. Actually that's why I am here. I have to rest of the day off and was wondering if you would like to spend the day out together? Maybe go do some stuff and then get some dinner?" "Yeah, I would love that Johnnie. I just need a few minutes to get ready."

Johnnie sat down on the porch while he waited for Tonya to get herself together. As a few minutes passed by Johnnie was still sitting on the porch waiting. He knew it wouldn't be that fast but he was willing to wait as long as it took. A few minutes to men are different than a few minutes to women. After several long, stretched out few minutes Tonya finally emerged looking as beautiful as ever.

"Wow! You look amazing Honey. Definitely worth the wait."

"Thank you," Tonya responded as her face lit up from her smile that always melted Johnnie's heart.

After a short pause while he was admiring her beauty, he finally came to himself and reached for her hand to help her down the stairs and continued to hold her hand as he walked her to the truck so he could open the door for her. Johnnie was thankful to be able to have this time with Tonya. With so many things going on all the time, it was moments like this that helped him to get through it and keep moving forward. His love for Tonya had always kept him from giving up. He was still determined as ever to build a future for them. He needed her and she needed him. Their lives were meant to be spent together.

Johnnie had no actual plan for their time together he was just kind of winging it but he knew he would find something for them to do. As he drove he had remembered a small waterfall he had been to a few times before when he was a child that would be a perfect setting for them to just relax while they spent time together. It was a beautiful spot filled with so many trees and flowers that were all in full bloom. The aroma of the flowers filled the air with a sweet fragrance as some of the bushes also added to the wonderful smell of the place they had come.

The whole scene was breath taking as the sound of the running water filled the atmosphere with such a romantic ambiance. Johnnie felt the place was perfect as he led Tonya over to a tree for them to sit under. Johnnie picked a spot that gave them a clear view of the waterfall under a nice tree that provided plenty of shade with gapes between some of the branches that allowed for the sun to shine through. The whole field was laid out with an array of flowers that provided a breath taking beauty that was vibrant and full of life from the water that was freely flowing from the waterfall. The river was full of many huge boulders and rocks for the water to flow around. Further down around the bend was a tiny island that supported a few trees and some grass. There were always some fish that would swim close to the edge and many of the visitors would sit by and feed them.

Tonya was in heaven. This was so unexpected and magnificently perfect. Johnnie had taken Tonya to the perfect place to just sit and spend some time together. They needed this moment together and it was perfect. No one else was there. They were all alone. They sat under the huge tree as Johnnie laid back against it with Tonya pressing against him. He wrapped his arms around her and held her.

"Oh Johnnie, this place is so beautiful. I love it here," Tonya said as she laid back against Johnnie with his arms safely wrapped around her. She hadn't felt this safe in a very long time as she comfortably nestled against him.

"I had forgotten about this place. It's been years since I've been here. My father used to bring me and my mom here when I was younger. They would sit under this tree together while I would be down at the water's edge playing with the fish. Mom would pack a picnic for us and we would spend the entire morning here and then have lunch on the blanket that dad would spread out for us. I still remember how much he loved my mother. They would just talk while laughing together and loving each other. I would feed the fish and sit and watch the waterfall sometimes I would walk down a little ways by myself and just explore the area. I can still hear my father's voice telling me to not go too far."

"You miss him don't you?" Tonya asked while she gently touched Johnnie's cheek.

"Everyday. There isn't a day that goes by that I don't think about my father."

"It must have been hard losing him at such a young age."

"Yeah it was. He was a great man. He loved my mother and me more than anything. He always knew how to handle things. I miss being able to go to him for advice."

"You been through so much already in life. I honestly don't know how you keep going with all that has happened to you and what you're still going through."

"It's not easy Honey but your love keeps me going. You mean so much to me Tonya. When we were apart there was a huge hole in me that hurt so bad. I desperately ached for you. You're my everything Tonya and I love you so much."

"Oh Johnnie, I love you too. I also ached for you and hurt for your love to just come and comfort me. I missed you so much and I am still deeply in love with you."

Johnnie had lovingly wrapped his arms around Tonya tighter as he softly whispered into her ear that he loved her too just before he gently kissed her on her cheek.
Tonya knew she still needed time to heal but in these moments it was too hard to slow things down. She needed this from Johnnie. She needed his love. She craved it so deeply. She had been lost without him and being with him was helping her more then he knew. His love for her was helping her to heal. She needed to know that nothing had changed in his heart for her and that he was still in love with her just as much as he was before. When Johnnie would take her to places like this and just loved on her, it made her feel special again. That was something she hadn't felt in forever. It was refreshing to feel this again. To feel special and loved by someone.

After a while, Johnnie got up as he pulled Tonya up with him. Taking her hand they went for a short walk down by the water. Tonya gripped his hand tight as she began to feel a bit anxious as it started triggering the memories of what happened to her in the park.

"Johnnie lets go back."

"Are you okay Honey?"

"No, I just need to go. Please Johnnie. Let's just go okay?"

"Yes of course."

Johnnie was concerned about how Tonya began to panic as they walked back to the truck. Once he got her back in the truck and they had pulled off, she began to calm a bit.

"I know it's going to take time Honey, but I'm not going to give up on us. Things will continue to get better, I promise."

"I know Babe and I'm sorry. I got a little scared. I really am trying."

"No Baby don't be sorry. This is something we have to work through together. But I promise we will get through all of this. Do you still want to go have dinner together?"

"Can we do it another day? I just feel like going home."

"Sure Honey."

"I'm so sorry, Johnnie."

"It's okay Baby. I know you're trying. I will plan a nice dinner date for us okay?"

"Yes that sounds great, Johnnie. Thank you for being so understanding."

"It's okay Honey."

Johnnie hid his frustration from her but he knew it wasn't her fault. He knew she was trying and he appreciated that. At least they were finally taking some good steps forward and he was happy about that. After Johnnie had gotten Tonya home he walked her up to the door and kissed her. They held each other for several minutes before saying good-bye.

"Thank you Johnnie for taking me out. It was so wonderful and the place you took me to was so amazing. I've never seen a more beautiful place. It was special and being with you there was special. We needed that together. I am sorry that I ruined it for us."

"No Baby, you didn't ruin anything. I enjoyed every moment with you. Please don't worry about it. I had a great time with you."

"Thank you Johnnie. See you soon?"

"Yes of course My Love." Johnnie was smiling as he kissed her one last time before leaving to go back home.

Things didn't end the way he had hoped but nevertheless it was still a wonderful time for them and they needed it so much as they continued to try to rebuild their relationship.

***

It was late. The work day had ended and the Two Brothers were home relaxing when Darryl decided to go to sleep. Randy was still up watching television when he began to feel a little hungry. There was nothing in the kitchen he wanted to snack on so he had decided to take a walk to the convenient store. It was located in the center of the neighborhood where the group wasn't far from. They all lived close to the entrance of the neighborhood and it was just a short walk for them to the store. Because it was centrally located all the neighborhood kids would hang around there and talk. It stayed open till midnight every day of the week and would reopen at six in the morning.

It was a quiet, dark night with hardly any movement outside at all. Randy was alone as he journeyed to the store. Darryl was fast asleep from the hard days' work but Randy was still a bit restless. He had decided whatever the group was going to do concerning this war, he was going to do it also. No matter what, they had always stuck together and he felt that this was no different. They had to stay together and back each other up, just like they had always done before. Maybe The West Dragons wasn't right in what they do, but this wasn't about them. This was about the group ending a life-long feud that needed to come to an end. Randy had struggled with this long enough and finally decided he was all the way in. He knew that the rest of the group needed him and he wasn't going to let them down any more. They never said anything bad about him but he knew it had to be a disappointment to them to leave him behind while they go off to fight their enemies.

As Randy was walking along and thinking, there was a car coming in the distance. They began to slow as they got closer to him until they finally rolled up to him. He saw it was some of the West Dragons and was curious as to why they was here on this side of the town when the group hadn't been with them.

"Hey Randy," a voice called out from the driver's window.

"Hey Auto. How are you?" Randy responded still surprised to see them here.

"I am good man, hop in Bro lets go for a short ride and talk," Auto said as the back door opened by one of the members who was sitting in the back seat.

"I'm good man. I am just going to the store real quick and then heading back home."

"No problem Bro. We can give you a ride, hop in."

"Well, okay," Randy said as he got in the back seat.

He was still not feeling very comfortable but he never had any issues with them so he reluctantly got it. As they drove a little ways they came to the park that was not far from the store, pulled in and slowly came to a stop. Auto had shut the car off.

"What's going on?" Randy asked with a bit of caution in his voice. It was evident that something wasn't right at this point.

"Get out of the car, Randy," Viper said to him as the rest of the gang got out with him.

Viper went around and opened the back door where Randy was sitting, reached in and pulled him out of the back seat.

"What is this about?" Randy had asked.

"We need to make an example out of you so the rest will know better than to back out of this," Viper said as he punched Randy in his stomach.

"We also need to re-motivate the rest of your little group," Snake said as he also started punching Randy as Auto also began to hit him until he fell down to the ground.

He tried to fight back but it was just too much for him. They were all over him and now began to kick him and stomp on him until he was no longer moving. Viper and Snake helped him up while Auto had thrown a rope over a huge tree limb. They put the other end of the rope around Randy's neck, pulled him up and tied it off leaving him there dangling. Auto pinned a sign on his shirt saying *The Hells Sinners* like Ricky ordered him to do so everyone would think it was them who had done this. Once they was finished they drove off and left Randy there dead, hanging from the tree.

When Darryl awakened early in the morning he went in to wake up Randy for work, but there was no one in his room. At first he thought Randy had woke up early until he had went out into the living room where his parents where. They had just woke up themselves and Thomas was getting ready for work.

"Where is Randy?" Darryl asked them as he was wondering why he wasn't in the house.

"He isn't in his room?" Christina asked.

"No. His room is empty."

"That's odd. I wonder where he went," Christina said as she grabbed the remote and turned on the television.

Her heart sank as it was all over the news about a young man who was found dead hanging in the park. She had no idea that it was Randy until the phone rang and it was the police asking for Mr. Hilton. "What is it?" she asked as she began to break down in tears.

"Is this Mrs. Hilton?" The police officer asked her.

"Yes I am," she responded and began to sob.

She knew what they were going to say because of the news on the television. Even though they had not released the name, she knew it was why the police was calling.

"Is Randy Hilton your son Ma'am?"

"Yes he is, what has happened?"

"I'm sorry Ma'am. We found your son in the park early this morning. It looks as if he was murdered. Can you and your husband please come down and identify the body?"

"What's going on Mom?" Darryl asked as he was standing there watching his mother sob on the phone. There was a pain in the pit of his stomach that something bad had just happened.

"Dad come here!" Darryl yelled out.

"Yes we can, we will be right there." Christina said as she hung up the phone and fell to her knees.

"What is it Darryl?" Thomas asked as he entered the living room and found Christina on her knees crying.

Thomas reached down and picked her up and held her. "Baby, what's wrong? What is going on?" he asked while holding her in his arms.

"Dad I think something has happened to Randy," Darryl said.

"Baby, who was on the phone? What has happened?"

"It's Randy! They found him dead at the park!"

"At the park? When did he go to the park? Are they sure

it's him?" Thomas asked hoping this was somehow a mistake.

"They are sure. They want us to come down and identify the body."

"This has to be a mistake," Thomas said as he was still trying to understand how Randy ended up at the park.

"I am going with you," Darryl said as he went to get dressed.

"No, Darryl. I need you to stay here just in case this is a mistake and Randy comes home," Thomas explained as he was still not willing to believe this was really happening.

The news had described it as gang violence because of the Hells Sinners name that was tagged to Randy's shirt. Darryl had no idea about this as of yet, but would soon find out. Thomas and Christina spent part of the morning downtown identifying the body at the City Hospital where they had taken Randy for examination to confirm whether or not it was murder or suicide. A police officer met them there to ask some questions about Randy and the situation that had occurred. Once they arrived and went to the front desk to get information, one of the nurses was paged to take them back to view the body to identify whether or not it was Randy. The police officer was waiting in the lobby for them to finish.

Their worst fears come true when they pulled back the sheet and saw Randy laying there. He was already tagged as a murder victim because of the bruises that was all over his body. Thomas and Christina just stood there holding each other as they wept bitterly. This made no sense to them.

All Thomas could say was, "He was home when we went to sleep."

"I am sorry for your loss," the nurse said. "Take all the time you need."

Thomas and Christina stayed there for several minutes trying to gather themselves together before slowly heading back to the lobby to go home. As they went to leave, the Police officer met them in the lobby with some questions.

"I'm sorry Mr. and Mrs. Hilton but if you don't mind, I do have a few questions I need to ask you."

"What kind of questions?" asked Thomas as the officer motioned for them to sit down.

"This appears to be gang related. Was your son Randy in a gang?"

"Are you serious? Of course not! My son would never join a gang."

"Yes, I understand that Mr. Hilton. The reason I am asking is because there was a gang tag pinned to his shirt."

"A gang tag. What do you mean?" asked Thomas as him and Christina was trying to make sense out of this conversation.

"My son was never in any gang, said Christina as she assured the officer.

"What gang tag?" asked Thomas.

"The Hells Sinners is a gang from Westbend Heights. The name of this gang was pinned to his shirt to let everyone know they had committed this crime."

"This just doesn't make any sense at all. My son was a good kid. Why would a gang do this to him?"

"I don't know Mr. Hilton, but that is what we are trying to find out. Do you know if there was any reason for them to be after your son?"

"I don't know anything about The Hells Sinners or whatever their name is. I have never even heard of them."

Randy and Darryl had never mentioned anything about their fight with Wayne and Ricco being against a gang. When the fights had started they wasn't a gang at the time but had developed into one after a while and Wayne had joined them.

"Okay Mr. and Mrs. Hilton. If you can think of anything at all, please give me a call. And if I happen to come across anything I will let you know. Thank you for your time. I will be in touch."

"Yes of course, Officer. Thank you very much," Thomas said as he led Christina to the car to take her home.

She was a wreck and he was struggling desperately to

keep it together himself. Darryl had called Johnnie and explained to him what was going on and that he and Randy wouldn't be working today.

Johnnie was in disbelief. *Who would have killed Randy?* "I better call Steve and let him know what is going on and that we won't be working today."

"Okay Johnnie. I will call you as soon as I find something out."

"Yeah do that. I will be here waiting. Do you want me to call George?"

"No. I am going to call him now while you contact Steve."

"Okay Darryl. Call me just as soon as you can."

"I will for sure Bro."

Johnnie could hardly believe this had happened. After calling Steve and talking for several minutes Johnnie went in and sat down with his mother and told her the horrible news about Randy.

"This can't be real Johnnie. Why would someone want to kill Randy? He was always such a good kid. Who would do this?" Sara asked while she sat on the couch crying. "Poor Thomas and Christina. They must be devastated. They are going to need our support. Darryl will also. Maybe we should all pitch in and make a nice lunch for them and bring it down."

"Yes, that's a good idea Mom. I will let you handle that."

As Johnnie got up to go wash his face from the tears, he received a phone call from Tonya.

"Johnnie, Steve just told me about Randy. Oh my, Johnnie, is this true? Did this really happen?"

"Yes Honey it did. I just got off the phone with Darryl. Thomas and Christina are downtown right now identifying the body."

"Johnnie this is horrible. Are you okay?"

"Yes I am okay." Johnnie said with a long drawn out sigh.

"Do you need me to come down?" Tonya asked as she was needing his comfort just as much as he was needing hers.

"Yes Baby, please come down. I need you with me," Johnnie said as he was fighting back the tears.

"Okay Baby, let me get myself together and I will be right there," Tonya responded.

She hung up the phone and went to take a shower. She needed to get herself together as she had awakened to the news about Randy and had called Johnnie immediately. After Tonya had got herself ready she went down to be with Johnnie who had received another phone call from Darryl. He explained how this was done by the Hells Sinners and was being investigated as a gang murder. Johnnie was beside himself. He couldn't believe it. There was no way The Hells Sinners could have known they were involved in this gang war. How could they have known? Who would have told them?

As Tonya came down, Johnnie took her out back to the patio so he could talk to her about this without his mom hearing their conversation. After he had sat Tonya down, he told her all Darryl had said to him.

"How did they know Johnnie?"

"I don't know but I need to talk to Ricky about this. Something just doesn't seem right about this at all. There is no way they could have known about us being involved in this war."

"Someone had to have said something."

"But who? And why? There was never any reason to mention us. It just doesn't make sense Tonya. Something isn't adding up here. I think before I talk to Ricky I am going to have another meeting with Jason."

"Yes that's a great idea Honey. If anyone would know how to get answers it would be Jason."

"Yeah, you're right."

Tonya sat with Johnnie crying as he held her in his arms. Everyone was in tears over this horrible tragedy. The mothers of Steve and George got together with Sara and prepared a meal for The Hilton family so they wouldn't have to be bothered with it while they grieved the loss of their son. Thomas and Christina would be busy with calling all of the family and also making arrangements as well.

Johnnie knew if The Hells Sinner had known they were involved then it would take things to a new level. They were all going to have to start looking over their shoulders and being way more cautious then what they had been. This had changed everything. Now it was definite they were going to have to finish this war.

That afternoon everyone who was available came over to the Hilton home with food so they would not have to worry about that. They were comforted by each family that was showing their support and love to the family in their time of distress. As they all sat together talking and eating, Darryl was in his room trying to figure out how he was going to handle this. Now The Hells Sinners had struck back and they took out his brother as far as he knew. This was something he just couldn't let go. He had to do something. But when and how was the question. Finally he came out to join the rest of the family as they were eating. Darryl was uncomfortable with everyone being here while he was grieving so his visit with them was cut very short as he headed back into his room after he had finished eating.

Later that night after everyone had gone and things settled down. Thomas and Christina were exhausted and finally went to bed to get some sleep. Darryl, on the other hand, was wide awake with anger in his heart. Finally he had decided this was it. He went out and headed for the bus stop. He had just made it to catch the last bus running for the night and headed to Westbend.

The bus ride was very quiet as Darryl sat there alone thinking about what he was going to do. Once he got off of the bus it was a bit of a walk to where The Hells Sinners club house was. When he finally reached the block where the club house was he quietly walked up to the house and fired two shots into the two members that where sitting outside keeping watch. At the sound of the gun fire members began to pour out of the house with gun fire. Darryl had emptied his clip into the door way at those who were coming out before they had fired back and riddled his body with bullets until he was dead. As he laid there, Wayne and Ricco realized who it was and knew he had come for revenge for the killing of his brother. The police had been questioning The Hells Sinners members all day before having to let them go from the lack of evidence on any particular member.

"What is going on with this? First we are accused of killing Randy and know Darryl shows up shooting at us?" Wayne asked as him and Ricco was trying to figure out this whole situation.

Ricco decided it was time for him and Wayne to go have a meeting with Jason to find out who was behind this. The only thing that was clear was someone had been setting them up. They knew they hadn't been behind Randy's murder but someone was and they were trying to pin it on them. The rest of the members had cleaned up the club house from all of the drugs and had shut it down before the police had arrived. No one stayed for questioning so it looked like the only ones involved were all dead.

In the meantime Ricco had enough of trying to find out who was hitting them and figured that whoever it was had also been behind the murder of Randy. None of this made any sense but he was sure going to find out. Jason had received Johnnie's phone call and set up a meeting for them two and now The Hells Sinners wanted a meeting over the same thing.

Later on that night Christina was startled when the phone rang. She was still trying to wake as she answered the phone. It was the police calling again, but this time it was about Darryl. She was in utter disbelief as she woke Thomas up. What was going on? Why was this happening? They couldn't understand as they received the news their other son had been killed as well. Thomas and Christina was in shock and didn't know how to handle this. It was just this morning they had received news Randy was murdered and now Darryl, who was supposed to be home, had also been killed. It had become obvious there was something going on they did not know about. It was in the middle of the night and now they had to get up and go identify another body.

How did God let this happen to us?" Christina asked Thomas.

"I don't know Honey. I just don't know."

Early the next morning it had gone through the community about the death of Darryl. Johnnie and the rest of the group were beside themselves. Johnnie had already had a meeting set up with Jason so he had to go take care of that and hopefully get some answers. Jason was smart enough to know that somewhere something wasn't right. He wanted to meet with Johnnie first so he put off The Hells Sinners until he had a chance to sit down with Johnnie and talk about what was going on. This time he didn't want anyone to know he was meeting with Johnnie so they didn't go to the Coffee House as usual. Jason texted him the address to the old warehouse he used for secret business.

Jason was waiting outside when Johnnie had pulled up. They walked inside together.

"Why are we meeting here?" Johnnie inquired of him.

"Well, the funny thing is this Johnnie, Ricco, from The Hells Sinners also contacted me to have a meeting about this very same thing."

"Really? What do they want to talk about?" Johnnie asked out of curiosity.

"I won't know for sure until I sit down with them, but from what I can gather, they wasn't behind Randy's death."

"How do you know?"

"Well, I don't for sure, but I will soon enough. It may be that someone else is behind this."

"But why? Who would gain anything from this?"

"That's a good question Johnnie and I promise you I will find out. I am very sorry for your loss my Brother. I will meet with them shortly then we can meet up again later and I will fill you in."

"So I came here to find out how they knew we were involved and you're telling me they may not have known?"

"Yeah. They are trying to figure out who is trying to pin this on them and why."

"You don't think it's Ricky do you?"

"It very well could be Johnnie. Once I find out then we will sit down and talk about how we are going to handle it if it is him."

"Okay. That sounds good Brother, keep in touch with me."

"I will for sure Johnnie, and don't worry about it. I will find out who is behind this."

"Thank you Jason, I will be waiting for your call."

Shortly after Johnnie left, Jason met up with The Hells Sinners and sat down with them as well. They too had only questions. This led Jason to agree with Johnnie's assumption that Ricky was possibly behind this. It was clear The Hells Sinners still didn't know who was hitting them or why and that Johnnie was also involved. Jason had to steer the conversation in a way to not reveal that to them. He didn't care if they knew who it was or not, but he needed to find out for himself. His next meeting was going to be with Ricky and he figured there he would find the answers he was looking for. If it was him and Johnnie was right, Ricky was going to pay for this.

CHAPTER 6

FUNERAL FOR TWO BROTHERS

Everything was getting out of control. Trust was becoming an even more serious issue for Johnnie and what was left of the group if they found out it was Ricky who had Randy killed. This was going to be tricky, trying to explain to the rest of the group without them knowing they may have been betrayed by Ricky. If they knew it was him, they may back out and all of this would be for nothing. So much was going on and he had no idea how he was going to handle all of this. He was fighting a war with allies who may have killed two of his own people. Two of his best friends and employees were now dead. This deal was getting worse all the time.

If Ricky had anything to do with this, he will surely die. This was all my fault. I should've never brought this to the group in the first place. How do I go on and keep helping them if they are working against us? If Ricky did this, I will give my life to see him dead.

After Johnnie got home, Tonya came by to spend some time with him. They needed to be comforted. As they sat out back talking about what happened, Johnnie realized that for now, he better keep this information to himself. Everyone's emotions were running very high, and he knew this wasn't the time to release this information to the rest of the group. Everyone on the block was very close, so they all had been showing their support to the Hiltons.

The Hiltons were struggling desperately to try and understand how this had happened and why God had allowed it. They had served God faithfully, and yet He had allowed this tragedy to happen to their family. In the midst of Christina ministering and encouraging Tonya, God had let her only two sons get murdered. How was this fair? Why had God not protected their family? Thomas and Christina were now struggling with their faith in God. They had always trusted Him to work everything out for their good, no matter what they faced. God gave them two sons and now, they had been taken away from them. How was she going to ever be able to continue ministering to Tonya when her two sons were lying dead in a morgue due to senseless gang violence, when her sons weren't even gang members?

None of this made any sense as to how two Christian boys could have got caught up in all of this. Johnnie knew it was only going to be a matter of time before they were going to question him about this situation. He was dreading it. What was he going to say to them? What was he going to tell them? How could he explain to these good Christian parents their sons had been caught up in a gang war? He struggled with the possibilities that could stem from telling them the truth. What if they gave the police the information that he gave them? He and Steve could be arrested for murder. There was no way to tell them without involving themselves in the situations that took place. Johnnie had always believed in being honest no matter what the cost, but this would ruin his and Steve's lives. He was going to have to find a way to deal with this without saying too much and without implicating him and Steve. They were not about to go to prison over this while The Hell's Sinners got away with another victory over them. They had raped Tonya and now, the Two Brothers were dead because of them. Whether they did it or not, it was because of their feud with them that cause their deaths. It didn't matter if it was them or Ricky; it was still their fault the Two Brothers were killed. Everyone was still in shock and in disbelief. The Hilton Family was a very good family who had always been there for everyone and always willing to help out when needed. They were model citizens and now people are talking about gang violence. The entire neighborhood was shook up over this severe tragedy. Thomas and Christina had been up since late last night and now it was after midnight and they were still awake. Although they both were extremely exhausted, they were unable to sleep.

    Johnnie and Tonya spent the night lying next to each other in the hammock. He wrapped his arms around Tonya as they talked and mourned. He hadn't heard anything back from Jason and figured he might hear something the following day. His mind was on so many things. He wondered how he was going to handle this with the Hiltons and with Ricky if it had turned out to be him, while making sure Tonya was okay. Hi plate was beyond full and he couldn't focus on work right now and wasn't going to be able to get back to it until after the funeral. He also had to hire at least one person, which was no problem. He knew George wanted to work.

***

    Thomas and Christina had a hard time falling asleep. Their faith had been tested beyond anything they could have ever imagined. They had so much faith in God and now, they felt so weak. Ann had always been concerned about George's participation in this war, even more so now that the Two Brothers had been killed. George did all he could to keep Ann calm during this war, but her concerns took on new meaning after the deaths of Randy and Darrell. She was even more worried about George than ever before. He had assured her no one knew they were involved, but now, as far as she knew, all of that had changed. That was also weighing on George's mind now. Things seemed even more serious now that they had been hit back. George's main concern was how they were going to protect themselves from The Hell's Sinners now that they knew about them. They had always stood their ground and wasn't about to stop now.

    It was a dark time for the group, who had now been placed in a horrible situation. They needed direction and

Johnnie himself wasn't sure what to do now. He couldn't tell the group what really had transpired. They needed to find a way to finish what they started without getting killed or going to prison. He had decided it was time to have another meeting to discuss how they were going to handle it if or when the Hiltons asked them questions about what happened.

There was no way Johnnie was going to go back into the system. He sure wasn't going to drag the rest of the group in with him. Three years in the system was more than enough and he wasn't about to lose his freedom again. He didn't want to have to lie to the Hiltons. After all, they deserved to know the truth, but at what price? There was no way to predict how they would respond to the truth, and what they would do if they knew. For now, he would avoid it and let Jason find out some more facts. Hopefully, all will come to light so he could figure out exactly how he was going to handle this if in fact Ricky was involved in the death of the Two Brothers, which he was sure that he was. Figuring out how he was going to deal with it was a different issue.

During this time, George and Ann spent all of their time together, comforting each other as their relationship had grown quite a bit. After the group had spent some time at the funeral home for visitations for the Two Brothers, Johnnie told them he needed to have a meeting that night to talk about this situation. During this time, Jason had reached out to Ricky after letting it settle for a few days. Ricky assured Jason they had nothing to do with it at all. However, Jason already knew they did and played as if he hadn't known. He was going to deal with this at a later time, but for now, decided it was best to let it lie so Johnnie wouldn't be put in any further danger until this war was over.

Jason had called Johnnie before they went to the funeral home. He instructed him to let it go for now and had assured him after the war was over, they would deal with Ricky. For now, the issue was set aside which was fine with

Johnnie. Later that evening, they all gathered together back at the camp behind Johnnie's house. Tonya and Ann were also present for this meeting. As they all gathered together, Johnnie stood up and spoke.

"As you all know, this situation has taken a turn for the worse, as far as we are concerned. We all knew the risk when got involved. The first thing I want to know is who is in and who is out."

"I'm in, Brother. I can't turn back in good conscious. They raped my sister, and now have killed two of my best friends. I won't stop until this is over with," Steve answered passionately.

"I'm still in as well. I feel like if we back out now, then they win again, and I am not willing to live with that," George said as he held Ann's hand tightly, hoping she would understand.

"George, let's think about this, okay?" Ann spoke up. "I mean, how far are you willing to go before enough is enough?"

"Ann, I know you're scared, I am scared as well, but we have to see this 'til the end and make sure that it is finished," George responded to Ann.

"I agree with George, we have to finish this," Johnnie added in agreement.

"To what cost, Johnnie? 'Til you're all dead? Are you willing to risk all of you being killed?" Ann asked in frustration.

"I only risk my own life, Ann. Everyone here has made their own choices from the beginning, even until now."

"He's right, Ann. We have all been in control of our participation," George said.

"Johnnie has always given us a way out if we wanted it. He even accepted Randy backing out and never complained about it or even made Randy feel bad about leaving this war," Steve said in his defense.

As they were all talking, Tonya sat quietly and just listened. She felt this entire war had started because of her, and in her own way, she felt guilty for the deaths of Randy and Darrell. She knew if this had never happened to her, they would not have been involved in this war in the first place. She wanted them out of this war, but couldn't bring herself to say anything voluntarily because of what they might think since they had went after The Hell's Sinner for raping her in the first place. She was very content, but Ann had to bring her into the conversation.

"What about you, Tonya? How do you feel about all of this?"

With a big, long drawn-out sigh Tonya responded, "I never wanted any of this to happen. I hate what is going on, I hate that I am not involved but I also hate they are. Had I known they were going to war with The Hell's Sinners over what they had done to me, I would have tried to stop them. However, I have heard everyone's point of view. Unfortunately, I have to agree with them. They can't back out now. If The Hell's Sinners know they are helping out in this war, then they have no choice but to stay in it and fight to make sure they win. If The Hell's Sinners are coming after us all, then it's better for all of us if we at least have a form of protection and some allies to assist us in this war, instead of being off on our own to fight against them by ourselves."

Everyone sat quietly allowing Tonya's words to sink in. She made much sense with her words. There is safety in numbers and there was no way that they could just fade out of this war now. Even with The Hell's Sinners in a state of confusion, Johnnie knew if they had backed out, Ricky might come after the rest of them as well. For now, he just needed to play the game and try to bring an end to this war without any further damage being done.

"One last thing we need to discuss," Johnnie said, as they all sat quietly. "We need to agree on what to tell Thomas and Christina if they should ask us about this."

"I don't think we should lie to them," Steve said. George, Ann and Tonya were in agreement.

"I think we say this and stick to this if or when we are asked. We tell them it was the group that we always had problems with in school, and they just happened to catch Randy alone and killed him. They already know Darrell went after them on his own, which allows us to keep our involvement out of the conversation. They don't need to know everything. We do have to protect ourselves and if we say too much, we could end up incriminating ourselves. None of us wants to go to prison. I think we only say about Randy and Darrell and leave ourselves out of it all together."

Everyone agreed to that as it did sound reasonable. They only needed to know about their sons and not about everyone else. So, as far as anyone knows, the rest of the group wasn't involved and it was best to keep it that way, so no one would risk their names coming up to the police.

After the meeting, the group sat around the fire and spent some time together reminiscing about some of their best times they all had with the Two Brothers. Everyone had special moments with Randy and Darrell. This was a very emotional time for them all as they remembered all the fun they had together.

Everyone hated not being able to tell Thomas and Christina the full truth, but some things were better left unsaid and well enough alone. There was no reason to incriminate the rest of the group unnecessarily. Perhaps, at a later time when this was all over, maybe then they could tell the full story. But for now, it was best to let it stay between the group. Johnnie knew at some point he would have to tell them. He couldn't let them live without knowing the full story. They deserved the truth and when the time was right, he knew he would have to tell them everything concerning the group and The Hell's Sinners. They owed it to them.

As the night came to a close, George and Ann wandered off to be alone, Steve headed back to the house while Tonya stayed a bit longer with Johnnie for some alone time. He held and comforted her. Tonya was terribly sad at all that had happened and needed to feel his arms around her. He remained strong in front of everyone, but it was getting harder to hold it all back. The stress of losing two of his employees, having to replace them and train two more people to do their jobs while mourning their deaths was hard for him to bear. He felt guilty as he took personal responsibility for their deaths. Losing two close childhood friends who were like brothers to him was too much. He broke down in front of Tonya. It had been a very long time since she saw him in this shape.

She knew in her heart when the time came for them to tell Thomas and Christina everything that happened, it would be him who would have to be the one to do it. She felt terrible about everything that he had to deal with. It was all on his shoulders and he would have to do it on his own.

Johnnie had already decided to not only hire George, but he was going to ask Ann if she wanted to work with George on the lawn care side of things. It was an easy job that he knew she could handle. Plus, this would put money in both of their pockets that would help them work towards their goals of getting married and getting their own place. He felt more at ease being able to hire people he already knew and trusted. With that being set aside, for now he was able to focus on Tonya and their mourning for their two fallen brothers. The rest of the night, Johnnie and Tonya held and comforted each other until the sun arose early the next morning. They were exhausted from another long night together that would result in them sleeping the day away after he walked her home.

Steve was still asleep when Tonya came in, but Tony and Tammy were awake. Tony was getting ready for work and Tammy was in the kitchen cooking breakfast when she had heard Tonya come in. Tammy asked Tonya if she wanted any breakfast, but Tonya was way too tired to eat. Tony and Tammy sat down together at the table to eat breakfast while Tonya went to bed.

It was exceptionally nice to be able to spend a nice quiet breakfast together as they usually never had any alone time before Tony went to work. As the two ate together and enjoyed being alone, Tony got up, turned off the kitchen light and lit a few candles, placing them on the table and shared the rest of their breakfast time romantically. Tammy was deeply touched as Tony had made this morning special for her. She always loved how Tony would take advantage of alone time together and create special moments for her. After a lovely breakfast with his wife, Tony was off to work and Tammy decided to get some cleaning done while it was still quiet in the house. After Steve woke up, he didn't feel like sitting around the house, but Johnnie gave him time off until after the funeral was over. After Ricky had received a phone call from Jason, he came to the realization that he better do a real good job at selling the murder of Randy to everyone as an attack by the Hell's Sinners. Ricky decided to order a few of his members to vandalize a few key places he knew Cypher would take notice of. He knew Jason was looking into the situation and needed to make sure he kept the pressure on The Hells Sinners while keeping the heat off of him and The West Dragons. Ricky wasn't exactly sure how much Jason already knew, but he did know if Jason found out for sure it was him who had Randy killed, that it might not be good for him. There was so much at stake. Everything he worked for was getting closer to being his and he wasn't going to allow the death of someone that he barely knew stop him from taking this territory and becoming the largest gang in Westbend Heights. To Ricky, Randy and Darrell had only been formalities to keep Cypher under his control. However Ricky hadn't anticipated Jason being that closely involved in Cypher's affairs, which was now a major concern to him.

***

The next day, everyone was up early getting ready for the funeral. This was an extremely hard day for the family, friends, as well as the entire community, which had been shook up over this gang violence. The Church was still in shock over the loss of two young men who grew up in their midst. It was hard to understand how something like this could happen to two young Christian men. Their death was a tragedy that was unimaginable for this city. It was common place over in Westbend Heights for senseless violence to occur, but this was Southbend Heights, where nothing like this had ever happened before. The group decided it was their duty to carry both caskets. Johnnie reached out to Jason and asked if he would help out to make up the last person they would need to carry the Two Brothers.

It was quiet as they all gathered together at the funeral home. Jason was there earlier than expected, as was his custom. They all gathered together to figure out where each person was going to be positioned. Ann and Tonya felt they also needed to be involved and opted to take the middle while Johnnie and Jason took the front and George and Steve taking the back positions. Sara, Tammy, Monica and Christina were together with a few other ladies from the Church. While Thomas sat with Tim and Tony, they talked about what the group must be going through. They knew this was very hard for Thomas and Christina, but the group grew up together and was all like real brothers and sisters to each other. For them, they lost family members.

Thomas was very concerned about Johnnie, who had been through so much in his life already. He kept a close eye on him to make sure he was going to be alright. This was a tough emotional time for all families, for they were all close to each other. Outside of the group, no one was really sure who Jason was. They had all assumed he must have been a childhood friend from school. They had never seen him before with the exception of Sara, who tried to explain to the other women that Jason was a close friend of Johnnie's who came to help out as a pallbearer. However, Sara knew very little about Jason and had called Johnnie over to explain in better detail how Jason was connected to this group. Everyone was so close, having a mystery person here was a bit of a talk for the ladies. Johnnie called Jason over to come join him so he could introduce him to the mothers. Jason knew how to be charming and took his time to meet everyone he was introduced to. They all were impressed with his style of dress and his mannerisms. Jason told them he was a business man who worked with many different people as a money handler and an overseer, which was pretty accurate, to say the least. It is what he did, he just didn't go into great detail about what kind of business and what kind of people. Jason had learned how to dance around questions and only say what he needed to appease people.

After Johnnie took Jason around and introduced him to everyone, it was almost time for the service to start. It was hard for Johnnie and the rest of the group to watch everyone crying while they knew what really happened. Tonya and Ann both cried, while Johnnie and George sat next to them and held them. This was the worst day ever for the group, who had never had to bury any of their friends before. Up until now, they had only experienced the hurt of Tonya being raped, which was bad enough and Johnnie going to juvenile prison. But having to bury the Two Brothers was way too much to bear. He and Steve pledged their lives to the destruction of The Hell's Sinners, but now, it was even more serious and the mission was even more real than ever before. Finishing this war became top priority.

The Pastor began the service with a short prayer for the family before he began to speak as soft music played in the background. Everyone bowed their heads as he began to pray.

"Our Father in Heaven, we humbly come to You as we all mourn the death of these two fine boys that You loved and cared for. It is my prayer, Lord that these senseless deaths will not be in vain. That somehow, some way You will work this out for the good. Let every heart be comforted as we all mourn the deaths of these Two Brothers. As Thomas and Christina mourn their loss, I pray that they will find comfort and peace in You Lord. In Jesus' Name, Amen.

"Darrell and Randy were two fine boys whom I had the pleasure of getting to know. They loved Jesus and enjoyed coming to church. They kept me on my toes. I never knew what they were going to do next. They were tough kids, but they were good kids. They were always ready and willing to serve and help people without any thought of themselves. This tragedy was senseless and undeserved. I mourn with the family as they grieve their loss. Thomas and Christina were wonderful parents who raised their children right and always made sure they were in Church. My prayers are with you as you grieve, that the Holy Spirit will comfort you."

Johnnie listened to the preacher talk about how Darrell and Randy's deaths were a senseless tragedy and all he could think about was killing Wayne. This was it for him, he had fought his life to try and not lose himself to the things that he was forced to go through, but this had pushed him over the edge. He had finally found his breaking point and death was sure to come of it. Fueled by anger and hatred, he no longer cared. He was going to become the cold-blooded killer that he fought so hard not to become. Revenge was now in his blood and hatred was deeply imbedded within his heart. Everyone was going to pay for this, Ricky included.

George was holding Ann, trying to calm her down, who cried uncontrollably. Thomas and Christina who were sitting on the front row had lost it as well. During the service, the pastor had opened the floor for anyone who wanted to say a few words about the Two Brothers. Johnnie, George and Steve all stood up and walked together up to the front to speak on behalf of their two brothers. They had felt it was only right to all go together as they had done all things together. By going together, they felt they were honoring Darrell and Randy. Johnnie spoke first.

"I grew up with Randy and Darrell. They were like my brothers. I loved them like they were my real family. We had so many good times together. We played hard together and fought even harder together when we needed to. They were true brothers and great friends that I was always able to count on them to have my back no matter what. They were both dependable workers who showed up every day, worked hard and never complained. They were a blessing to my life. They were the kind of friends you can never replace. They were faithful and I always knew they would be there for me whenever I needed them. Randy was a fun person to be around who would always tried to lighten the mood with his wonderful sense of humor, while Darrell was a bit more wild and always ready for some wild fun," Johnnie continued. "They were exciting to be around and always kept things interesting. I will deeply miss my brothers, but I will never forget them. They are forever in my heart and in my memories." After Johnnie finished, then George stepped out and began to speak.

"These two brothers were two of the best friends anyone could have ever asked for. Johnnie talked about them being dependable and that, they surely were. This tragedy is a loss to us all. They were amazing friends who will deeply be missed by us all. Johnnie said everything. They were all of this and so much more. They loved their friends and would do anything to help others. I will always love them." As George finished, Steve began to speak.

"I met these two brothers when I moved into the neighborhood. I was new and didn't know anyone and they all came down to meet me. Immediately, I knew we was all going to be good friends. They accepted me right away and the rest is history. I loved them very much. They was always there for me and made my life a lot more fun. I will miss them. My heart aches for their loss, as we mourn with Mr. and Mrs. Hilton. I will never forget the many times we had shared together. In a world that seems to be so fake nowadays, they were the real deal. They knew how to be real friends. This tragedy will not go unpunished. Justice will prevail. We will all suffer this loss together. They came from great parents and it showed in their character. We will forever love them."

As the boys returned back to their seats, the pastor had come back up to finish the service. There were no dry eyes in the room. They all felt the words from the Johnnie,

George and Steve as they had honored their brothers. After the pastor had finished, everyone came by the casket to say their last goodbyes to the Two Brothers. Once the room had emptied out, the group took the first casket out and placed Randy in the back of the hearse, then returned to bring out Darrell. Tonya and Ann were desperately trying to keep it together. This was something they felt they had to do as a group and they weren't going to let them down. They fought as hard as ever to hold back the tears as they walked the Two Brothers out.

Once they had finished, Johnnie, Tonya and Steve sat on one side of the limousine as George and Ann sat on the other side with Jason, who had helped out as well. Johnnie held Tonya while George held Ann as the two broke down on the way to the cemetery. As they pulled into the cemetery, Tonya and Ann tried to regain their composure as they tried to pull themselves together. Once they had carried Darrell and Randy to their final resting place, the pastor finished the service.

"As we come to pay our last respects to Darrell and Randy, as we lay them to rest I will now share a few Scriptures with you. In Ecclesiastes three, verses one through eight, it says 'There is a time for everything, and a reason for every activity under heaven. A time to be born and a time to die, a time to plant and a time to uproot. A time to kill and a time to be healed. A time to tear down and a time to build. A time to weep and a time to laugh, a time to mourn and a time to dance. A time to gather stones and a time to scatter them. A time to embrace and a time to refrain. A time to search and a time to give up. A time to keep and a time to throw away. A time to tear and a time to mend. A time to be silent and a time to speak. A time to love and a time to hate. A time for war and a time for peace.'"

As the pastor was reading those verses, it all rang in Johnnie's ears as it greatly spoke to his heart. It was all true, and he had hoped at some point he would be able to put off this hate and they would all have peace after this war was finished.

"Also we find in Second Corinthians, chapter four, verse sixteen and chapter fifteen verse eight, 'For which cause we faint not; but though our outward man perish, yet the inward man is renewed day by day. For our light affliction, which is but for a moment, works for us a far more exceeding and eternal weight of glory; while we look not at the things which are seen, but at the things which are not seen: for the things which are seen are temporal; but the things which are not seen are eternal. We will see these two brothers again when we meet them in Heaven."

After the service ended, they all went back to the funeral home. The group had spent a few moments alone talking before joining everyone who had already left the cemetery to go to the hall for repast. Everything had happened so fast, they couldn't believe it was over already.

After talking and sharing, they headed to the repast where they would spent the next few hours before heading back at the camp area. There was a sense of relief once it was all over with. Everyone felt as if they could breathe and relax as they sat by the fire and reminisced about the times they had all shared with the Two Brothers. They all needed to find healing and peace from this entire ordeal. There had been so much killing and death, and so much more was to come. This war was far from over.

As the night went on, Steve left to go home as Johnnie and George spent the night holding Tonya and Ann as they wept their final mourning. It was now time to let go.

CHAPTER 7

TIME TO REGROUP

The next day, Johnnie decided to take one more day off before making everyone go back to work. They stayed up late and needed the rest. It felt weird having this all behind them now, but it didn't change the fact a huge part of their lives was missing. His blood boiled with anger for more revenge. He felt somehow no matter what he did, they always seemed to find a way to win against him, to hurt him more than he hurt them. Killing them was the only way to make things right. They would all suffer for Wayne's mistakes. He had always been able to hold himself together, but now it all seemed to begin to unravel. The only thing that would satisfy his hate and lust for revenge would be the death of his enemies.

The need to spill their blood was starting to force Johnnie to cross over into a killer. The times he had killed before was out of necessity, but now he was hungry for it. He began to thirst for their blood, he wanted to kill them all. As he tried to relax, he went through all of the messages that were piling up from the work that was left undone. They were way behind now, so he began to write out invoices and stack them from priority to what can be put off until they got things caught up. The painting side of the business was really picking up and he didn't want to lose that. Had he not invested so much with the lawn care, he would let that go. He had more than enough repair work to keep him busy for months. One thing for sure, if he was going to keep all three businesses going, he was going to need another truck. However, he didn't have the money to pay for another truck, but he did know where to get it. A quick call to Jason might solve the problem, but before he did that, he needed to find a decent truck for sale at a reasonable price.

After going over his budget and determining about how much he could afford to borrow, Johnnie went to the local convenient store to get a newspaper to see if there was anything for sale. He never been in debt or owed anyone anything before so for him to borrow money was a tough decision to make. However, he needed to have another truck. This war took a strain on his finances with the things he had to pay for, for him and the group as well, as the time missed from work due to funerals and leaving early to go on hits. Not counting the week off when he took the entire group over to Westbend Heights for a week, paid for the food and everything plus the guns he bought from Jason.

As much as he hated to admit it, they needed to focus on nothing but work for a few weeks before resuming this war again with The Hell's Sinners. He couldn't afford to lose any jobs. They all now was depending on him as an employer and he needed to make sure that he had plenty of work for them. It began to weigh heavily on him about making sure they had work and to continue to build his business. His business was still in the growing and development stage, and now was not the time to neglect it.

After he got a newspaper, he returned back home, sat at the kitchen table and began to look through the want ads to see if he could find a good truck at a decent price. There were several he came across, but quite a few were priced so high, that he could not afford to borrow at this time. But there were a few that had potential. After calling about the trucks that were available in his budget range, he went and took a look at them to determine which truck would fit his needs. They needed to be somewhat cheap but dependable at the same time. He was going to have to use it five days a week with lots of wear and tear from the tons of hauling and driving that it would need to endure on a daily basis. The first truck he looked at was in great shape for what he needed, but it was also the most expensive one of the three he was looking at. The second one was in pretty good shape, but he knew he would have to put some money into it. The last one was decent, but it had a little too much rust for his liking. After taking time to consider the possibilities, it was time to see if he could get a loan from Jason to make the deal. After a quick call, he was on his way to meet him.

Johnnie was all too familiar with the Coffee House where Jason liked to do simple business. Not that it mattered to Jason, he liked to keep his routine just to keep them busy. All of his real big deals were done at an old abandoned warehouse across town the police had no idea about. It was good to sit and talk with Johnnie again, so Jason was eager to meet up with him and discuss business. They did business in the past with guns, but this was much different.

As Johnnie came in and sat down, the two began to catch up with each other before getting down to business.

"It's always good to see you, my Brother," Jason said.

"Likewise. I want to thank you for helping out at the funeral. We all appreciated that."

"It's no problem, Johnnie. We will discuss those details at a later time though. So what's going on Bro? What can I do for you?" Jason asked just before the waitress came to take Johnnie's order.

"Can I get you anything?" she asked Johnnie.

"Yes please, I would just like a black coffee." After she left, he began to talk to Jason about his truck situation.

"Well, Bro, I need a favor from you. My business is growing and I need another truck. But as of right now, I am getting low on funds from having to take too much time off. I need to get things back on track and I can't do that with only two trucks."

"I see. So, how much are we talking about?"

"Well, I know it's a lot, but I need three thousand dollars."

"No, that's not that much, Bro. I can handle that easily. This is business though, with a loan I need to charge a little on the back end. But for you, I will keep it light. For three thousand, I will charge you thirty-two hundred on the return."

"That's not bad. I can handle a few hundred dollars." he said as he agreed to the terms of the loan.

"Plus I will follow you home to drop off your truck and take you to go pick up your new one. Fair enough?"

"That's a deal. Thank you, Jason. I really appreciate this."

Johnnie still had money, but he knew supplies and payroll had to get done as well, and making this new truck legal which he could take care of outside of the loan. But the next few weeks were going to be extremely busy. He needed to make this money back to get this loan paid off quickly.

After Jason had followed Johnnie home and took him to go get the new truck, this was a good time to talk about the Ricky situation while the police wasn't watching him and trying to listen in on his conversations.

"So, I am very sure Ricky was behind the killing of Randy. I need you to remain calm about this situation and stay focused on what's important here. Once this war is over, we will deal with our friend, Ricky. Don't worry about that, but for now, you need to act as if everything is cool."

"Yeah, I got you. As long as it gets taken care of."

"It will, my Brother, it will." As they arrived to where the truck was, Jason took a good look at it and felt that the deal was right on the money. After making the purchase, the two parted ways as Johnnie went to go get everything done to make this truck legal so they could use it in the morning. The rest of the day was spent getting everything set up for the following day.

He was ready to sit back and enjoy the rest of evening with his mother, who was watching television. They haven't had a chance to talk about the Two Brothers and now it was time to do so. Sara loved them very much. She had considered them as family. There were many times when they practically lived at her house. They spent so much time back at the camp, it was like their second home. Johnnie knew his mother had been grieving hard over this loss and he needed to be there to comfort her as well. They spent the rest of the evening talking.

She had cried a lot, but now that she was talking to Johnnie about it, more tears came. She had mourned them, but had not had the chance to talk about them and get the closure she felt she needed. She wept bitterly as they shared stories and reminisced about the many times they had sleep overs and cookouts. Sara felt deeply sorrowful for Thomas and Christina, who had been such great friends and a huge support to her when she lost Mark, and again when Johnnie was taken away to juvenile prison. Thomas had gone to visit Johnnie while he was in there whenever he had time to do so. Christina would sit with Sara quite often so she wasn't all alone.

The next day, Johnnie called Steve to come down and pick up a truck for him to go and do the painting jobs that were stacking up. Once Steve arrived, he sat down with him at the back patio to go over the invoices, as well as his need for him to train his new employees for the painting part of the business. He needed Steve to be able to help him with repairs full time once he got things set up with George, to where he would be able to handle the lawn care. He knew he still needed one more employee, but hadn't decided on who he wanted to bring in. He had used Timothy and Nate on and off when he was behind and was giving great thought about bringing them both on full-time to work with George. But for now, he needed to get Steve situated.

"I need you to come every morning, grab the truck and go get Tonya and Ann as they will now be working with you. I need you to fully train them and get them set up to be able to run this on their own, so I can have you with me doing repairs. Here are your invoices for the week, teach them everything. Let them take turns driving the truck so they can get comfortable with it. Teach them how to bid jobs and where to get supplies at, as well. For the next two weeks you will be working specifically with them and training them. We are so far behind right now that I can't afford to even take a day off for the next few weeks. If you want to pick up some extra hours on the weekends helping me do repairs I could use the help, but it's up to you, you don't have to if you don't want to. I know we are going to already be working long hours as it is."

Steve was excited about being able to train Tonya and Ann. He was ready for this responsibility that Johnnie was giving him.

"That sounds good. I will go over everything with them and be very thorough. Two weeks should be good enough to train them. These are a lot of invoices, what does next week look like for us?" Steve asked as he wondered how far behind they were.

"About the same, not quite as heavy but close. Plus you will have more days. I know I stacked it heavy, just get as many done as you can."

"Yeah we will for sure. Let me get going then so I can pick them up and go get the supplies we will need so we can get this day started."

"Okay Steve, be safe and have a good day."

"Thanks Johnnie, I will see you later tonight."

After Steve had gone, Johnnie called George to come down. Once George arrived they also talked for a bit as Johnnie explained to George what his expectations were concerning him and the lawn care.

"I want to train you over the next two weeks to run this lawn care. I need to hire two more workers and business is growing and we are far behind. I am thinking about Timothy and Nate. What do you think about working with them?"

"I would like that. I get along great with both of them so it should be a good fit I think," George said.

"They have done some work for me with the lawn care on and off as I needed, so they have a good idea of what to do. I will work with you this week and train you and then next week bring them on as well to help us get caught up, then after that, you three are on your own."

"Sounds good to me. What is Ann and Tonya going to be

doing?"

"I have Steve training them for the next few weeks on painting so they can take that over, and Steve and I will be back to repairs after he gets them fully trained."

"That's great. Ann loves to paint so that will work out much better for her than doing lawn care. You will find she is very good at it. She has helped other people do some painting around their houses and she loved it."

"That's good, then she has some experience already. That will make it easier for Steve, and hopefully they will be able to get more done then. Every morning you will come down and pick up the truck and trailer, then go get Timothy and Nate and then get the things you need like gas and whatever. I will have the invoices ready for you when you get here."

"Okay, what time do you want me to be here?"

"By seven-thirty so you can be on the first job by eight."

"Okay, that's no problem at all. They don't live far from us, so picking them up is a quick trip, plus there is a gas station right by their house, so that makes everything convenient for us."

"I will call them once we get everything ready for the day. I will have you drive so I can call them and see if they want to come on full-time."

"Nice, there will be three of us. I think that will be good."

"Yeah it will. You will find that switching on and off will give everyone an easy day every week."

"I like the sound of that, especially if we are going to be working long hour," George said.

"It will get easier once we get all caught up."

After their talk, they needed to get going to get the fuel they needed for the day. While George was driving them to the first job, Johnnie made the two phone calls. He needed to see if Timothy and Nate were interested in working full-time for him doing the lawn care with George. These two were not a part of the war and had no idea it was even going on. So for Johnnie, he now would have two employees that could just work five days a week without the interruption. Timothy and Nate had always worked hard for him when he had used them in the past.

Once he finally got off the phone, he was excited to let George know they would be starting the following week as full-time employees. George had never been a supervisor before, but Johnnie had great confidence in him that he could do it. He would do all of his business calls while George would drive. Business was picking up even more and he spent a lot of time during the rides to the next jobs returning calls he missed while working. He had always recorded all the information in a notebook that he kept in every truck and would make up invoices every night before going to bed. His reputation for getting jobs done right had been growing and now he had more work than he could handle due to being behind while new jobs were steadily coming in.

Having three crews would help out tremendously and they all would be able to focus daily on one thing, and when there was times there were no repairs to do, he and Steve could split up and help the other crews so they would be able to get more done and get a bit of a break. Johnnie liked for them to be able to get off early on Fridays. He hated working late on Fridays and not being able to get to the bank. He would work them twelve hours a day Monday through Thursday, and then be done no later than three on Fridays, sometimes earlier if they had all of their invoices done for the week.

Whenever Johnnie had a chance, he would call and check up on the other crew and see how things where coming along. During their lunch break, he got a call he hadn't wanted to take but needed to as Ricky was trying to get in touch with him. This was the third time he had called and Johnnie had been putting off calling him back but knew he needed to take this call and see what was going on.

"Hey, Ricky what's up?"

"Hey, Cypher. How did the funeral go?"

"It was as good as any funeral can be."

"Right. How soon before you will be ready to ride with

us?"

"I need a few weeks to get things caught up on my business. I have fallen too far behind and need to get things where they need to be."

"Are you thinking about backing out?"

"No one is backing out Ricky, you need to chill on that. We have real jobs and need to get some work done before we can get back into this with you."

"Hey, relax Cypher. I am just asking, is all."

"Yeah, well I honor my word and my commitments, as well as the people I work with."

He had a way of warning people and the statement he had made to Ricky was a clear indication that he knew more than Ricky thought.

"That's good to know. Well stay in touch and keep me posted on your return," Ricky said, as he was now thinking about the conversations he had with Jason and was wondering just how much these two really knew.

"I will for sure. See you soon."

"Who was that?" George had asked being curious by the way the conversation sounded.

"That was our good friend, Ricky. He was wondering when we were going to get back involved in this war."

"Things didn't sound like he was happy."

"I don't care if he is happy or not. Our jobs come first. Then we will get back on track with the war."

Things were definitely wrong and it was obvious, but Johnnie was only willing to say so much. He didn't need George knowing what he knew until the time was right. And right now wasn't the time for that. For now, Johnnie needed to keep everything going in the right direction and keep everyone on board with each other so they could finish this war. He already hated this war continuously dragged on. This was not at all what he had expected and he was getting fed up with Ricky also. It was getting harder to hide his emotions and he needed to try to keep them buried for now. He was sure George had picked up on that now and he needed to act as if things were cool. But underneath it all, he wanted to kill Ricky in the worst way and that was very hard to hide.

After lunch, Johnnie and George got right back to work. He hoped George would forget the conversation he had just witnessed. The rest of the day, he made sure to keep every conversation away from that phone call and on business matters instead. If nothing else, he at least wanted to make it seem as if it was something between him and Ricky that was of no concern to anyone else. He knew this was going to be hard to keep from the group, but he had to, at least for now. This whole ordeal was not good for Johnnie. He had always been open and honest with everyone, and now he had secrets from Thomas and Christina, as well as the rest of the group, which took its toll on him. Everything seemed to keep getting deeper and soon he would have to find an end to all of this.

Later that night, Ricky sent a car load of his members to vandalize the Hardware Store where Cypher got his supplies. Once again, he had instructed them to tag the place with The Hell's Sinners mark as to try to convince Jason and Cypher that it was them who had killed Randy and not his own people.

As Auto and Viper went out to accomplish their assignment with a few other members, they passed by a car that was sitting on the side of the road where two men were sitting inside talking, but they could not see who it was. However, the two individuals saw them clearly. After the car had almost disappeared out of sight, Gunz slowly turned around to follow them from a distance. They stayed far enough behind that Auto had no idea they were being followed. Gunz turned off his lights when they got close to where Auto parked the car in the hardware parking lot.

"What gang is this that we are watching, Jason?"

"That's the West Dragons," Jason replied.

Gunz and Jason had been watching this area for a few days and were waiting for them to show up and try to cover their tracks to throw Jason off, but he was already on to them. Gunz normally wouldn't put himself in the affairs of simple street thugs, but he liked Jason and was eager to start training him to eventually work with him.

"Why are you taking interest in them?"

"Well, I am curious to see what they tag on the building that they are breaking the windows out of."

"Why does it matter?"

"Because I believe they are doing things and putting the blame on The Hell's Sinners. And some of those things are very much my interest."

"I see. Well, I don't care. I wanted some time to talk with you anyways. These past few days we have discussed many things about me and you working together as a team."

"Yeah, and I love that idea, but when are we talking about doing this?"

"It won't be for a while Jason, we need to replace you first before we can move you up. But I do know that Pauli has his eye on someone already, which is why I am here with you."

"I'm good with it. I like everything that we talked about."

"That's good, Jason, because soon you will be moving up the ranks. You're a good learner and when you went down you did your time like a real trooper. You never ratted anyone out or gave up any names. You took it like a soldier and Pauli was very proud of you."

"Yeah, well I ain't no snitch and never will be. But don't get it twisted, G. I don't have a problem killing someone either. I will put someone down fast if they try and test me."

"My man! That's what I am talking about. I love that edge about you. You take no crap and deal it straight. You got that killer's heart that many don't have. That is going to get you promoted. Pauli sees it, too. He's been watching you just like I have."

"Good to know. Look, see there? That's what I was waiting for. They tagged it as 'The Hell's Sinners.'"

"Yeah I see that, what do you want to do?"

"Nothing, for now. I will deal with them when the time is right, I just needed to see this for myself."

"Okay, so are we done here?"

"Yes, let's get out of here before they see us. I don't want them to know that I am onto them."

***

The next day, Mr. Smith, the Hardware Store's owner called Johnnie.

"Johnnie, my store was vandalized last night."

"How bad is it, Mr. Smith?"

"It's bad, Johnnie can you please come this morning and look at it?"

"Yes, I sure can. Give me a bit and I will be there."

When Steve came, Johnnie wanted him to go pick up the girls and meet him at the store while he and George got loaded up and headed there as well. Mr. Smith was outside looking over the damage when Cypher had pulled up.

"Johnnie, thank you so much for coming right over, I really appreciate this. Look at this mess. Look at what they did. Why would anyone do this to my store? I don't bother anyone, Johnnie. Why would they do this to me?"

"Don't worry about it, Mr. Smith. It's just some thugs, is all. We will take care of it and clean this up and fix your windows."

"Thank you, Johnnie. I have glass already ordered and it's on its way."

"No problem, Mr. Smith. My painters are on their way here as well."

"I have paint in the store they can use, just have them do the whole wall please and make it all one color. Everything you need to fix, the window frames and whatever materials you may need is in the store as well."

"Will do, Mr. Smith."

"Johnnie, you're a good man. Your father would be so very proud of you. Just tell me what I owe you when you're done."

As they finished talking, Steve had pulled in with Tonya and Ann.

"Look at this mess," Steve said, as he walked over to Johnnie. "I take it we are going to paint that wall."

"Yes, you three are going to do that while George and I fix these windows. Go inside and get the paint from Mr. Smith. He is expecting you."

"Sure thing. Looks like someone is sending us a message."

"Yeah, well I already got this under control, no worries about that."

Steve took the girls in with him to get the paint. As Ann and George were kissing each other, Tonya gave Johnnie a hug and kiss.

"Too bad we don't have more time. I would like to give my boss a few more kisses," Tonya said as she walked away to help Steve with the paint.

"A good way to get a raise, huh Tonya?" George said jokingly as he let Ann go as well so she could go help them.

"I don't a need a raise, my man takes very good care of me," Tonya said as she smiled at Johnnie, who now had a very deep red face.

"Oh, Johnnie is embarrassed," George pointed out.

"Get our tools out of the truck, George," Cypher yelled back to him to regain control while George was laughing.

"Ha! Ha! Sure thing 'Boss Lover Man'," George said as he was still laughing.

"I do believe you were having a moment with Ann as well there, 'Sir KissALot'. Now shut up and get things ready."

Johnnie walked around the building to make sure it was only a few broken windows and some spray painting that had been done. After Steve and the girls came back out with all of the paint they would need, he grabbed Tonya to steal one more kiss before they got to work.

"Maybe we will talk about that raise later, Honey," Johnnie said.

"Mmm, looking forward to later, My Love."

"I am, as well. Would like to have some alone time with you at some point this week."

"I would love that, Johnnie, we need that," Tonya agreed.

"Okay, Babe let's get this done so we can get on our other jobs for the day."

After Steve and the girls got all set up and started painting, the glass truck pulled up. Johnnie and George went to talk with the glass people with Mr. Smith.

"Good thing that they didn't do any damage to the inside of the building," Johnnie said to Mr. Smith, as they watched the glass man unload both pieces of glass that he needed for the two windows.

"Yeah I guess it isn't as bad as it could have been," Mr. Smith responded, as he took the glass man inside to pay him.

Johnnie and George cleaned up both window areas and began to tear it all apart to rebuild it and put in the new glass. Johnnie went into the store to get some of the materials they would need to get started on the rebuild. George swept up all the debris from the mess that was created by them and The West Dragons. By the time he returned, George had everything almost cleaned up already.

"Looks good, George. Help me with this, I want to teach you how to build window frames while we have the opportunity to do it."

As they began to repair the frames and get it all ready for the glass install, Steve and the girls were making good time on the paint job they were doing to cover up the gang tag. Mr. Smith had been so good to Johnnie, it was important to get this done for him as quickly as possible. Mr. Smith allowed him to come get things that he needed many times and paid him later after he got his checks from his customers. He never skipped on a bill.

Once he got the first one done, he let George do the second window before setting the glass inside the first window. It took longer than they had hoped. Johnnie wanted to get it all done in just a few hours, but time seemed to be flying by and they still had a stack of other jobs waiting for them. It was already going to be a long night, and now with this added job, they were getting a much later start then they had planned.

After finally getting it all done, they got everything cleaned up and put away. Johnnie went in to talk to Mr. Smith about the bill while George helped Steve and the girls finish the painting.

"The windows are all finished, Mr. Smith. They are just about done with the painting. Why don't you come and take a look at it before we go?"

"Okay, Johnnie, thank you."

As they both went outside and looked at the windows and the freshly painted wall, Mr. Smith was very satisfied with the work that Johnnie and his crew had done for him.

"Everything looks great, Johnnie, how much do I owe you?"

"Nothing, my friend. You have been very good to me and helped me to get this business started, just consider it as a thank you gift from a friend."

"Awe, Johnnie, you truly are a good friend indeed. I loved your father, and I want you to know that I love you as well. Your father was a good man and a good friend. I am so proud of you, Johnnie. More and more I see your father in you. He would be so proud of you."

Johnnie struggled to hold back the tears from the words spoken by Mr. Smith. He had longed to be like his father and those words echoed in his soul as they were spoken to him. Excitement swelled up in him at the thought he was being compared to his father. That was his dream. It was his goal since before he had lost his father to that tragic accident that had taken his life.

"Thanks Mr. Smith I appreciate you saying that. I miss him so much, you know."

"Yes I do, too, my friend, I miss him as well."

Johnnie had always appreciated Mr. Smith, but they had never had a moment like this before.

"Your father knew how to honor people as well. That's a great trait that you got from him, Johnnie."

"He taught me how to value people and honor those who help you. My father would never turn his back on a friend. I suppose I never will either."

"That was what made him such a great man, Johnnie. Never lose that. You honor your father by doing what he would've done if he was still here."

"That means a lot to me, Mr. Smith. Well looks like they are finishing up, call me if you have any more problems."

"Yes, I will Johnnie, and thank you again for your help. It is most appreciated."

"Any time."

Johnnie went and helped them get everything cleaned up and put away so both crews could finally get back on track and get some of the work orders done.

"Steve, just go as far as you can. If you don't get them all done, then just pick up where you left off in the morning."

"Okay, Johnnie, see you in the morning."

After Johnnie and George were able to get some jobs done, they took a late lunch break. While they were eating, Johnnie checked his messages and had seen Jason had sent him a text letting him know he needed to talk to him and wanted him to call after he got home. He texted him back to let him know he would be working late but also he needed to talk to him as well and would call after he got home. He figured right away this might have something to do with their first job this morning at the Hardware Store.

Jason sent that text early. Perhaps he knows something already. Maybe, we were wrong. At this point, Johnnie wasn't sure if it was Ricky or The Hell's Sinners. *If it was Ricky, then he has gone a long ways to cover his tracks and try to convince us that it was The Hell's Sinners. On the other hand, if it is The Hell's Sinners, then they not only know that we are helping the West Dragons, but have now officially declared war against us.* Either way, he knew he had better find out which one it was, and fast. Not knowing who it was for sure was leaving them vulnerable and it was going to be harder to protect themselves if they didn't know where the attacks were coming from.

Lunchtime always seemed to fly by and Johnnie already wanted to be done for the day. There were so many jobs that needed to get done and he knew he had to press through and work on getting them finished. They had taken all the smaller jobs today so they could get as many done as possible. But tomorrow they would have to work on some of the bigger jobs because he couldn't afford to lose any of those contracts. He felt they could still get a lot of jobs completed today and would be able to hopefully get two to three of the bigger jobs done tomorrow.

These long days were going to be tiring, especially with working through the next few weekends to get some of the repairs done as well. No time to rest until things got back on track. It was way too easy to get behind and so much harder to get caught back up. He hoped two weeks would be enough to get caught up because he couldn't keep putting Ricky off. They were in a war, and it did require their participation. He knew if he was going to win this war and finally end things between him and Wayne, he would have to refocus on it very soon and make it a priority once again.

He was at a place in his life where he was trying to move forward, but had come to the realization he would not be able to do so until this war was finally over. He knew it was affecting his business. His war with The Hell's Sinners was wearing him down and it was taking too much energy away from the things he was trying to do with his business and with Tonya. Once he was finally finished with this war, then he would be able to get everything going the way he had wanted it to.

Now that he and Tonya were starting to get back to where they belonged, he was starting to think about marrying her. He knew that he and Tonya had a long ways to go, but he loved her and was so very excited that she was starting to show him love again. It felt so good to be able to hold her and kiss her like he used to. He needed her. She was everything he had ever wanted and that had never changed. He was more confident now they would get through this together and be able to have a life together after all.

Later that night, Johnnie was very tired and didn't even

want to eat, but his stomach was hurting and he needed to at least put something in it. So much was on his mind, as he sat there picking at his food while thinking about the phone call that he still had to make. *George did a great job today. If he keeps working like this, then next week won't be so bad. Hopefully we can split the crew up and double our work.* Johnnie realized he better spend the rest of the week getting the larger jobs done so that way, they could split up next week and get the rest of the smaller jobs done.

After finishing his dinner, he went to his room to call Jason and see what he had for him.

"Hey, Jason are you busy?" Johnnie asked as Jason answered the phone.

"Nope. I was just laying here trying to rest while waiting for your call."

"Yeah, I am sorry it's so late, I actually just finished eating dinner, to be honest."

"Late dinner, huh? Business must be going good for you then, got you a new truck and working long hours."

"Yeah, well we are behind due to obvious reasons. So what do you have for me, Brother?"

"Well I got good news and bad news. I know who killed Randy for sure and who vandalized the Hardware Store."

"Yeah, we spent most of the morning cleaning that up and fixing the windows. So who was it? You know it was tagged as The Hell's Sinners right?"

"Yes, I sure do, Bro. I watched them do it last night."

"So, it was The Hell's Sinners then?"

"No, it wasn't. It was Ricky's crew, The West Dragons. I saw Auto and Viper with a few others do it. I haven't said anything as of yet, I am going to play it off as if I believe Ricky for now."

"I want to kill him, Jason."

"I know you do, but you have to stay cool for now. Let me work this, Brother. Trust me, in the end I will take care of this."

"I want him Jason."

"I can't let you do that, Brother. Gang code alone will

bring that whole crew down on you. You don't need that after fighting this war. Just let me deal with this and you will have your revenge. I promise."

"Okay Bro, I trust you. But I want to be there when it goes down, I need to see it."

"I got you, Bro, no worries there. I will get it all set up and have you there when this is all over with."

"Sounds good."

"Okay, Bro, we talked too long about this on the phone, I need to cut this conversation short now."

"Talk to you later, Jason, and thank you for all of your help."

"No worries, there, I am always here for you."

"Same, Brother. Talk soon."

It was going to be another sleepless night now that Johnnie had something new running through his mind. He was going to have to try to keep this under wraps until he and Jason could deal with it. He couldn't help but feel everything was closing in on him. As he was lying there, he had thought about how grateful he was for everything Jason was doing for him. If there was a bright spot in this mess, it was having Jason watching over him. He had been his best friend since The House. He was closer to him than he was with George. Johnnie and George grew up together and had always remained close friends, but when you spend three long years watching each other's back on a daily basis, that brings you closer and the bond between him and Jason was evident.

He had made a name for himself in The House and was respected as well. Surely, Ricky must've known that if he ever found out that it was him who had killed Randy, he would surely come after him at all costs. Ricky might have been a leader of one of the biggest gangs in the state, but he still feared him and knew better than to cross him. Now it was too late and all he could do is try to cover it up in hopes that he would never find out that it was him. He had always wished that he and Jason could've spent more time together since they were both released from The House, but they were always so busy, that getting time together was nearly impossible.

Jason had grown into a very powerful young man on the streets. He was feared just as much as he was respected. Even to the point where no one would even dare to challenge him. He was now the man and having him as a friend was more valuable than money when you're in a mess like he was in. He felt that he owed Jason so much for always being there when he had needed him. With Jason being so powerful, Johnnie felt he could never measure up now to be of any real help to Jason. There was no way to repay him for how he was helping him.

But for Jason, there was no need for such thoughts. Johnnie was his only real friend and family and that was more than enough. He was the only person who Jason trusted and he had always known that when he needed Johnnie, he would be there for him. There were things he had talked to him about that no one else ever knew.

Johnnie knew things about Jason that were very personal and he confided in Jason, as well. If anyone could keep a secret, Jason could and he was quite sure of that. *The things he knows and have to keep to himself has to be a daily struggle.* At least it would be for him anyways. He hated secrets but understood the situation he was in had required it for the time being. He was so confrontational when things weren't right, that it was in his nature to go after Ricky, but he knew he had to trust Jason in this situation.

***

Early the next morning, Sara decided to cook breakfast for the group. It had been so long since they sat down and ate breakfast together. It was a nice surprise to everyone, as they gathered together around the table like old times. The two empty chairs was a reminder there were two people missing from the group. No one said anything, but it wasn't hard to see everyone kept glancing at the two empty seats where Randy and Darrell use to sit. Nobody wanted to bring this moment down. It had been way too long since they all sat together and ate. Nate and Timothy were absent as they hadn't started work yet. Ann sat between George and Tonya.

Everybody had been working so hard, that having this time together felt very good. They all missed the times they had stayed back at the camp and Sara would cook them all breakfast in the morning. Those were great times when there was no war, no stress and everybody were still here. At times, when it got quiet and their minds all drifted to the memories of Randy and Darrell, Cypher would start talking more about work to keep the conversation going.

After a nice long breakfast, they talked before they headed into different directions. Everyone was a little more upbeat after having breakfast this morning. The work day seemed to fly by as they were working very hard to get as much done as they possibly could. Steve and the girls were getting a lot of the painting jobs done. In some houses, they were all able to take a room a piece and work three rooms at a time until they were done. Steve was real good about sticking with the game plan whenever they would figure out what was the best way to get a job done quicker. Meanwhile, Johnnie and George had been taking on the smaller jobs after rethinking the game plan and waiting until Nate and Timothy joined them. It would be a lot easier to do the bigger jobs with them helping than trying to do it with just the two of them. George was coming along just fine and was now getting into the groove of things. Johnnie became more comfortable with him every day. He decided he would go ahead and work through the next week with George and the other two, and just keep working through the weekends doing the small repair jobs.

Everybody had kicked it up into high gear and was pushing as hard as they could. After another long hard day, Johnnie was exhausted. He got home late and sat at the kitchen table working on the finished invoices. His mother had made him some hot tea.

"Nothing like a refreshing shower and some hot tea to

relax," Johnnie said as his mom sat down with him and talked while he finished things up.

Hot tea was something he had picked up from Jason and now his mom began to enjoy hot tea as well. Tonya went straight home and got cleaned up before bringing her invoices down for him so she could stay and visit.

As Tonya came in and joined them, Sara poured her a cup of hot tea. They sat for a while before Sara excused herself. It was late, but once Johnnie had finished his work, he took Tonya out back to relax with him on the swing. It was so nice to be able to sit with her under the clear night sky. The stars were shining over them while they held each other. They reclined on the long tan wooden swing that had a long green cushion tied to the back and another one for the seat. Tonya had turned her head so he could kiss her. Time went by way too fast. A few minutes had now turned into a few hours and it was way past time for some sleep for them both, but they severely missed each other, and neither one was willing to let go.

Early the next morning, as Johnnie awakened. He was still holding Tonya who slept against him all night. She had slept so good in his loving arms. He, on the other hand, woke up with a kink in his neck and his back was hurting from the hardwood swing's arm rest. Tonya slowly began to open her eyes and smiled as she woke up in the arms of her love.

"Good morning, Honey," he said to her as he had leaned down and kissed her.

"Mmm, good morning, Baby. Wow we must've fell asleep out here. What time is it, Babe?"

"I don't know, Honey, but we should probably get up and get ready for work."

"Okay, Babe. Do you want to help me load up the truck before I head home?"

"Yeah, that sounds like a good idea. You and Steve can just take off from there. Let me cook us some breakfast first, Honey. Then we can get you all loaded up."

"Yes, Baby, that sounds like a wonderful idea."

Tonya got up and watched as he slowly got up off the swing. She could tell he was in pain from the way he had slept.

"Are you okay, Baby?"

"Yeah, I'm fine, Honey, I will work this out as the day goes on."

Cypher led Tonya into the house and cooked breakfast for her and his mom, who was surprised to see Tonya and Cypher already making breakfast when she came downstairs.

"Well, look at you two."

"Good morning Mom."

"Good morning, Sara."

"Good morning, you two. Did you both fall asleep out back last night?"

"Yes, we did. We just woke up."

"You look a little rough this morning, Johnnie," Sara said to him as she watched him moving much slower as usual.

"Yeah, that swing isn't very comfortable when you fall asleep on it."

"I can imagine. How did you sleep Tonya?"

"I slept better than he did, I suppose. I don't hurt like he does this morning."

Tonya was setting the table while Johnnie cooked. Sara poured coffee for everyone. Both ladies sat at the table while Johnnie served them. As they all ate together, Sara began to tell them just how happy she was that they were trying to make things work out.

After breakfast, Johnnie and Tonya went out back and got her truck loaded up and her invoices together. Tonya leaned out the window and kissed him goodbye and headed home to get ready for work. Johnnie got himself together and took some extra strength aspirin to ease the pain.

"Love can be rough sometimes, Johnnie," his mom jokingly said to him as she watched him take a few pills for the pain.

"It's worth it."

"I'm just happy to see you two working things out."

"Yes, me too, Mom. Me too."

George had soon pulled up and was ready to get going. Johnnie was dreading this day, but he had no choice but to get going. George had looked a little rough as well.

"Long night, Bro?" Johnnie asked.

"Yeah, I spent some time with Ann after work. She stayed longer than we had planned."

I know how that goes. Tonya and I planned to spend some time together last night and we both fell asleep on the back patio. Wasn't very comfortable either."

"I can imagine. How are things going with you two?"

"It's been pretty good, actually. Much better than I had expected. She has been very loving towards me again."

"You two will make it, Bro. You have always been so good together."

"Things will get a lot better once we are done fighting this war."

"Yes, I do have to agree with you there. We will all be glad when this is over. Ann is more worried now than she was before since the death of Randy and Darrell."

"Yes, I know. But if we stop now, then they died in vain. I am not willing for that to happen."

"I'm not, either. I personally would like to kill Ricco myself."

"Why is that?" Cypher asked, being curious why he would pick Ricco over Wayne.

"Darrell hated Ricco. I want to get revenge for him."

"Yes, he did hate him. They had some good fights."

"Yeah, well I just hope it's my bullet that will take him out."

"This war, with these long hours has really taken its toll on me, to be honest George. I feel like I am tired all the time. If I want any real time with Tonya, then I have to sacrifice even more sleep."

"When are getting back into that?"

"After we get caught back up on work."

"That's what I thought. Are you still going to work the weekends?"

"Yes, I have to. I have so many repair jobs stacking up, that I seriously need to get done. I'm not going to work you guys though; you're going to need the down time."

"I understand."

"We will still get out early Friday. I want to spend some time with Tonya and get my banking done."

"That sounds good to me, Bro."

Johnnie relaxed on the way to the first job, but it did him little good as his body ached and his eyes were heavy. It was going to be a long day and staying motivated was going to be the real task. This week was about done and he needed to finish his goal so that next week he could get everything caught up and then split the group up to get more done and work less hours.

***

While everyone was working, Thomas was still on leave from his job. It had been a real struggle for him since the burial of his two sons. His faith in God had been shaken tremendously, and he was now questioning everything he always believed in. Christina was doing her best to hold on to her faith during this trying time. She needed to feel God's comfort as she tried desperately to cling to Him while Thomas, on the other hand, became bitter towards God for letting his sons die. He felt God had failed him by not protecting his sons. The Hilton home had once been so vibrant with life and excitement had become a quiet home. Thomas and Christina barely talked to each other now. Their home was now filled with so much anger and bitterness.

The rest of the group hadn't been by since the funeral because they were so swamped with work. Johnnie felt bad that no one had stopped by. He was planning to visit them just as soon as he was able to get a break. Right now, everyone was so caught up in work and no one had any time to do much of anything else. Christina was going to ask Tonya if she wanted to go to Church with her, but hadn't been able to get in touch with her since the funeral. She hoped to touch bases with her before Sunday. Thomas decided to step away from the Church for a while and Christina didn't want to go alone. She hadn't been there since the death of her two boys and she needed to get back. This was too hard of a time for her to not be in Church. She needed that comfort to pull her through this.

Tonya had been so busy and so tired, she had not yet returned any of Christina's phone calls. She knew she needed to touch basis with her and was planning on doing that Saturday when she had some time off. Christina was very important to Tonya, and she had felt so bad about blowing her off. She was just way too tired to have a serious conversation that could last a while. She needed Christina as well, but knew she needed time to finish mourning for her sons.

   Johnnie was also feeling he needed to spend some time with Thomas, but he dreaded it because he felt responsible for Randy and Darrell's death. However, he wasn't about to ignore the fact that Thomas needed Johnnie to be a good friend to him, just as Thomas had been to him when he lost his father and when he was in The House.

   Tonya finally called Christina and was eager to go with her to church that Sunday. Johnnie used that time to talk with Thomas instead of doing repairs once he found out Thomas was staying home alone. Once Christina and Tonya were gone, he walked over to see Thomas. He was hoping to guide the conversation so he wouldn't have to answer any questions about the murder of his two friends. As they talked, he knew Thomas was seeking some answers and he was doing his best to try and give him what he had needed.

   "Why did they kill my sons, Johnnie? You have to know something," Thomas said, as he sat there, with a blank stare in his eyes. Cypher hated to respond to this, but he could see that Thomas was lost.

   "We had been having problems with this gang for a while. It's the same kids we've been having trouble with for a very long time. They were the ones who raped Tonya and who also killed Randy, which is why Darrell went after them."

As Thomas listened to Johnnie, his anger began to rise up with in him.

"You mean to tell me that the bullies you all had been having trouble with in school killed my two sons?"

"Yes, Sir. We know it was them by the gang sign that was left behind."

"You didn't tell the police who it was?" Thomas asked, puzzled that Johnnie was not doing more to help the police to solve this crime when he had some answers.

"It's not that simple. We know they are a part of that gang and we know they was behind it, but we don't know for sure if they did the actual killing. We don't know who all was involved in the actual murders. All we know is what gang did it, and the police already know that much."

"But you know more. You know they were behind it."

"Thomas, all we know is that they are a part of the same gang that killed both of your sons. That's all we know," Cypher hated keeping the rest of the information from Thomas while pretending to believe that it was this gang who killed Randy, but he had to protect himself and the others. "I wish I knew more, Thomas. I am waiting for the police to find out who was the actual shooters as well."

"Why did they do this, Johnnie? Why couldn't they just leave you guys alone?" Thomas asked as he sat there and cried with tears streaming down his face.

"I don't know," Johnnie said as he desperately tried to only say what he had to.

After a long morning with Thomas they met Christina and Tonya for lunch. Afterwards, he and Tonya spent the rest of the day together. Tonya was excited to share her experience with Johnnie, who listened to her as she told him all about the service and the inspiring message she had heard. He was always interested in different beliefs, so he patiently listened to Tonya as she shared with him. He was intrigued by her excitement as he listened while thinking about what a powerful sermon this was that made her so excited.

He became more curious about what the environment must have been like to get her this excited. Christianity seemed to really affect Tonya in a positive way and she seemed to be getting some real help from it. He did find the message to be inspiring as well. He always felt so good after Thomas would visit him in The House. While being in there, he read about a lot of different religions and was quite aware what they had believed.

After a long work week and doing repairs on Saturday, Johnnie was feeling exhausted, but he had one more week to go and was happy that Nate and Timothy was joining the team this coming week. Steve would be letting the girls completely take over the painting now and would focus on repairs while Johnnie would work with George and the crew for a few days to get them all in the flow and see how they worked out together. He hoped to rejoin Steve and get back to working on repairs to get all caught up so they could go on a hit with The West Dragons.

Everything was taking its toll on Johnnie and this war was pressing. Nothing would have pleased him more than to finally have The Hell's Sinners wiped off the face of the Earth. It was hard trying to keep everything together when his mind constantly raced between so many things all the time. It became more complicated dealing with The West Dragons. The attitude of their alliance seemed to have changed and there was definitely a shift from allies to users who would attack their own friends just to get what they wanted. These were frustrating and dark times for Johnnie, who was constantly fighting the past while trying to build a future. However, a new week was upon him and it was time to bring in two new employees and get them trained. George would be picking up Nate and Timothy before meeting up with him.

When Tonya came to get the paperwork, she showed up a bit earlier than usual. She was still excited about the service she went to with Christina and wanted to share some more of it with Johnnie, who wasn't ready to hear it this early, but listened anyway. Tonya became more interested in this religion than what he had wanted her to. He didn't want to think about God while he was in a war and killing people. It just didn't seem right to him to try and believe in God while fighting his enemies. But he knew it was important to Tonya and it was helping her, so no matter what his feelings were, he would let her tell him everything, and afterwards they would focus on business. However, he did love how much Tonya was being helped and how there was some excitement in her life again. It was encouraging to see her coming back to life after the longtime of being isolated and depressed. She was no longer having thoughts of suicide and was beginning to return back to her old self little by little. He couldn't deny it was having a real impact on her life.

After their morning talk, he kissed Tonya and got ready for George who would soon be on his way. Once George and the others got things loaded up, he took Nate with him and George and Timothy went together, as they both were going in different directions and would meet up with each other later. He felt it would be easier to go out to the farthest places and work their way back in. It was going to be a long day, but at least they were doubling up on the work load and covering more ground at one time.

He and George had to take time to teach Timothy and Nate how to properly weed whip before they could both get started mowing. He made a side bet with George on who would be at the lunch spot first. They always tried to stop and eat at noon unless they were on a job. Both Nate and Timothy picked it up rather quickly and were working hard. Everything seemed to be working out as planned and the week went by quickly.

Johnnie was back on track, and everyone was now finally on their own. Tonya and Ann ran the painting part of the business and was doing great. George was proving himself to be a very good leader, and Steve and Johnnie were getting all caught up on the repairs. The money was coming in real good for him and he paid Jason the rest of what he owed him. Everyone was making good money and he finally had a good handle on everything. It was just in time for them to get ready to go back across town and meet up with The West Dragons and make another run.

Johnnie was feeling more at ease with his business and less at ease with Ricky. He was going to make sure his group stayed together at all times and no one was going to split them up. He didn't trust Ricky at all and had given thought to just killing him, but he knew he had to trust Jason on this one. They had discussed some things concerning this very thing when Johnnie met up with him to pay the rest of his money. Jason reminded him about their previous conversation concerning this and why he had to let Jason handle it. It was frustrating to him, who was used to handling his own problems and now having to bite the bullet and let someone else take care of it for him proved to be difficult for him.

As the weekend approached, Johnnie decided to take Tonya out on a nice date since they had worked so hard that week. Things were still edgy for Tonya, but slowly she was getting better every day. Christina and Tonya had been spending some time together, talking and praying. It really had seemed to be making a huge difference for Tonya. Sara had been going over and sitting with Christina during the days so she didn't feel so alone, although Thomas was there. Sara was a real comfort for Christina. Sara felt good being there for Christina, but she too was mourning the death of the Two Brothers. It was hard for Sara to see the kind of shape that Thomas was in. Sara loved them tremendously. She and Christina would talk for hours about them and share stories with each other. Sara even would sit quietly while Christina would pray and hold her afterwards as she would cry.

Johnnie wanted to start going out with the group on Fridays first, then go back to the camp area for the rest of the night. He had everyone meet up at his house before going home so they all could get their paychecks. Sara had been doing payroll for Johnnie now and was very good at it. She loved being a part of his business and enjoyed having something extra to help occupy her time. She was able to save the rest of the money from Mark's settlement, and Johnnie paid all the bills and bought the food for them while paying Sara a few hundred dollars a week for doing payroll for him.

Everyone met up at the pizza restaurant and was finally able to begin their weekend. Johnnie had a few tables put together so they could all have dinner together. After a fun time at dinner, they went back to the camp area for the rest of the night. Nate and Timothy had only been back there a few times before.

The following day, Johnnie decided to spend the entire Saturday with Tonya. They went to lunch and then to a movie afterwards. Tonya was feeling anxious at first, but settled down after lunch and started to really enjoy herself. Later that evening, they dined at a nice restaurant followed by a quiet evening out back on the deck where they cuddled for the rest of the night.

After a wonderful day together, Cypher walked Tonya home and returned home for a good night's sleep. Everything had gone as planned the entire week and Johnnie felt relieved things were back on track with the business. He was enjoying the time he spent with Tonya. Everyone was still adjusting to the loss of the Two Brothers, but work became a good distraction for them. They felt a sense of responsibility for what happened to them.

Johnnie took it the hardest because the war was his idea, which had cost him two of his childhood best friends. He knew things weren't as they appeared and he couldn't wait to get this over with so that he could deal with Ricky. But for now, he had to keep it cool and act as if all was well.

And all the while, it was eating away at him.

CHAPTER 8

KEEPING THE SECRET

It had been a long two weeks for the group but they all made it through and business was doing great. Johnnie, along with George and Steve knew this following week would bring another trip to take a run at the Hells Sinners. They was ready for it. Every hit meant they were getting closer to ending this long feud and hopefully bring peace to their group from all they had to deal with because of them.

Steve couldn't wait to finally fulfill his revenge on them. So much was going on with Johnnie as he was working hard to rebuild his relationship with Tonya. As Monday came and Johnnie was out with Steve doing repairs he received a phone call from Ricky who was wanting them to go on a run to spot some of The Hells Sinners who have been posted up on certain corners selling dope. This would be a good opportunity to catch some of them apart from the rest and eliminate more of their rivals.

Johnnie wanted to continue to keep it hidden they were working with the West Dragons because he knew they would come after them in their own territory and the three of them would now be able to handle them on their own as long as they did it this way and wasn't caught. His trust with Ricky had now been shattered and he wasn't sure how long Ricky would keep this a secret. For now they still needed each other and that was the only thing that made Johnnie at ease about this whole situation.

Steve was also becoming uneasy with the West Dragons. He was beginning to sense something wasn't right. Being only three of them now, Johnnie was starting to wonder just how much help Ricky was going to think they were now.

As they finished their work day early so they could meet up with Ricky, Tonya had decided to see if Christina wanted to meet up for some one on one time. They still needed each other. Tonya was still struggling with what happened to her and Christina was so terribly sad over the loss of her two sons. They had become a source of strength and comfort to each other. Tonya loved that after they spent some time talking, Christina would pray for them. The prayers Christina would pray had always made Tonya feel better and much more encouraged. She was new at this and had not prayed for anyone before, so this time Christina would ask her to pray as well so she could start to develop her own prayer life. As Tonya prayed it was very short and was filled with pauses as she tried to think of what to say. Nevertheless, she was learning and Christina was proud of her.

While they were spending time together Ricky had everything set up with Auto to go pick up Johnnie and his group to make this hit. Ricky gave strict instructions to rob them after they had killed them. As they were on their way to where The Hells Sinners were posted on their corner, Johnnie was very quiet as his thoughts was on the situation they was heading for. Finally as they drove past them they turned the corner just up ahead to come around for another pass where they would open fire on them. Johnnie and Steve along with George let off the shots hitting all three that stood there together, just before they all jumped out and took everything that was on them. George kept the gun for himself but the drugs he wanted nothing to do with, the same was for the other two. Dope was something they never wanted any part of.

They were three dead gang members closer to ending this war. On the way back they gave Auto all the drugs but the money Johnnie kept for himself to use to fund this war instead of taking it from the business fund. He then had him take them back to their place instead of going back to meet up with Ricky. As they was on their way back they had come across a few more of The Hells Sinners who were walking back from the store and was not paying attention to the traffic that was passing by. Auto had circled back around and dropped them off a bit ahead of them. All three stood by the corner of a building that was at the end of a block and waited for them to walk by. They had faced the other way as to conceal their appearance and to appear as just some friends hanging out. As they began to walk past them, Johnnie and Steve grabbed and started hitting them while George began to switch back and forth between the two hitting them both and beating them down until they laid unconscious.

"We can't let them live," Johnnie said as he pulled his gun and shot one while George shot the other.

As soon as they were finished Auto pulled back up to pick them up and get them out of there as quickly as possible. After dropping them off a few blocks away from Johnnie's, Auto returned back to find out The Hells Sinners had hit them as well. The Club House was riddled with bullets as a few of the West Dragons laid dead on the front lawn. They had finally realized who it was that had been hitting them and had now retaliated. It was also suggested Johnnie may have been helping them but Sisko dismissed that for lack of evidence and the fact that someone other than them had actually killed Randy.

There was still a lot of confusion between everyone as to what really happened and no one knew for sure who had done it other than the ones involved. Jason and Johnnie knew but for now, they were keeping that knowledge a secret until a later time when they could deal with it properly. The confusion however played into the West Dragons' hand as well as kept Johnnie and the rest of the group safe for now.

***

Meanwhile Tonya and Christina were sharing stories together about how God was moving in their lives amidst all that was going on and after all that had happened. The presence of the Lord had filled that home as they prayed and talked. They could feel God's peace in the home that had once been filled with so much sorrow. As they cried, it was as if their tears were washing away the pain they felt.

Tonya wished Johnnie had been there to experience this moment. She knew what he was going through and all the struggles he had been facing. The hurt and turmoil within him almost seemed to never let up. She could feel he was losing hope this war would soon end as it continued to drag on and on. The struggles Johnnie faced daily was real and undeniable. Johnnie was tired of fighting and wanted peace in his life.

Christina wished the same for Thomas who was going to be back at work the next day and had not been in Church since the death of his two sons. He had been left feeling hopeless and lost after his two boys had been murdered. Every day for him was as if he was just drifting through with no direction or purpose. Christina hated watching Thomas drift into darkness as most days he would just sit and not say anything. He barely even acknowledging Christina when she would try and talk to him. He wanted to be left alone. Even at work he hardly spoke to anyone unless he had to and would often go off on his own at lunch time. He would even at times get up and walk away when someone would come over and sit next to him. The inner struggle of his faith was surreal as he felt so alone and helpless. It was as if he had been abandoned by everything he once believed in. *Where was the God who had promised to comfort him? Where was his God who had promised to protect him and his family?*

Christina also felt alone since Thomas stopped talking to her like he used to do. They used to share everything together and now her husband just wanted to be left alone and wouldn't even hold her when she needed it. After his talk with Johnnie he stopped visiting with him and made excuses why he couldn't talk when Johnnie would try to make time.

Johnnie had his own struggles and let it all fall away to the side as he didn't have the energy to try and help Thomas. It was too much for him with all he was facing himself to try and reach someone who didn't want to talk anymore. Johnnie was very sad for Thomas and knew that he needed help, but he just didn't know what to do in this situation or how to reach him at this point. This was going to have to be between Thomas and his God. Johnnie could do nothing but just hope for the best that he would be able to shake this off and come back to his own self. Johnnie didn't know much about God, but he had studied some books. Although he felt that after reading on so many different things that Jesus did seem to be the best way because no other religion had offered any real salvation apart from human efforts. And only Jesus was referred to as Lord. However for Johnnie, he felt religion was something he really didn't need. He never could understand how any God, no matter what religion it was, would have allowed all of this to happen to him. For him, God was an afterthought, something he only thought about when someone else would bring up the subject or some topic about religion or angels. All he cared about was getting through this war and building his business and at some point getting on with his life. The normal life he had always wanted with no wars to fight and no struggles and turmoil to deal with. Just a good ordinary life for him and Tonya. That was all he had ever wanted. That was his only goal, to make that dream come true.

   God had blessed Tonya as she worked hard and became extremely good at what she was doing. Business was growing and she was building a solid reputation for excellence in her work habit. Tonya had become a perfectionist and made sure everything she did was right as she didn't want to let Johnnie down. The respect he had with his company was continuing to grow and he never left any job undone, and everything was always done right. Johnnie never believed in cutting corners. Everything needed to be done right the first time. He never wanted to lose hours having to redo a job because it wasn't the way it was supposed to be. He knew it would only cost him money and time wasted that could potentially cause him to lose customers.

Johnnie was very strict about his work ethic and the work ethic of is employees as well. He built this business from a small company that just mowed lawns in the neighborhood to a full blown business now with four trucks and his own equipment. Small repairs where becoming bigger jobs now as his reputation grew.

Tonya was now running the painting part of the company and the jobs were coming in as fast as they could get them done. Tonya and Ann worked great together and was fast at everything they did. They worked out who was faster at what and designed their work day around each other's strengths. This helped them to work more efficiently and faster so they were able to get more done in less time.

Johnnie and Steve were steady in their work doing all the repairs that came in, which was now quite a bit. George was growing into a fine leader and Nate and Timothy were turning out to be great employees as well. They worked hard and loved what they were doing.

Sara enjoyed handling payroll and being a part of the company. Johnnie would have meetings every so often to go over issues and progress, as he was good about letting his employees talk about things they needed or things they wanted to see happen with the company. Every meeting they had, Sara would cook dinner as they would sit around the table and discuss business. Johnnie valued his employees' opinions and wanted to allow them the opportunity to voice and express their ideas as they grew in their positions. This allowed each person to feel more important in what they did, knowing they could try new things and see what worked better for them.

Johnnie believed in his employees and didn't mind them trying new techniques that better suited their style of how they did things, just as long as it didn't compromise their quality of work or slow them down. Johnnie remembered his father saying people have a different way of doing things and you have to be flexible when working with other people. He also knew that he wanted his employees to learn, grow and try new things if it made the company better. Johnnie himself was not above learning from his workers. He knew everyone was valuable and brought something to this company. It was never all about him being the boss but he respected his workers.

 Johnnie wished he could spend all of his time working and building his business but that idea was soon shattered when he got a phone call from Ricky, explaining to Johnnie how the Hells Sinners had retaliated against them. Up until this point they had been lucky in that it had been kept quiet about who was doing the shootings and as of yet, no one knew how they had found out it was the West Dragons who had been hitting them. The real questions for Johnnie now was if whether or not they also knew about him and his group being involved or if they would piece it together with Darryl coming after them for the death of Randy. Surely they would have to consider the possibilities and if so, what did that mean for Johnnie and his remaining group? They had been extremely careful in trying to hide their involvement but now all of that could have been exposed. No one knew if anyone had told them and if someone did, how much they told them would be the next question. They could never be too careful. At some point, someone might see them or there could even be a traitor in their midst who is now telling them what's been going on and who all was involved. This was more of a concern for Johnnie then it was for the West Dragons. *What if the Hells Sinners come here looking for us?* Johnnie hung up from Ricky who had very little information to give to him at the moment. He hated loose ends just as much as he hated not knowing what was going on. It was always important for him to be able to control certain situations but with no real information, there was no way to prepare for any possible attacks against him and the remaining group that was involved in the war. The fact that Jason hadn't called him yet meant there was no real information that had come his way or not enough to make a phone call to him. As soon as he was alone, he would be giving his old friend a call to see just how much he knew concerning this situation. As for now though he would keep this a secret until he had something solid to share with the group. He didn't want to cause any unnecessary worrying until he had real answers to share with them.

They would have to be even more careful because the Hells Sinners would be watching the West Dragons. They would have to work out a new meeting place to be picked up and dropped back off. They couldn't afford to let the Hells Sinners find out where they lived. Certainly that would put everyone at risk, even their families. He wasn't about to risk the safety of their families which meant they needed to be so much more careful in keeping not only their involvement a secret but where they all lived as well. It was bad enough that the West Dragons knew but if the Hells Sinners ever found out, that would be even worse.

***

It was late that night and Thomas was sitting up alone thinking about all that had happened as great sorrow filled his heart. As he sat weeping bitterly, he began to feel the warm Presence of the Lord as his heart was filled with God's love. God began to heal his broken heart and restore his relationship with Him. Thomas couldn't understand why God had let his boys die but he knew God loved him and his boys. He sat in God's Presence and the Lord healed him. It didn't matter anymore that he didn't know why, all that mattered was God loved him and his heart was being healed. After a few hours of crying and praying Thomas got up and went to bed. He finally rested as he slept.

The next morning when Christina had awakened, she could feel that something was different in their home. It wasn't until Thomas got up that she understood what happened. Thomas held Christina as they wept and held each other. It felt like forever since Thomas had held her and loved her like this. She so desperately needed it. Their marriage had taken a strain since the death of their sons and now it felt as if things were starting to turn around for them and for their marriage. Christina began to have hope again as she held her husband for the first time since the funeral. The man she had loved and thought she was losing was now back in her loving arms. Thomas kissed her as he held her and loved her. Christina's heart was once again filled with so much love for her husband she no longer felt alone. The house finally started to feel like a home again.

"Oh Thomas, I have missed you so much. You don't know how much I have needed this," Christina said as he held her in his arms.

"I am so sorry Honey. Everything will be okay. I miss my sons but I miss God more. I miss you Honey. I love you so much."

"I love you too Babe," Christina said as Thomas kissed her again.

"I need your love so much. I just couldn't go on much longer without it. It was so hard seeing you like this, knowing what kind of man you are and how much sorrow had filled your life. I've been so desperate just for you to touch me and love me," Christina said while Thomas was holding her tight to him.

"Oh Baby, I love you so very much. I will never let you go. I promise. I need you just as much as you need me. We will get through this together," Thomas promised her as they stood together.

"Yes Baby, together. I have felt so alone. I never want to feel that way again. I need you to love me, to comfort me. It's so good to have my loving husband back. I truly have missed the way you take care of me and love me. I have missed your touch, the way you wrap your arms around me and just love me."

"I never meant to make you feel alone Honey. I just couldn't deal with losing both of our sons. I am sorry for not putting you first and making sure you were okay."

"Oh Thomas, I know you love me. I just need you to hold me and let me feel it. Stay with me today. Please, just stay with me today. I need this. I have longed for this since the death of our two boys."

"Yes Baby. I will call in to work and let them know I won't be in today. Today I am all yours my love."

Thomas did just that. He called into work and took the day off to be with his wife and gave her the loving attention she needed. The whole day was spent just cuddling with each other as they sat together throughout the entire day and just held each other.

***

Johnnie got home late and was really tired but he wanted answers to the phone call he received from Ricky and there was one person he knew would tell him the truth no matter what. As he sat down and drank some hot tea while trying to relax a bit, he grabbed the phone and called Jason.

"Hello," said the voice on the other end of the phone.

"Hey Jason, how are you?"

"Hey Johnnie I am good, how are you my friend?"

"I am good. I was just calling to see if you had any information about the hit that was put on the West Dragons by the Hells Sinners?"

"Yes I do. It took longer than I had expected for them to figure it out but they finally did. As far as your group, which I suppose is why your calling me. Well, Johnnie as of yet, they have no idea that you guys are involved in it."

"That's good. I would like to keep it that way for as long as we can."

"Yeah. Well now that they know who has been hitting them they will be keeping a close eye on them so you're going to have to be even more careful."

"Yeah I am already working on that part as we speak."

"It's going to get harder now Johnnie, so prepare yourself for it."

"I know. Thank you for being here for me. I always

appreciate you."

"No problem Johnnie, keep your head down and be careful."

"I will Bro. I thank you for your help."

"It's cool Bro, stay safe and stay in touch."

"I will Jason, have a good night."

After hanging up Johnnie sat there for a few and thought about it as he finished his hot tea before getting into the shower. He felt relieved they didn't know about him and the rest of the group but he also was uneasy about how much more difficult things were going to become now.

As the group got together later, Johnnie shared with them the new information he had received from Ricky and Jason. As they discussed it, they were quite aware of how difficult this was going to make things and how much more they were going to have to be careful to continue to conceal their involvement. They knew eventually this was going to happen, but they were hoping for more time before it did.

Tonya became very afraid that it was getting too risky for the group and she feared eventually something was going to happen to Johnnie like what had happened to Randy. They felt as if they were now treading on thin ice. Tonya starting talking to them about backing out and leaving this war behind. They all agreed they wanted to, but they knew at this point they were going to have to see it to the end. It was better to finish this war then have to start a new one with the West Dragons.

At least this war they had a pretty good chance of winning and they weren't fighting it alone. They knew that the end was much farther away than they had hoped it would have been at this point. It was hard to count the cost in a situation like this. They hoped for the best and wanted this to end quickly but the reality of it all was that no war ends quickly. They had all paid such a great price with the loss of the Two Brothers and to back out now would dishonor their deaths and no one was prepared to do that.

As much as Tonya hated to admit it, she knew they had to finish this. There was no other way. However it was taking its toll on more than just Johnnie. George and Steve were also becoming weary from the long hours of work and the stress from fighting this war at the same time. No one thought it would be easy but they sure didn't expect it to drag on this long and go this far. In theory it sounded much simpler then what it really was. Even though they made so much progress in the fight, the war was far from over.

Johnnie began to wonder how much of what they had missed in this war had effected its progress. There were a few too many hits they didn't go on they were scheduled to participate in. But for them, the death of Darryl and Randy was devastating and they had to not only be at the funeral, but they needed time to recover from their loss as well. For Ricky and the rest of the West Dragons death was a very familiar thing and dealing with it was much easier since they lived it every day. But for Johnnie and the rest of the group, that was not the case. The death of the Two Brothers was a very hard blow to the group and they needed time to mourn for the loss of their fallen brothers. The inner conflict they were facing was tremendous. The longer this war went on the worse they all felt about it. None of them felt that it was worth it any more. But they were way too deep to back out now. The price they had already paid was more than what they were willing to pay, but it was too late now. All they could do was try to keep moving forward and see this thing through to the end. If they could go back and do this over, none of them would have taken on this war, including Johnnie who always felt responsible for getting them involved in this in the first place.

***

Later as the week went on, things began to be more normal for Thomas and Christina. Thomas decided he was going to take her out on a date when the weekend arrived. He knew she needed it and he really did as well. They needed to work together on rebuilding everything after the loss they suffered. Thomas had made reservations for the two of them to get away for the weekend and just spend some time together. There was a nice hotel he made reservation at that had a wonderful suite with a Jacuzzi and a fire place. It was a romantic place with so much for lovers to do together. As Thomas was making reservations he found a nice jazz club that he booked a reservation for dinner. Christina had no idea what Thomas was doing. He wanted to surprise her with the most wonderful romantic weekend. He knew she deserved it after sticking with and not giving up on him when he had given up on everything. She never wavered in her love for him even when he was at his lowest point, and now he wanted to reward her for her faithfulness to him. She stood by him when he was ready to give up on life when she needed him the most and he had failed her when she desperately needed him to comfort her and love her.

Her boys were gone and her husband would barely even talk to her. She was so lonely and depressed having to grieve all alone while her husband just sat there as if nothing was even around him. She could have found comfort or love in another, but she didn't. She was going through this on her own and never thought of even leaving him and he knew that. His love and respect for her was more now than it had ever been before.

She had more than proved her love for her husband and Thomas didn't take that lightly. He owed her the world and was going to start with a romantic weekend away that she had richly deserved. He was going to go all out and make it the best weekend she ever had. He knew he had failed her when she needed him the most and he wasn't ever going to do that to her again. She deserved better from him and he was going to be the best husband that a man could possibly be.

***

Meanwhile with a good work week just about behind them, Johnnie was also thinking about taking Tonya out on the weekend once he got things wrapped up with the West Dragons who was prepared to go on another hit. They had already done so much damage to the Hells Sinners but retaliation was in order for the West Dragons after they were hit by the Hells Sinners. It had to be unexpected though. They knew the Hells Sinners would be waiting for them to come with another attack after being hit by them. Johnnie felt his group should do things a bit differently and let the West Dragons do their hit the way they wanted and then they would come behind it while taking them out as they caught them on the streets. This would help to keep Johnnie and his group from being caught helping the West Dragons out.

As Johnnie was going over this with Ricky they began to work out the details together and set a designated driver aside. They couldn't use Auto for that anymore because he was needed on the drive-bys. After they finished talking and got things worked out, Johnnie got a hold of Steve and George to let them in on what was going on with what they would be doing now, which made them feel more at ease about the situation.

***

As the night came to a close Christina went to take a shower before getting ready for bed. While she was preoccupied, Thomas went into her closet to get the sizes of the dresses she wore so he could get her a nice dress for their getaway as a surprise. He knew she would love that and it would be such a nice surprise to help get things back on track. Christina loved when he would surprise her with gifts or a romantic night out. As Christina was getting out of the shower, Thomas hurried and got ready for bed as well. It had been an all-around good day for everyone.

With the new way Johnnie was going to do things with the West Dragons meant he could schedule his own hits and not be so stressed over trying to get his work done so he could meet up with them. This way he could take a short day when they had most of the work done for the week or even go out at the beginning of the week and then work a few late nights to get caught back up. He knew it would be good to keep switching it up so the Hells Sinners wouldn't pick up on a certain time frame when hits would come. Johnnie wanted it to be completely random to better hide themselves and keep from getting caught or set up because of a routine. Everyone felt more at ease about that. Ricky was free to not have to try to get Cypher's group lined up with his group. He could just go and do what he needed to do and then let him do what he needed to do with no conflicts.

***

As the week was winding down and everyone was ready for a few days off to relax and just have some fun, Johnnie was putting together his own plan to put a hit on the Hells Sinners. He went over the plan with the West Dragons driver they were letting him use. Together they figured out the best plan of action and what would be the best route for attack.

***

While Thomas was working on building his weekend plans for Christina, he had stopped off on his way home and bought her a nice black dress and a necklace for the weekend. He wanted to surprise her with them for the dinner reservations he made at the Jazz Club.

***

Everything was all set and all they had to do now is pack and go. Johnnie had been so busy working and putting this hit together, he hadn't had time as of yet to plan what he wanted to do with Tonya. Once Johnnie got everything set up with this hit, he called to set up a meeting with Jason to go over the plans and get his opinion on it. He trusted Jason's opinion more than anyone else's when it came to stuff like this. He knew Jason would know if this set up for the hit was good and how to carry it out with extreme perfection. His reputation was growing as a major player even though he would never be able to be a made man. Yet at his young age, he was feared by even some of the top Bosses. Being he was Pauli's boy, no one could touch him either. Pauli was proud of Jason and loved that everyone was afraid of him. As far as Pauli was concerned it was good for business.

   Cypher had made quite the name for himself as well and Ricky was tired of trying to control him. He knew he had stepped over a line that he might have to pay the price for. Ricky felt he was on thin ice with Jason and still wasn't sure if he found out it was him who killed Randy. He felt it was a great possibility. If Jason did know then his relationship with Jason and Cypher would be greatly at risk. Ricky was afraid of Cypher and had been since they were in The House together. Everyone had great respect for him but they knew he was not afraid to go after anyone who crossed him. For those who were involved in the death of Randy was desperately trying to keep that under wraps. Ricky knew he had messed up and now the only thing he could do was try to continue to lie about it.

   Jason had a way of making you feel like he may know something but at the same time keep you wondering if he really did or not. Jason never got in a hurry to deal with an issue unless he had to. But a situation like this, he would keep you guessing until it was time to handle it, no matter how long that took. Jason had learned to be patient with his training from Mr. Ling which allowed him to be more in control. For Jason, it was like a game. He would let you think you got away with something and then out of nowhere he would show up and deal with you. One time he even let this guy walk around for months after he had crossed him and then one day no one ever saw him again.

   Cypher had proven himself now as a more serious killer

as well. His fighting skills was one thing but he was quite handy with a gun now also. Outside of Jason, they had never seen someone so fearless or aggressive in his attacks. He was real good at hiding his fears and always gave off the appearance he had no problem killing his enemies, but secretly he hated it. He hated the fighting and the killing. He only did it out of necessity. However, he found himself feeling too comfortable now with killing someone who had crossed him. He knew every time he went out, he was losing apart of himself with every hit he made. Revenge had ate at him. It was changing him little by little and he could feel it. For now he embraced it in fear that if he didn't he wouldn't be able to finish this war. He needed this edge. He needed to stay in control. Even though he often wondered just how much it was changing him and if he would be able to find his way back to himself after this was all over.

 For George it wasn't that simple. He wasn't able to handle it like Johnnie. He started smoking weed to try and coupe with what was going on. Ann didn't like it at all but never told anyone. She hated George was starting to get high more and more as this war consumed him. He hid it from Johnnie and the rest of the group and made Ann promise to never mention it to Tonya. She loved George and would never tell anyone in fear she would lose him. George promised to stop after the war was over but the truth was he was getting deeper into it than he planned and it was slowly becoming a major part of his life. George thought he could control it but it was starting to control him instead. Ann was worried about it but never pushed because she knew how hard this war had been on George and the struggles he was going through because of it. All of them couldn't wait for this whole thing to be over so they could get back to living the normal lives they all had wanted. But for now, George would keep his struggles a secret that only Ann would know about.

 For the Hells Sinners things were about to get more heated with Cypher's new plan of attack. They would never see this coming. Jason had given Cypher all the areas to post up at and wait for their attack. With this new plan Cypher felt this would push the war closer to an end.

Every night Tonya would pray for the group. She feared none of them would make it out of this war alive and even if they did, how much would it change them?

For the Hells Sinners the pressure was mounting. On top of being hit every week, the Police were still pressing their investigation into the deaths of Randy and Darryl. They didn't have much to go on with the murder of Randy other than the gang tag that was left by the West Dragons to pin the murder on them. But since they hadn't actually been involved in the death of Randy, the police didn't have any real leads other than that. And as far as Darryl was concerned, no one was talking so all the police had was proof the Hells Sinners had shot and killed him but they had no one as an actual suspect. The information Johnnie and the rest of the group gave to the police only helped to prove that it was the Hells Sinners who did it. The only other lead they had was the group had given them Wayne and Sisko's name along with Ricco. But they still was not able to trace anything back to those three and they all had alibi's proving they was elsewhere during the time of the murders. They pulled all three in and held them as long as they could while they interrogated them. They were quite aware since they were released the police was keeping an eye on them.

That was one of the main reason why it was so hard to catch who was hitting them. The West Dragons would sit and watch the police as they were camped outside and watching the Hells Sinners. Then they would wait about fifteen minutes after the police drove by the Hells Sinners' Club House when they would leave, they would speed by and fire off shots at them and bail out fast before anyone could chase after them. They watched the police long enough before they started hitting the Hells Sinners to get their timing down on just how long they had before the police would come back around. Everything was precise, but it was obvious they could have only done that a few times before the police would stake out and wait for it as well as the Hells Sinners.

Cypher was very smart on the way he thought as opposed to Ricky who would of got them all caught by taking one to many chances. He was always trying to change things up on the way they went about hitting them. They never did anything more than two times before changing their tactics, and would even sometimes alternate between tactics to keep the Hells Sinners confused. No one knew the extent of Cypher's involvement except for Ricky, the top leaders as well as Jason who knew everything.

Nothing ever got past Jason as he was keeping a close eye on Cypher as well as both gangs. Jason was real good at keeping his involvement quiet and playing both sides so he could help Cypher better plan his next attacks. The information Jason was giving Cypher allowed him to move more freely and set things up so they could make swift hits and move out quickly. Everything was timed and well planned out before executed. This was why the Hells Sinners never knew they were involved in this war.

They could never catch them and Cypher never left anyone alive to go back and tell. Every hit was done with perfection. He was learning from Jason just how to pull things off without anyone knowing who did it. This allowed for Cypher to only hit his targets and keep from innocent causalities. It really made him mad Ricky didn't care who got hit just as long as he wins this war. For Cypher, he only wanted his enemies and didn't want to hurt anyone else, especially if they had no involvement what so ever. This war was personal and anyone not involved didn't need to be effected by it. To him, Ricky seemed too careless when it came to hitting the Hells Sinners in public places.

There were times when he thought about killing Ricky, but he kept thinking about what Jason told him about not being able to handle another war, and he was right. This war had taken its toll already and had cost the group way too much. There was no way Cypher was going to throw them into another war after this. Once this war was over, that was it. Whatever happens to Ricky would have to be Jason's doing and nobody else's. Once it was done, then and only then would he tell the rest of the group what really had happened to Randy and Darryl, but not until Ricky was dead.

***

As the week finally came to a close Thomas had everything all set up and was ready to take Christina for her weekend getaway. He knew she would be excited as soon as he got home and told her to pack her things for the weekend. As soon as Thomas came home from work he kissed Christina and told her to go pack while he went to get a shower. She couldn't believe it. They were going to get away. She needed to get out of this house and this was the perfect timing. Things between her and Thomas had really turned around and she was ready to be away with him and just focus on the two of them. She had no idea what all Thomas had planned for them but it was going to be great to be away from home for a bit and clear her mind instead of sitting and looking at the walls that hung the pictures of her two boys.

As soon as Thomas was out of the shower, he hurried and packed his clothes and was ready to get out of there. Christina was eagerly awaiting him to finish packing so that they could leave. She knew there was a sense of urgency with Thomas. She made sure she was ready and waiting for him so they could leave just as soon as he finished packing. After Thomas loaded up the car they headed off to a nice restaurant for some dinner before driving to their hotel. Not only was it great to get out of the house but Thomas was taking her out of the city as well.

***

Meanwhile Johnnie had his own plans but first he needed to handle some business with the Hells Sinners before he could enjoy the rest of his weekend. As soon as work was done and everyone was ready, he wanted to meet up and go over the plans for the nights' run against their enemies. He had everything all planned and was ready to put it into action and make it happen. George and Steve were ready. They liked the idea of being on their own now with only a driver from the West Dragons. They were getting tired of the way they were being treated by Ricky also and this was the way they wanted it from the beginning. Had they done this from the start, the Two Brothers may have still been alive and Johnnie knew it. But that will take care of itself in time, for now it was time to focus on the Hells Sinners and pay a little more retribution to the ones who had caused them so much trouble for years.

Ricky had sent them HK as a driver just in case things didn't go as planned. Hit Killer would be there to back them up. Meanwhile as the Hells Sinners was getting ready for a huge party at the club house, little did they know there was another group that was about to lay a hit on them as well. The Death Clicks hated them and wanted to see them taken out and decided to hit them again. They didn't know later on that night the West Dragons was also planning a hit and so was Cyphers group.

Rockit and Toxic had picked up a van Nuke had stolen the night before that they had hidden. It was mid evening and everyone was starting to show up at the club house when the van Rockit and Toxic was in came fast down the street. Toxic opened fire at the Hells Sinners with an AK forty seven hitting five members and killed three on the spot while leaving two laying there struggling to stay alive. The Hells Sinners were confused because they knew it hadn't been the West Dragons who did this hit on them.

About an hour later Johnnie and his group posted up and watching three of the Hells Sinners hanging out at a corner and selling drugs in their territory. Once the coast was clear, HK hit the gas pretty hard and flew up on them before they could respond as Cypher and Steve opened fire. George had gotten out and started shooting as well and was already on them, going through their pockets while Steve and Cypher also was now out and getting everything they could from them. They kept everything but the drugs, which they gave to HK to take back to Ricky for resale. The money and guns they kept for themselves. Cypher wanted nothing to do with drugs whatsoever, but the money and the guns were always needed. As soon as they got everything they took off before anyone saw them.

While HK was dropping them off, the West Dragons was already on their way to put another hit on the Hells Sinners. Not knowing that the Death Clicks had already hit them. When they rolled up on the club house, they were surprised to see a lot of the Hells Sinners standing outside keeping watch. They figured this was a good time to get a lot of them at once. They did not know the Hells Sinners were already waiting and prepared for it. It was their custom to stand guard after a hit by them or a hit put on them. For the West Dragons they saw this as an opportunity but it wouldn't work out as planned as the Hells Sinners was armed and ready. As the West Dragons went by they soon found themselves in a shootout as bullets riddled the vehicles they were in. Both of the passengers in the car were hit and killed instantly but not before they were able to fire off some shots. This time two of the West Dragons died in the drive by, while only a few of the Hells Sinners were wounded.

It wasn't till late that night that the Hells Sinners was made aware of the other hit that was put on them by Cypher and his group. The only thing they didn't know was it was Cypher who had done it. They supposed it was either the West Dragons or the Death Clicks. The rest of the night Johnnie and the rest of the group stayed back at the camp and hung out all night.

***

Thomas and Christina had a wonderful dinner and finally reached the hotel where they would be spending the next few nights. As they got all settled in and was enjoying a nice quiet evening next to the fire place on the soft bear skin rug, Thomas had pre-ordered some room service for the night. They were not drinkers so instead of champagne, Thomas had them bring some chilled sparkling juice on ice with a plate of strawberries and some fine chocolates. The whole night was perfect as they laid next to each other sipping on their sparkling juice and feeding each other fresh strawberries and chocolates. This romantic night was just what Christina needed.

***

As the night came to a close and Saturday had come, Johnnie was up early preparing for his day and making plans for him and Tonya. There was a nice place he wanted to try that just opened up. Tonya loved when Johnnie would take her out to dinner. He called to make sure they could get reservations so they wouldn't have to wait in line when they got there.

***

That night Thomas was also taking Christina to dinner at a fancy Jazz club he had reservations for. While Christina was in the shower Thomas went out to the car and got the package out of the trunk he had the store wrap for him. When Christina got out of the shower she saw the package wrapped as a present sitting on the bed with a card waiting for her with a smaller box on top of it. As she opened the card and read it she began to get very excited. The card read: *My Dearest Love Christina, I can't go back and undo how I was but I can promise you that this day forward, everything will be different. I love you more than anything and I need you. Please forgive me for being absent when you needed me the most, but I am forever here and will be here forever. Yours truly, Your Loving Husband Thomas.*

Her face lit up as she smiled just as big as she had on their wedding night. Thomas came up from behind her and wrapped his arms around her and lovingly held her as they kissed.

"I love you so much Christina."

"Oh Thomas, I love you too. More than you will ever know."

"Oh Baby, trust me, I think I know," Thomas said as he kissed her again.

Christina very excitedly took the small box and opened it and pulled out the diamond necklace.

"Oh Thomas, it's just beautiful. Thank you so much Honey."

"Open the other present Honey," Thomas said as he was excited for her to open both presents.

Christina hurried as she opened the bigger box and pulled out a beautiful black dress that was the perfect size.

"Oh Thomas, this is just wonderful."

"I have more for you. These presents go with something I have planned for us for later on tonight.

***

Meanwhile Johnnie settled his plans and called Tonya to let her know they were going out that night and then just relaxed for a while before going to pick her up.

***

Thomas and Christina were out all day sightseeing and shopping together before stopping at a nice diner to grab something to eat before going to a museum. Later on in evening, Thomas took Christina back to the hotel room so she could put on her new dress and get ready for their dinner plans. She was absolutely stunning as she came out of the bathroom with her new dress on. Thomas had turned her around and put her new diamond necklace on as she watched in the mirror. After kissing her on the cheek, he took her to the Jazz Club where their table was ready and waiting for them. Christina couldn't believe it when they pulled up to the Jazz Club.

"Oh Thomas, you shouldn't have. This is just too much."

"Baby, you're worth it." Thomas replied as he parked the car and walked Christina to the door where there was a man waiting to open it for them.

The place was beautiful. Their table was up in the front where Thomas had requested. The small round table had a single candle lit in the middle and the chairs were close to each other so they could sit next to one another and hold hands or wrap their arms around each other while the music played. It was a dark setting with just a few lights on the dance floor.

The food Thomas ordered was magnificent. Everything was perfect and went as planned. After having a nice dinner together while watching the band play, Thomas took Christina out on the dance floor and danced with her while the band played a nice slow song that was perfect. He held her close to him. After returning back to the hotel Thomas and Christina spent the rest of the night by the fireplace once again.

***

Johnnie and Tonya enjoyed the new restaurant and afterwards, they went back to Johnnie's and relaxed together on the back patio as they usually did when the rest of the group wasn't around. They held each other all night and fell asleep in each other's arms until morning.

CHAPTER 9

THE STRUGGLE CONTINUES

   It was a great week that had just came to a close. The aroma of romance had finally settled as everyone was back to work and refocused on making money. For Christina and Tonya they were still glowing from the weekend with their men who had surprised them with a nice time. Thomas went all out and made Christina so very happy. She had been losing hope in their relationship but was now floating on cloud nine. For Tonya, any time she got to go out with Johnnie made her night. Things had been so distant for a while but things where really getting hot between them two again. Johnnie couldn't be happier with the way things were going and was hoping it would continue.
   Everyone was happy to see these two getting things back on track with each other. Especially Sara who was thrilled these two were working everything out and getting their lives back together. It had been such a hard time for Johnnie who needed Tonya now more than ever. Life was hard enough for him and Tonya was the one person who always helped him keep it together. For so long she had helped Johnnie through his struggles and helped to keep him focused. Having her back was a great motivation for him and it also helped to relieve some of his fears. Sara always hoped these two would settle down together and get married. Life with Johnnie wasn't easy, but she loved him. It was always hard to watch the things he had to go through. Especially knowing that it wasn't his fault. Things just always seemed to happen to him. Things that were out of his control.

Being with Johnnie meant Tonya had to go through all of that with him and it was very difficult at times. The House was the hardest for her when they had to be apart for three long years and now this war she felt partially responsible for. Tonya wished they never got involved in this. She felt her guilt and shame was being put on display as long as this war was going on, but the boys refused to give up.

Steve would never relent even if he had to go after them alone. There was no way they were ever going to get away with what they had done to his sister. He would give his life to see they all paid for what they did and Johnnie was no different. He paid the ultimate price for this war and knew that at some point things were going to end. He could no longer live with what they cost him without bringing retribution to the cause.

Death just seemed to be a part of Johnnie's life and there was no way around it. Everything he had faced in life he had to go through. There was no ignoring any of it and trying to wish it all away. It all had to be dealt with and he faced everything that had come his way. His struggle to not lose himself continued as his hate was eating away at him while slowly chipping away at who he was and who he was trying to be. It just seemed to go on and on, no matter what he did to try and better his life. He knew life was hard but his always seemed harder than everyone else. Tonya had kept reminding him there had to be a reason for all of this hardship, and maybe God was preparing him for something great. However, that didn't make him feel any better during the moments when he had to do things he really didn't want to do.

Meanwhile Ann had a single cousin who had just moved there and was getting settled in. She was very pretty and she and Ann had always been real close. Ann was excited to have her close to her now so they could hang out all the time. She had a nice personality and was easy to get along with. *She maybe someone that Steve would like.* Ann talked to George about her.

"My cousin Debra just moved here and I can't wait for

you to meet her. You will absolutely love her George. She is so nice and I think maybe she would be a good fit for Steve you know."

"Well I can't wait to meet her and maybe we can set up some kind of double date once she gets settled in."

"Yes Honey that would be great I think. Steve never gets out to meet anyone with everything you guys have going on, and so maybe this would be a wonderful opportunity for him to finally get to be with someone."

"Yes perhaps they will hit it off if she is as nice as you say she is. Steve is a really good guy and I am sure he would treat her right."

"Yes he really is, he was so good to me and Tonya when we would work with him and very patient with us as he trained us. He was always so very respectful to us. I want to introduce them once she gets unpacked and settled in to her new house. George do you think Johnnie would hire her to help us? We could use an extra hand and she doesn't have a job right now."

"I could ask him I suppose. The Painting Business has been picking up and some extra help could be needed."

"Yes it has and we have been swamped. Work is steadily coming in and we are booked right now with three weeks of solid work."

"I will talk to him later on today and see what he says."

"Okay, thank you Honey. I am sure she will appreciate that."

Johnnie wasn't interested in all the match making stuff but another employee for the Painting Business would be helpful. After George called him, he agreed to meet her and talk to her about possible employment with his company. Tonya and Ann had done so good at their jobs the business was growing and so was their reputation. The money was certainly coming in and everyone was getting paid pretty good. Everyone was doing good and no one ever complained about the jobs that had been done.

Johnnie waited for a time when Tonya could be there to meet with Debra since she would be working under Tonya.

Johnnie felt it was important to incorporate his leaders into the interviewing process so they could get a good feel for the new employees. However, it was something he had not done as of yet and this would be the first co-interview because he hadn't hired anyone that he hadn't already known. He wanted his leaders to be active in every process of their side of the business. He wanted Tonya to be there to see if she felt it would be a good fit for them.

Johnnie learned from his dad about how coworkers needed to flow together and how personalities was important when making sure people would be able to work good together. Mark had always taught Johnnie things that most parents would never think of teaching their sons at that age but he was good at teaching people and wanted to prepare his son to be successful as early in life as he could. When he had time to just talk with Johnnie, he would tell him things that were going on in his life and how it was effecting him. He did that in order to help him understand how to handle situations and how to deal with people. It had been Mark's plan to bring Johnnie up in such a way he would be able to stand on his own and not have to depend on a corrupt system. Mark saw how advertising had changed and how companies had now used marketing as a way to be dishonest in how they promoted their products. He watched the system use marketing as a way to lie to people and manipulate them so they would purchase their products. He remembered when it was not allowed to lie in commercials when promoting your business or products, how marketing had changed all of that and how honesty and integrity was instead replaced with greed and corruption. Mark wanted Johnnie to be wise about how things worked and how to stay clear of lies and tricks that would cause him to fall into that kind of corruption.

Johnnie never forgot anything his father taught him and when building his own business he used his memories to guide him in his decision making process. Mark taught Johnnie the importance of being honest with people and giving them the truth so they could depend on him and allow him to be able to grow whatever he had decided to do into something successful with a solid foundation.

While Johnnie was continuing to build his business, on the other side of the city Ricky was struggling with his bad decision to kill Randy. He knew it was a mistake he may have to answer for. Those who went on the hunt that night also knew it was a huge mistake and was nervous about what could easily be the consequence for Ricky's decision. He had hoped by putting the Hells Sinners' tag on it that no one would even question it. But the plan was not well thought out and the police had very little to go on. Ricky hoped the extra pressure put on the Hells Sinners would have been too much for them during this war. But the truth was, all the police had to go by was the tag of the Hells Sinners that was left by the West Dragons and that wasn't enough to put anyone in jail. Ricky should have tried to pin it on certain individuals instead of the whole gang. The police had no real suspects to pick up on charges. All Ricky could do now was just wait and see how this was going to play out. Those who went on the hit was staying very silent about it because they all knew Jason was asking questions and no one wanted him to find out that they were involved.

Viper never wanted to even go on this hunt for Randy in the first place. He knew it wasn't right to do such a thing to allies who were helping them and he had strongly disagreed with Ricky about the very idea of doing this to Cypher's group. He was next in command and thought about making a secret meeting with Jason to tell him the truth in hopes to spare him and the rest who had been ordered to go with him to kill Randy. But for now Viper would wait and see what would transpire before making that kind of decision. The fall out with the rest of the gang for going to Jason about what Ricky had them do could be catastrophic in his ability to take over the gang. He feared they would view him as a snitch and no longer have trust in him, and right now there was so much at stake he needed the gang to believe in him and have faith in him. He couldn't run this whole territory without the complete support of the whole gang. Ricky had really fouled things up for them and Viper knew it. But this was Ricky's decision and Viper wasn't going to go down for something he didn't even want to do. He liked Cypher and had highly respected him. Even though Cypher was one man, the whole gang had feared him. And if it all came out the backlash could be major. No one wanted to have to deal with Jason and Cypher at the same time. That was definitely playing with fire. The only thing that had worked out in Ricky's favor concerning the death of Randy was the police was watching the Hells Sinners almost constantly which made them have to be more cautious in what they did and when they did it.

The police was almost always making their presence noticed by the Hells Sinners. They wanted them to know they were watching them to hopefully add enough pressure to cause them to slip up. Nobody wanted this kind of heat on them, especially during a war they were losing. The Hells Sinners had suspected the West Dragons had set them up and had actually committed the crime but had no proof to go on. All they had was the fact they knew they didn't do it and the West Dragons had been the ones hitting them all along. They had felt the West Dragons had done it to limit the Hells Sinners ability to retaliate against them. They still had no idea Cypher and the rest of his group had been involved from the beginning and even now they still didn't know Cypher was also hitting them.

As long as they didn't know, it allowed Cypher to move freely and not have to deal with it on his business or in his neighborhood. Cypher could keep the fight on the Hells Sinners territory and out of theirs. Which not only gave them a better advantage but it kept them all safe. The longer they could push their secrecy the better things would be for them and their families. They knew how these gangs operated and how they would go after whoever they could get just to get their revenge. They had no honor and he knew that. He would continue to press this war and let Ricky deal with the consequences of it while he focused on making his life better. They way he saw it, Ricky deserved whatever he got, along with the rest of these gang bangers who didn't value human life whatsoever. They were ruthless in their killing of innocent people who just happened to get in the way of their bullets. They had no remorse for the innocent kids and mothers they gunned down for no reason, other than being in the wrong place at the wrong time. He hated them for that. He wanted them to die in this war for the things they had done to other people and families.

***

As they week went on and Debra had gotten herself settled in, she invited Ann and George over for a dinner.
"Wow this place looks great Debra," Ann said as she was looking around.
"It really does. Unpacking must have been a beast," George added while looking at a collection of figurines Debra had in a wood corner case with glass windows that was tall and slim.
Debra loved little porcelain figures and had collected many different kinds. It was her hobby to collect things to display. She had many cabinets full of wonderful things she collected. A smaller one was full of all kinds of different little glass animals. As Debra gave them a quick tour, the house began to fill with the wonderful aroma of what Debra was cooking for dinner. She had baked some fresh bread earlier that day and now had a chicken in the oven with carrots and potatoes. Dinner was almost done so Debra sat them down in the living room while she went and prepared the table for them in the dining room that was just off of the kitchen.
"Johnnie would love the paintings," George said to Ann as they waited for Debra to return from the dining room.
"Yes he would indeed. They are all so very vibrant and colorful," Ann added as they looked at the walls that where covered in so many paintings.
The cherry hardwood floor extended from the living

room, through the kitchen where there was a nice cherry island in the middle of the room and into the dining area with a nice wood table with wooden chairs. After Debra finished preparing the table she returned to take them into the dining area where everything was ready. As they entered into the dining area there was a pan in the middle of the table with the chicken and all of the sides waiting for them as the steam rolled off of the pan.

"It smells so wonderful Debra," Ann said as they all sat down.

"Well thank you Ann. I hope you both enjoy it."

"I am sure we will, everything looks so delicious," George said as he fixed Ann's plate for her and then Debra's before getting his own food.

The whole evening went well. George and Debra liked each other just as Ann had hoped. As they sat and talked after dinner, Ann brought up the topic of meeting Steve. She had been waiting all evening to bring it up and was now finally discussing it with her. George had mentioned how Steve was such a great guy and a very hard worker while Ann focused more on talking about how handsome he was as well as his personality. Steve was a very nice guy, but he didn't talk as much as the rest of them did. He was more reserved in his conversations, but did appear to be a good listener.

Debra was excited to meet him as well as meet with Johnnie and Tonya for her interview. She thought it would be so much fun to work with Ann. She met Tonya a few times before when Ann would come to visit. Her and Tonya sometimes would go there together and spend some time visiting with Debra. They seemed to get along pretty good so Ann hoped she would become a good addition to the team.

Johnnie didn't really care just as long as she got along with everyone and worked hard and did a good job. He allowed Tonya to pretty much run the whole painting operation on her own. She had proven to be a good leader and a very hard worker. All he did was give her the invoices so she knew where to go and what to do but she set her own hours now and knew just how much she had to do every day to keep on pace and not get behind. Tonya liked the idea of working long hours on Mondays and Tuesdays and getting off early on Fridays. It seemed to work out good that way and no one had to worry about getting paid.

 Sara started making sure payroll was done Thursday nights and Johnnie would hand out checks first thing in the morning so they wouldn't have to come back and get them after work. Instead they could go right to the bank as soon as they were done for the day. Johnnie liked keeping things efficient and not wasting anyone's time. As long as they got the jobs done, he didn't care. He trusted his employees and rarely ever had to get on anyone. They all worked so hard for him and he valued their hard work and would often reward them for it. He was happy to have another employee that Ann and Tonya was already familiar with. He felt this always made it easier for someone to get into the flow of things if there was already a relationship there.

 After Johnnie and Tanya met with Debra and accepted her as a new employee, he went over just a few simple things with her so she would know what he would be expecting. She was excited to have this new job and to be able to work with her cousin and her friend. This made her feel more comfortable and she was eager to start right away. Debra had come from money and her parents had bought her the house, but she had to pay the bills and keep things up, so for her to already have a job after just moving in was a true blessing. Johnnie paid his people very good so with not having a house payment she would be able to pay all of her bills without struggling.

***

 Johnnie was beginning to feel this war was finally starting to have the progress they had hoped for. The Hells Sinners had taken a huge blow they couldn't get a grip on.

They were losing this war mainly because it took them too long to figure out who was hitting them. Normally they would have suspected the West Dragons but Jason had been clear about there not being a war between the two and there was supposedly a temporary truce between the two gangs. They had no idea he had allowed this war to happen because of what they did to Tonya, and he was behind the order for them to be taken out.

Jason had been stealing the money that was supposed to go to Pauli as a tribute from the Hells Sinners and was killing whoever they sent to deliver the money and made it look as if he never met with them. But when he talked to Pauli he made it seem as if they just wasn't willing to pay anymore which allowed him to okay this war.

Pauli would never allow anyone to get away without paying tribute. It was like a service fee for being able to operate in his territory. Either way Pauli wanted his money. If they wasn't going to pay then he would allow the West Dragons to take their territory. All the Hells Sinners knew was someone was killing their delivery person and taking the money but they would have never guessed that it was Jason who was doing it. Jason was saving the money to help build up his finances while using the fact Pauli wasn't getting his money from them as a way to justify a war between the two rival gangs.

Johnnie had known somehow Jason had worked this all out but he didn't know how or the extent to it. All he knew was Jason was making sure that certain things had happened to allow it to begin and after that he was only involved at certain times to make sure things went according to plan. Jason had been leading the war without anyone knowing it, and was making sure things had went in the direction he wanted it to. Many times the Hells Sinner had come to him about being hit and he played it off that it might have been one of the smaller gangs who was trying to make a name for themselves, but wasn't quite sure at the time as to which gang it was. Now that the Hells Sinners finally knew for sure who it was, they struck back before going to Jason. They knew they were going to have to go talk to him about it, but they had to retaliate as soon as possible and made sure they did it fast and hard.

After which Sisko called for a meeting with Jason to have a sit down about this war they had been thrown into. There was no way Jason hadn't known about this and they knew it. He knew everything before anyone else did, and the fact they now knew who it was that had been hitting them then Jason also knew as well and they knew it.

Jason agreed to meet with them and have the sit down, but he only wanted to sit down with the Hells Sinners for now and denied them a sit down with the West Dragons. He first wanted to make sure he could conceal his involvement first before allowing the two rival gangs to have a sit down with him together. Jason would have to play the devil's advocate in this situation and try to spin it as if at first he was unclear as to who was hitting them but after finding out he had allowed it only because Pauli was unhappy with the money situation. As Jason sat down with Sisko and Ricco, he only allowed the two to come, he began to explain the situation to them.

"Thank you for meeting with us Jason. I was hoping for a sit down with the West Dragons as well, but at least we get to talk to you about this situation."

"Well I already know what you're wanting to know so let's not waste any time. First off I was unsure of who it was that was hitting you. But when I did find out and went to talk to Pauli about how I should handle it, he said to allow it to take place as punishment for having not received his payments from you."

"Jason as you know that is not our fault and we have been looking into it and trying to find out just who had been taking the money and killing our people. Now we believe it is very possible it was the West Dragons who have been doing it all along. We know it was them who had set us up for the killing of Randy as well. We believe they have been behind all of it Jason."

"Pauli doesn't care about any of that. He wants his

money, whether it's your fault or not. He doesn't care."

"Why didn't you tell us when you found out that it was them? You knew we had inquired of you many times concerning this situation."

"I had just found out myself Sisko. It appears that your info came just after I had learned the truth myself."

"So what now? What are we supposed to do? We put a hit on them last night to retaliate for what they have been doing to us. It is not fair they get away with what they have done to us."

"This is your war not mine. You see to it. I have no stake in this war whatsoever."

"That's fine Jason but we still want a sit down with them to expose the truth."

"I don't feel that is necessary at this time. You know who it is that is hitting you, so I suppose you deal with it."

"Trust me Jason we are going to deal with it."

"That's good, now is there anything else you would like to discuss?"

"Yes actually there is. What do we do about the payments?"

"That's your problem, but I would suggest that you come up with the money pretty quickly. You are way behind in these payments and Pauli is going to add interest on top of what you already owe him."

"Jason you can't be serious. Do you know how much we already owe him?"

"Yes actually I do. You're about a hundred thousand behind and now you can add another twenty percent to it."

"So now we owe a hundred and twenty thousand?"

"That is correct Sisko."

"This is crap Jason! That will eat up a lot of our profits that we have."

"There is nothing I can do about it."

"Fine! Let's go Ricco, we have work to do."

Jason watched as they left before he left as well. There was no way he was going to make things easy for them. He knew that hurting them financially and causing added stress to their situation was going to help the West Dragons and Cypher and his group as well. Now they had to worry about the West Dragons, the police and now Pauli as well all at the same time. While Cypher was also a problem for them that had not yet figured out. The West Dragons and Cypher had gotten away with it for a while and the damage had been done. It was going to be almost impossible for the Hells Sinners to recover enough to win this war. They had been hit on every side and Cypher was still getting away with it.

Later on that night, Jason called Johnnie to let him know about the meeting he had earlier with the Hells Sinners. Johnnie had just gotten settled in for the night when the phone had rang.

"Hello?" "Johnnie, are you busy?"

"No I am free to talk. What's going on Jason?"

"I had a meeting earlier with the Hells Sinners."

"Yeah? How did that go?"

"It was interesting. They still don't know you're involved. They only know that the West Dragons been hitting them and that it was them who had killed Randy and tried to pin it on them."

"We need to deal with that Jason."

"Yes I know, and we will in due time. That I promise."

"Well it's good to know that they still don't know about us. So we are pretty much safe for now."

"Yes. Just as long as you keep making sure that no one survives the hits when you go out after them."

"Yeah so far we have been good with no one escaping."

"Well keep putting pressure on them, because right now they are getting it from every side and it's starting to take its toll on them."

"That's good."

"But also be careful Johnnie, the police are watching them all the time. You have to make your hits in between if you don't want to get caught."

"I understand, thank you for the heads up."

"No problem. Okay we have talked too long about this. I

will talk to you later if I have any more information for you."

"Definitely appreciate that Bro."

"Later man," Jason said as he hung up.

Johnnie was relieved to hear this news and he was certain to pass it on to the rest of the group. He knew they needed to be at ease. He knew they would ask about Randy if the Hells Sinners didn't know about them. He would have to explain it away as a separate incident without telling them about Ricky. Either way it's always good when you're the one who is winning.

The West Dragons knew a hit was coming again and had been waiting for it. It had been a few days and all was quiet but they knew the Hells Sinners were desperate and would feel the need to mount another attack against them to try to even up the odds. The police were still keeping their presence felt as they remained posted up outside of the Hells Sinners' club house. They couldn't make a move while they were watching them. They had to wait them out before going on a hit to keep the police from following them. The West Dragons were also posted up a block down watching and waiting for the police to leave as well. A few blocks down the other way was another crew from the West Dragons waiting in a truck Auto had stolen early that morning from a nearby city. As the night went on the police finally left to clock out for the night. There was always a thirty minute window before the other officers would arrive.

A few minutes after they left, the Hells Sinners left in a car and was heading towards the West Dragons' club house. A few blocks down as they were crossing a side street, the truck the West Dragons were in sideswiped them. At the same time the other car that also was full of West Dragons drove by fast and shot up the house. In the meantime the crew in the truck had gotten out and fired shots at the Hells Sinners members that was in the car killing them all while the other car came up behind them and picked them up as they sped off. It was another successful hit that ended very good for the West Dragons. They killed six more members of the Hells Sinners as two was lying dead back at the club house. Four that was in the car all had been shot to death.

   The police were already on their way but by the time they got there, the West Dragons were long gone and already back at their place hanging out as if nothing had happened. Except for Auto and another members who took his car and followed Auto to go get rid of the car they used for the hit. After wiping it down, he set it on fire in an empty field far from where they hung out. By the time Auto showed back up, the police were there asking questions. Auto and the other members played it cool like if they had just showed up for the first time and tried to ask the police what was going on as if they didn't already know. They police grabbed them and started asking them questions as to where they had been and where they was just coming from. Auto told them he just came from his home and didn't know what was going on. Since the car they had pulled up in didn't match the description of the vehicle that was used in the drive-by shooting, they had no choice but to believe them for now. They figured they wouldn't get any answers from the West Dragons but they hoped to maybe at least find the vehicle they was looking for. With the police doing their investigation at both clubhouses, that guaranteed for tonight there wouldn't be a hit by the Hells Sinners. It was another failure on their part that continued to add to their frustrations.

   For the group on the other hand, work was going great. Johnnie scheduled a team breakfast meeting to go over some things and also as a way to introduce Debra to the rest of her coworkers. It was a nice morning. Johnnie felt having the meeting outside on the back patio would be a great idea. Before everyone arrived, Johnnie went to the doughnut shop and picked up a few dozen donuts for the teams breakfast meeting. Sara had a fresh pot of coffee prepared for the group to go with their donuts. Once everyone arrived and were all sitting out back together on the patio, they began to eat and talk. Johnnie finished up his breakfast and was getting ready to go over things with them. After taking another sip of his coffee, he got everyone's attention and started the meeting.

"First I want to thank you all for coming. I know we don't have these very often and probably should have them more then what we do. Before we get to the business side of things I want to introduce you to Debra. She is our new employee with the painting crew."

Johnnie paused as everyone was saying hello to her. George and Ann had positioned themselves to where Debra was sitting next to Steve.

"I would like to thank you all for the great job you have all done. The lawn care business has been doing a very good job at keeping with pace and getting everything done, as well as making sure everything is cleaned up on every job. I am pleased to say we have had absolutely no complaints whatsoever. You're doing a great job working together and getting things accomplished. Is there anything you want to add George?" Johnnie said as he continued the meeting.

"Yes I would. I want to thank my crew for their hard work and dedication to excellence. I am very proud of them."

"Thank you George. I am very proud of your crew as well. Would either of you like to say anything before we move on?"

"Well I am very happy to be working with George and also for this company. I appreciate you giving me a chance Johnnie, Nate said as he was drinking his coffee.

"Yes I am as well. George is a very good leader and I like how he keeps things running smooth," Timothy added before Johnnie moved on to the next area.

"The Painting Business has been swamped with work. And I am very pleased to add people are recommending you to others. I commend Tonya and Ann for being able to take over this part of the business and keep it growing. You two have done an amazing job which has allowed me to hire another employee. The two of you have been working very hard and have done a great job of getting everything done and not falling behind. I know you have worked some long days and I really appreciate that so very much. Is there anything you want to add Tonya?"

"Yes I do. I am so very pleased with my crew, Ann has worked so very hard and also she makes sure everything is done right the first time so we don't have to come back and fix anything. Debra has joined our team and has not only fit right in but has got right into the flow and has been doing such a great job with everything that we have asked her to do. She works fast and hard just as we like it. I have no complaints at all."

"Would you like to add anything Ann?"

"Just that everything has been running so very smooth and Debra has been a great addition and Tonya has been such a great leader. She allows us to have fun while we work and it just makes the day go by so much easier. We have very little frustrations and everyone's personality has been great."

"Would you like to add anything Debra?"

"Yes please. I am so very thankful for the opportunity that you have given me Johnnie and I really enjoy working for and with Tonya, and Ann also. It's a fun job and we keep it fun. I truly enjoy being here."

"Well as you all know I work mainly with Steve doing repair work. Business there has been so busy and Steve has been a great coworker/employee. We have very little problems at all, and when we do, together we have been able to solve the problems by working together and thinking together. Is there anything you want to add Steve?"

"Well work has been very steady which is great. This company has grown in every area and we all have been making very good money. Johnnie you are a fantastic leader. You not only are patient but you know how to handle situations. You lead by example and never ask any of us to do anything that you're not willing to do yourself. It has been a pleasure working with and for you. I hope we have many more years together my friend."

Everyone agreed with Steve as he talked about Johnnie's leadership and how he was such a great leader.

"As you all know this company has grown so much over the past year and as it continues to grow, I hopefully will be able to continue to give raises and bonuses. It is important as an owner and leader of a company to hear from his employees. You're the ones out there making it happen. It's good for me to allow you time to express your feelings, wants or desires. Together we make this happen. You're all valuable. Everyone here has a very important role to fill. I am not only pleased with your work ethics, but I am also very proud of each and every one of you. We sadly lost two great employees to senseless violence. Nate and Timothy both had big shoes to fill and have come in and kept things going just as they were when Darryl and Randy were working with us. I am thankful for the roles you have filled with this company in spite of the tragic loss to two of our great coworkers. They will forever be remembered."

A few of the employees had added an "amen" to that statement about the Two Brothers. Everyone teared up a bit at the mention of Darryl and Randy. They truly had been greatly missed.

"Other than that, just keep up the good job and don't be afraid to come to me if there is a problem or something that you need. We are all in this together. Finish your coffee then take a light day today. We are all doing such a great job that we can have an easy day and then tomorrow make sure you get off early as you usually do on Fridays. Have a nice easy few days and then enjoy your weekend. Thank you for your hard work and dedication to making this company what it is. The success of this company rest on your shoulders, and you all have done a fine job."

As Johnnie brought the meeting to a close he allowed them to chat for a bit while drinking more coffee. It was nice to relax and enjoy part of the morning together before heading out to get things done. Johnnie was so proud of the business he was building and the employees who had been working so very hard for him. There were no weak links on any team and everyone loved working together. Johnnie was blessed to have such great friends who respected him enough to work hard for him and not try to take advantage of their friendship. Johnnie made sure he took real good care of them. Johnnie knew he had real good employees and trusted them.

They trusted Johnnie as well. It was true, he was a great leader, and they knew they could follow him. He worked just as hard as they did and never used being the owner as a way to take it easy. He was sweating just as much as the rest of them did while working just as hard as them. He knew if he wanted them to continue to respect him he had to give it his all every day while working side by side with them.

Everyone has those lazy days but Johnnie pushed through it just like his employees did. Integrity was everything to Johnnie and he wanted the same respect his father had and he knew that didn't come easy. But day by day, he was earning that very respect he had so desired and longed for. Never taking any short cuts whatsoever as he knew his father wouldn't have either. Johnnie still wanted to make his father proud even though he had been gone for so long now, and he would never stop striving to be just like Mark. No matter how hard it was or how long it took, one day he was going to make it and have the life he had always dreamed of.

CHAPTER 10

THE WAR RAGES ON

Every time Johnnie had moved forward it seemed as if things kept trying to push him back. The good days were always followed by something bad it seemed. There had been some evil days that had been upon him. He was always trying to stay in control during times when everything was out of control. He knew he could not allow situations and circumstances to dictate who he was or who he wanted to be. Bad things happen and he just had to roll with the punches. He felt as if he had no choice but to let life take him wherever it led him, whether good or bad. He seemed at times to have very little say so in the matter.

He often wondered about people who would say that life is what you make it. Perhaps they had never lived in his kind of reality. A reality where things just happened and you couldn't control it. Perhaps they were living in a dream land where reality was an afterthought. No one would purposely create this kind of life for themselves where they lost so much so early and so often. People wasn't always honest and he knew that for sure.

How could he dare to believe such a thing as life is what you make it when he was in the middle of a war that he never wanted and had cost him so much? Do these people really believe that? It's absurd to believe that one could always be in control of everything that happens to them. What about the millions of homeless people who lost their jobs due to major companies giving their jobs to other countries? Was life what they made it when a corporation they committed their lives to, took everything away from them and gave it to someone else that had never even bought their product? How I would laugh at the senseless bumper stickers that said buy American if you want American jobs, while the whole time they was selling our future out and giving it to other people outside of our country. How are we so easily fooled into supporting the ones who have screwed us? How many families have been ruined due to big businesses taking what was theirs and giving it away to people who never fought to make these companies successful? And for what? To be kicked out and left behind with nothing? These companies never cared about the homes that was destroyed so they could save some money. Yet they want us to stay loyal to them while they sold us out. What about their loyalty, what about their commitment? They have billions of dollars and willingly hurt American families just to make more money. The greed and the corruption was always surrounding us, and making it hard to believe in people any more.

A corrupt system that sent me to juvenile prison for protecting me and my mother. How could they not understand that it was self-defense? Or did they even care? I killed a cop's friend who was abusing my mother and I lost three years of my life. There is no real justice. Everything is corrupted. Gangs like the Hells Sinners and the West Dragons are all over the place and no one does anything about it while they senselessly hurt innocent people. I would wish they all would die. All of this pain and for what? So these useless criminals can make money by hurting others. Ricky will have his day. Retribution is coming to them all. The Hells Sinners will pay with their lives for what they have done and so will Ricky. I will not let any of them get away with what has happened. I will find my justice, even if it has to come by my own hand. I will receive my retribution and I will punish them all for what they have done.

It was beginning to get even harder to keep a positive mind in the midst of such turmoil for Johnnie. He embraced

Cypher as an alter ego to help him cope with what he was doing. For Johnnie, it seemed to make it less real at times if he was Cypher instead of Johnnie. Cypher could do things Johnnie couldn't. Cypher could be the ruthless killer when needed and Johnnie could be the business man. However, at times, it was hard keeping it all together. The lines could so easily get blurred while his focus was being distorted. It was mentally trying as he tried to keep the two separated. At times it became more complicated but it was necessary to keep the two under control. For the group he was always Johnnie but for the West Dragons he was always Cypher. The more he embraced Cypher as his alter ego, the more aggressive he became when stepping into that role.

And that was something everyone noticed. He was becoming more and more feared by his allies then they had ever expected. Ricky was now becoming extremely fearful Cypher would eventually find out about what he had done and kill him. Ricky knew there was nothing he could do but try to keep it a secret in fear of what would happen to him. He knew he couldn't touch Cypher because Jason would come after him if he ever did. He was trapped now in his fears and secrecy. With Jason poking his nose into the death of Randy, it was very likely he would eventually be exposed. There was no way he could even dare to think of touching Cypher for that would surely expose him. There was only one way out of this and that was to keep lying in hopes he could keep this matter covered up.

Later on that week Cypher had set Steve and Debra up on a double date with him and Tonya. Steve seemed to like her and she had been a little flirty with him as well. They looked as if they would be a nice couple together. It was at the end of the week they would get together for a nice time out so the two could spend some time together outside of work and get to know each other a little better. Johnnie loved taking Tonya out on dates anyways, and knew that would be fun to have a new couple with them. He would have invited George and Ann, but they had already made plans for themselves but promised they would go out with them the next time. It would have been nice for the whole group to go out together but nevertheless they would all have fun just the same.

Johnnie had a can he would put extra money in to save for date nights with Tonya. It was money that was left over from the week's budget that didn't have to be used. Every time he had saved money from discounts, he would add that extra money to the date can. Whenever he could take Tonya out that was the highlight of his week. They had come through some tough times together and now things were really getting good again and Tonya was working hard at trying to get passed the incident, and Johnnie was trying extremely hard to keep her happy as well as comfortable.

Steve had always been so busy he had never taken the time to date anyone before and this was all very new to him. He was enjoying it. It was a good feeling to him that he had never experienced before. He knew why Johnnie wanted to kill every one of the Hells Sinners for what they had done to his sister. As the night went on and he was really starting to like Debra, he could get a better understanding of just how much Johnnie loved his sister as he watched them interact together. The feelings he had for Debra were new so he could imagine how much Johnnie was in love with Tonya who he had been with him for most of his life.

All the time he had known Johnnie, there was something between him and his sister, but it was different seeing them out on a date together, in a different type of setting away from the group. They were more romantic together and had a different kind of spark they seemed to have hidden when they were with the group. It was special, and the love was more intense than he had ever seen between them two before. Being out with them on this date really helped him to see just how deep their love for each other really was. He understood why Johnnie would risk his life for her and kill for her. Watching them dance together was like magic. Neither of them ever stopped smiling as Johnnie held her close to him and their eyes seemed to pierce each other's as they kept constant eye contact with one another. It was deep and intense for sure, the way they looked so heartfelt into each other's eyes with such deep love and fondness for each other.

    Debra had noticed it as well and was so very deeply touched by it. Johnnie and Tonya was absorbed by each other's love that everything else had faded in the background as they held each other in a loving embrace while dancing together as if they were the only couple on the dance floor. It was so easy for the two of them to get lost in each other and almost disappear in public and become oblivious to everyone else that surrounded them. The love they had for each other was unfathomable. The way they looked at each other was so lovingly sensual as if there was a hunger between the two that could cause them to devour each other in their passion.

    For Steve this was all new but he was enjoying it. It felt good to be with someone, to have someone. Up until now, he had never really cared. Being in this moment had awoken something deep inside him. As he returned his focus back to Debra he could feel there was now something different. He was effected ever so deeply by the whole experience. He already liked Debra but now it was different. Something had sparked within his heart for her that he had never felt before, and he wanted more of it. For the first time in his life, he had felt real love for someone as he began to crave the feelings that he was having for her. She was beautiful and had such a nice personality. Steve was enjoying her company and moved in closer to her as they danced together. It was such an intoxicating sensation as he held her closer to him. He was falling for her in this very moment and he knew it and he wanted it. He needed it. He began to feel that need for her as he held her tightly while dancing with her. And she felt good in his arms as he wished for the moment to never end. He didn't want to let her go and she could feel it too.

    Debra adored Steve and felt pleasure in his arms as she took such great delight in being with him. She had savored every second she spent in his arms. She wanted this to develop between the two of them. Steve wasn't a great a dancer but he held her tight and moved slowly in a small circle that created an intimacy along with the music in the dark lighting.

Johnnie smiled at Steve as he could tell they were enjoying themselves. It was obvious the two liked each other as Johnnie had whispered in Tonya's ear.

"Look at them two, they can feel it. They want to be with each other. Look at how their eyes meet and how they stare at each other, that's love in their eyes. Steve wants her."

Tonya smiled at Johnnie and nodded in agreement.

"She is right for him. I really like her, and my brother needs to be with someone. I hate him not having someone and not being able to share with someone what we have always had together."

Tonya and Johnnie both were watching them a brief time before they all went back to the table once they saw they had brought them their food. Steve hated to release his hold on her, but it was time. He could have went without food just to stay in that moment. He wasn't ready to let her go at all, he wasn't ready for that feeling to end. Debra wore a short black sensual dress that was revealing her sexy thick legs that was highlighted in her black high heel shoes. Steve loved the way she looked. He had seen plenty of sexy women before but there was clearly something different about Debra. She had ignited the flames of his passion that began to burn within him.

As they sat at the table, eating and talking, Steve could no longer resist the uncontrollable urge to touch her as he slipped his hand under the table and gently ran his fingertips across her smooth, soft skin. He touched her leg and she welcomed his touch. She let out a soft sigh as he touched her while she lovingly looked deep into his eyes. She smiled as he felt on her leg. Her soft, silky skin felt nice to the touch as he continued to rub her leg under the table while trying to eat his food, hoping no one would noticed but it was all too obvious. He brought attention to what he was doing while his best friend and his sister was observing them. He was not experienced enough to not bring an awareness to what he was doing. He couldn't help it. He needed to touch her sexy legs. They had been calling to him all evening. Beckoning him to touch them and he could resist no longer.

"So will you two be joining us on more dates?" Johnnie asked to break the attention Steve had unknowingly brought upon himself. Debra, who being more experienced, was quite aware of it.

"Yes, I would like that. I mean if Debra wants to?" Steve said while being slightly embarrassed.

"Yes I would love to," Debra responded while smiling at Steve.

"Perfect, then how does next Saturday night sound?"

"It sounds perfect," Steve said as Tonya and Debra was also agreeing.

The night was going by fast and Steve knew at some point they were going to have to go but he had wished for this night to never end.

"The food was amazing," said Debra as she took her last bite.

"Yes it was. I am so full," Steve responded while taking a drink to wash down the bite he had just taken.

"This might just become our new spot," Johnnie said as he reached over and grabbed Tonya's hand. She smiled back at Johnnie as she gripped his hand.

"I would love that Baby. This is such a nice romantic place." "

"Yes it is Baby," Johnnie said as he leaned in to kiss her.

Steve and Debra looked at each other and both had felt a little uncomfortable. They weren't sure if they should share a kiss also. Finally Steve went for it as he also leaned into a kiss with Debra who was accepting his invitation to share a kiss with him as he pressed his lips against hers. It was their first kiss and they had shared it with Johnnie and Tonya who was now smiling at the two of them.

"Looks like we have a new couple to double date with,"

Johnnie said to Tonya who was so happy that Steve had found a nice girl to be with.

"I certainly hope so," Tonya said as she responded to Johnnie while watching Debra kiss her brother.

Debra's face became as red as the table cloth at their words. Steve was still kissing her, who had now pulled away realizing he got caught up in the moment and perhaps may have kissed her too long. He was now also a little embarrassed himself.

Johnnie raised his glass of wine to present a toast.

"To new love. Let it flourish like a fresh spring flower," he said as he looked at the new couple and then turned his attention to Tonya. "To never failing love that endures forever," he said as they all took a sip of their wine.

Then Johnnie returned his lips to Tonya's for one more kiss after toasting their love for each other. After finishing their food, Johnnie took Tonya back to his place to spend some time out on the back patio like they always did when they wanted to be alone and hold each other. Steve had taken Debra home and dropped her off before calling it a night, but not before he gave her a nice long good night kiss. The whole night was perfectly romantic. Steve was thankful Johnnie and Tonya had invited him and Debra out with them. His first taste of love was amazing and the rest of the night he laid in bed thinking about her until he finally had fallen asleep. Steve knew this was something real and couldn't wait to see her again. The night had dramatically affected him as she was also effected by the way Steve had touched her and kissed her.

After she went into her house, she laid down on her bed and thought about how Steve had touched her under the table. She was craving and wanting more of his touch. No one had ever handled her that way before and when she was being held by him, she could feel herself falling for him. But that touch had set her skin on fire. She had never felt her whole body tingle like that, at a simple touch of a hand on her leg. But it was the way Steve touched her and it felt so good as she laid there thinking about it.

Johnnie had spent the rest of the night holding Tonya as they talked about their relationship as well as Steve and Debra's new relationship that was beginning to develop.

"What a great way to start a relationship isn't it? A nice romantic night out with great food and some slow dancing," Johnnie said while lovingly holding Tonya in his arms.

"It sure is. I rather enjoyed it myself, the food was excellent and the music was perfect. I always love when you take me dancing like that."

Johnnie smiled as big as ever at her words. He loved taking her dancing also, and she was right, the music was perfect. All night they slowed danced and held each other. It was beautiful in every sense of the word.

"I really am happy for my brother. I know he really liked her a lot and I think she likes him as well," Tonya softly uttered as she indicated her approval of her brothers new relationship.

"Yes I agree. I think they hit it off very good, and they really seem to make such a great couple together. Your brother is a really good guy Tonya. I am happy that we became close friends like we have. He truly is like a brother to me."

"Steve liked you the moment we all first met. It was good for us to meet you all when we first moved in. It made the transition so much easier. I was thankful that you all had come down to meet us. Actually I have a confession to make. That day we met, when I first saw you, I was attracted to you. There was something about you that drew me in to you. Honestly I have loved you ever since. You're my soul mate Johnnie. You always have been." She leaned in and kissed Johnnie as he held her.

"Tonya, wait here for a minute, I will be right back."

Johnnie went into the house and hurried back to Tonya. She had shifted in her seat presuming he was going to come and sit right back down with her and continue to hold her, but he didn't. Instead Johnnie had reached down and took Tonya's hand and pulled her to her feet. Looking deep into her eyes he kissed her and then got down on his knees and pulled out a ring that he had bought a while back and then proposed to her.

"Tonya, My Love, it's always been you. My whole life I have never been with anyone but you. You were my first and only girlfriend. I have never till this day ever touched another woman, and the only lips I have ever kissed is yours. You are and always will be my only love, my true love, and I want it to stay that way. I never want to be with anyone other than you. You are all I need and all I have ever wanted." Johnnie still holding her hand in his took the diamond ring and put it on her finger. "Tonya My Love, will you marry me?"

Tears ran down Tonya's face as she was so overwhelmed that after all that had happened, the man she had always truly loved still wanted to marry her.

"Oh yes Johnnie! Yes I will marry you!" Johnnie stood up and held her in his loving arms and then kissed her while wiping away her tears.

"Oh Tonya, I've waited for this moment my whole life. I have never wanted to be with anyone else."

Tonya knew they were meant to be together and no matter how hard she struggled at times with what had happened, she knew Johnnie and her was supposed to be together. She loved Johnnie more now than ever. He had proven his love to her a thousand times over. She had no doubt he would love her forever, never leave her, and she loved him more than anything. She could not deny her own heart. She needed him just as much as he needed her. Their hearts had always burned for each other and nothing that happened could have ever quenched that flame that burned ever so deeply within their hearts.

Tonya knew that Johnnie's love for her was real and she also knew he would never stop until he obliterated everyone who was involved in hurting her the way they had. The Hells Sinner would be erased from life before he would ever stop coming after them, and Tonya knew that. As much as she hated it, she had to accept it as it was. They had brought this upon themselves but she truly hated Johnnie was involved in this war and was always fearful that at some point he would get hurt or end up in prison for the rest of his life. But there was no stopping that train now. They had forced Johnnie's hand and they would die by that hand.

   The rest of the night Johnnie held Tonya as they fell asleep in each other arms until he had awaken early the next morning. She looked so beautiful and peaceful as she slept in his arms. He gently ran his fingers through her hair as he watched her sleep. Loving her as he held her while she rested in his arms, taking a deep breath as he breathed her in. *Finally we're engaged.* He smiled as she laid peacefully in his loving arms. Johnnie gently touched her cheek as he leaned down and kissed her ever so softly, not wanting to wake her. Tonya stretched as she slowly began to awaken smiling as she looked up into his eyes as he was still holding her. She laid her head back against his chest as she was not yet fully awake and didn't want to move from his loving embrace.

   "Good morning my Darling Fiancé," she said as she laid against him while basking in his love for her.

   "Good morning Baby," he responded as he continued to hug her while embracing her as she laid back on him.

   "Are you hungry my Sweet Love?" Johnnie inquired as he was feeling famished from a long night that had rolled into the early morning.

   "Yes Baby I am," she responded as her stomached growled.

   "Okay Baby, let's get up and get some breakfast and see if Mom is up also."

   Tonya sat up so Johnnie could get up and go in the house, but she laid there for a few more minutes until finally getting up and following him into the house. Johnnie and Sara were both in the kitchen working together to cook breakfast as Tonya joined them.

   "Baby, sit and relax. I can help her," Tonya told him as she took over helping Sara cook breakfast while Johnnie sat at the table and drank some hot coffee Tonya had poured for him.

"Everything smells so good," Johnnie commented as he sipped his coffee.

Tonya was still smiling and the excitement of being proposed to was still very vibrant and noticeable.

"What's with you two this morning?" Sara questioned as she was watching the two of them. They could not keep from smiling as they kept looking at each other.

"Johnnie asked me to marry him last night!"

Sara was overwhelmed with excitement as she grabbed Tonya and hugged her so tight.

"Oh Tonya that is so wonderful! Congratulations!" Sara said as she then looked over at Johnnie who was smiling while sipping his coffee.

"It's about time Johnnie," Sara said to him.

"I know Mom. I wanted to wait until the business was where I wanted it to be and the money was right. Everything has been growing the way I wanted it to and well, now is the time I suppose. I love her more than anything and I am tired of waiting to be her husband." Tonya walked over and kissed him then stood next to him with her arms around him.

"It is time. We have been through so much and we are still together. I love him more than anything as well. This is where I need to be, with him. I know I still have my hard times, but I love him and he has been so good to me, so supportive and ever so patient with me. Even when we weren't talking, he still waited for me and remained true to me. I can never be more thankful having such a wonderful, sweet, loving man. So of course I had to say yes!" Johnnie pulled her down onto his lap and kissed her.

"I couldn't be happier for the two of you. I knew this day would come. I have been waiting for it for a long time. You two were meant to be together. You belong together. This is such an amazing morning. Oh my! I am happy for you both. Let me take you two out to dinner tonight so we can celebrate."

"That sounds like a great idea Mom."

"Yes it does, I would love that Sara," Tonya added as she sat with Johnnie.

"You can call me Mom now Tonya. We are going to finally be family."

"Awe Mom we have always been family," Tonya said to her as she got up and hugged Sara who was in tears. They briefly held each other before returning their attention back to the food that was starting to overcook.

"It's a little too over done," Johnnie told them as he laughed. "No worries, I will go and get us some donuts. You two relax and talk for a bit while I run out to get us some breakfast."

"Okay Baby, hurry back," Tonya spoke as she kissed him before he left.

As Sara and Tonya sat at the table drinking coffee together they began to talk about Mark and Johnnie.

"Mark would have been so happy to see you two getting married."

"Oh Sara, do you really think so?"

"Yes I do. Mark would have loved you. He would have been so proud of Johnnie for everything he has accomplished. But most of all, he would have been proud of Johnnie for wanting to marry you and do things right. Mark was such a romantic. The way he loved me was like nothing I have ever experienced before. It was intoxicating the way he used to come up from behind me and gently touch my skin as he kissed all over my neck. Just thinking about his soft lips against my skin to this day gives me chills."

Tonya sat smiling as Sara was talking about Mark, because she knew exactly what Sara was talking about. Johnnie would do the same thing to her and get the same result from Tonya that Mark used to get from Sara.

"Oh Sara, he sounds just like Johnnie. Now I truly understand where Johnnie gets it from."

"Yes Johnnie is much like his father. Mark was an incredible lover. He knew how to set my whole body on fire with such great passion that I could barely contain myself. Mark was everything to me. He was such a strong man, too. I always felt safe with him. He was never afraid to fight or defend me. He always protected me. One time there was these bullies that Mark didn't like and they didn't like him either, and one of them had a thing for me. Well, we were out on a date one night and they were there at the spot where Mark had taken me. This guy that wanted to be with me came up and tried to grab me in front of Mark. Oh boy, was that a huge mistake. Mark laid him out with one punch in front of everyone. The next time we saw him when we were out again, he had four of his other friends with him. He started running his mouth to Mark about the things he wanted to do to me. I mean it was so disgusting and disrespectful. Mark at first was trying to let it go until he got real obscene about it, and there was people everywhere hearing the things he was saying. Mark got up and walked over to him and said this is between me and you, and looked at the other four and told them to stay out of it. Of course they said they would but once they started fighting, it was only a few seconds into it that Mark clearly had the upper hand and the other four jumped in on Mark. They beat Mark up, but they all was hurt from that fight. They didn't know what they had got themselves into. They may have won the fight, but not before Mark hurt every single one of them. They never messed with me or Mark again."

"Wow Johnnie is so much like his father. Christina told me a little bit about Mark and how Johnnie was so much like him. But he really is."

"Yes Tonya, he really is. Even right down to the way he looks at you. It's exactly the way Mark used to look at me. That is why I had no doubt that at some point you two would be getting married. Johnnie is a lover and a fighter, and so was Mark."

While they were still talking, they heard him come in the front door. The two of them sat smiling at the thoughts they were having about their conversation.

"Donuts are here!" Johnnie announced as he walked into the kitchen and sat them on the table. He couldn't help notice the two of them with their smiles beaming so big. "What did I miss? You two look like it was a very good conversation."

"Oh Johnnie we was just talking about you and Mark, and about how you two are so much alike."

Johnnie let out a huge sigh as he thought about that statement and how he had wished it was true.

"I am not like my father. He was a great man." Johnnie was putting the donuts on their plates and had served them.

"Oh Johnnie there are things I haven't told you, but when I do then you will understand just how much of Mark is in you," Sara told him as he sat down with them.

"It's true Johnnie, even Christina has told me the same thing," Tonya added as she took a bite of her donut.

"Then tell me," Johnnie said.

Tonya was getting everyone some fresh coffee before returning back to her seat as they both told Johnnie everything that was said and how he resembled his father way more than he thought. Johnnie needed to hear this and it was time for them to tell him. He always used his father as a way to measure himself as a man. He felt he had fallen short of what his father was, but the truth was, he was just like Mark and it was time for him to know that. As they told Johnnie everything they talked about and how even Christina had told Tonya other things about Mark as well. Johnnie, for the first time, felt proud of himself. He had always assumed he wasn't even close to being the man his father had been. Mark was his hero and now he finally saw everything he had done and was doing didn't make him different from Mark but rather brought him closer to being what his father had been. That had always been his goal. He sat there almost in tears now realizing he was like his father and that he hadn't failed Mark at all, like he supposed he had done. Johnnie was over whelmed with such great emotions as they all sat talking before he could not hold back the tears any longer.

"Oh Johnnie," Tonya said as she got up and hugged him. Johnnie rarely showed this side of himself, because to him crying was a sign of weakness. The truth is that crying is just a part of life, and Johnnie was feeling vulnerable as he wept in Tonya's arms as years and years of frustrations and disappointments came pouring out of him. Sara also joining them as she embraced Johnnie as they both understood what he was feeling with all that he had been through.

Sara had never known just how deeply Johnnie had been struggling with this. She always known he was trying to be like his father, but in her eyes he had been. She had no idea he never saw it the way she had.

He had accomplished a lot but he felt this was his greatest accomplishment. Even though he didn't really know just how much he had accomplished because it was so hard for him to not focus on all the bad stuff that he had been through in his life. Even though he was not that old, he had been through a lifetime of pain and hurt already, and was in the middle of a huge war. However, with all of that considered, he had built a successful business while dealing with all of this. Which in itself was a huge accomplishment. And everyone was very proud of him for what he was doing and how he was helping the group to become successful as well. He had put his heart into everything he did, whether good or bad. He really was a great fighter just like his father as well as an amazing lover. After breakfast Tonya went home for a bit to get freshened up before returning after a few hours to spend the rest of the day with Johnnie and Sara.

For Sara, this was the perfect day. Her son finally got engaged to the woman Sara had already considered as her daughter, and now they were going to spend the entire day with her and then have dinner with as well later on that evening. After Tonya had returned, Sara pulled out some old scrap books with photos of Johnnie as he was growing up.

Johnnie sat with them and explained different things about the time periods of each photo. It felt good as Johnnie walked down memory lane and reminisced about some of the good times in his life that he had almost forgotten about. After they had finished, they talked until lunch time when Sara and Tonya made lunch together while Johnnie went to get a few movies for them to watch together after lunch.

Later that evening, Sara took them out to a nice restaurant to celebrate their engagement. While they were eating a man had approached their table who had been looking at Sara since they had come in. As he began to speak to Sara, Johnnie interrupted him and stopped him immediately.

"She isn't interested man," Johnnie said as he shot the man a glare that let him know he meant business.

"Hey relax kid there is no harm in me just coming over to introduce myself to this fine looking lady." Johnnie started to get up before Tonya grabbed his arm to hold him back down.

"I said she isn't interested, now go back to where ever you came from."

"Well you're a feisty young man aren't you?" Shaking his head as the scowl on his face became more serious.

"Listen my son is right. I am not interested, so please let us be, we are celebrating their engagement and don't want to be bothered with anything else."

"Okay, no problem. You need to learn some manners kid."

"Why don't you teach me some old man," Johnnie responded and before the man could say anything Tonya had interrupted.

"Look, you really don't want this problem. I don't know you but I do know my man and if you pursue this any further you will regret it. Now, if I was you I would just walk away before you get embarrassed." The man had looked at Johnnie and saw in his eyes Tonya was right.

"My apologies," the man said as he walked away.

Sara grabbed Johnnie's hand and thanked him for stepping in immediately. Sara thought the man was attractive, but she was nowhere near ready to date again.

This wasn't the time or the place for her to be meeting someone, as she had also felt that it was rude of him to come over and interrupt their celebration.

After a wonderful dinner the three of them went back to Sara's house for a night cap of hot tea. The night was winding down and was coming to a close. Sara was exhausted and was ready for a good night's sleep while Johnnie and Tonya stayed up for a bit to relax together before she went home.

The next day it was back to the grind. Work was keeping them all very busy and they were loving it. The money was coming in better than ever and everyone was doing so good. Johnnie was building such a strong reputation for his business and everyone respected just how much he was accomplishing. He ran a tight ship and his workers did every job right without cutting corners. Never had Johnnie received any real complaints, but rather they always told him how well his workers did. Johnnie was proud of his team and always tried to show it with free lunches or even sometimes taking them all out for dinner. Every quarter Johnnie handed out bonuses to all of his employee's according to how their division was doing. He knew they were working very hard for him and he knew the importance of showing his appreciation to them for all they had done for him and for his company. They were the backbone to his success and he knew it. Their hard work and late nights were what was making this company standout as one of the best.

Johnnie rarely took credit for the success of his business but instead he always gave credit to just how hard his people worked and how they paid great attention to every detail. He loved his crew and always made sure they had everything they needed to get the job done. They never lacked for anything, he took care of their personal needs as well. He paid them more then what any other business paid for people in their position, but he could afford to do so, because they always had tons of jobs to do. In spite of all he was going through with this war his business continued to grow and flourish.

   The community had favored him because they knew and loved his father and they could see the same qualities and workmanship in Johnnie as they did with Mark. They knew he would make sure everything was done right and they would never have to ask him to come back and fix something that wasn't right. He took pride in that and always made sure his people did as well. Integrity was a must if you worked for him. You had to be dependable and trustworthy. If he could not trust you to work on your own and get things done right, then you had no place in his company. He demanded leadership from every one of his workers no matter what your position was. Because of that, he started taking all of his employees to leadership conferences. He would never demand leadership from his people without providing the right training so that they could do it. The next day after every leadership conference Johnnie would hold a leadership meeting, where he had everyone share and talk about what they learned and how it impacted them. They would all discuss how they thought they could implement things into the business.

   Johnnie did pay them the top salaries, but he also expected more out of them. They were the best and he made sure they all continued to grow, even himself. He wanted the best for his employee's but he also wanted the best out of his employee's. It was always his goal they grew together as a company. In his meeting he always gave everyone a chance to express their thoughts and ideas and even their criticism and what they wanted to see change within the company. Johnnie valued his employee's thoughts and ideas. He was their leader but he was not so far above them that he became a dictator. He wanted their insight and their input. He wanted them to be able to express their feelings and take ownership of their positions and do their best, and he felt the best way to do that was to allow them to express themselves and really be a part of this company as a leader and not just another employee. This is what helped make this company better then every other company, because every employee on staff took personal ownership of what they was doing. They knew they were responsible for every outcome and it was up to them to either be the best or find a new job.

There was no room for slackers with Johnnie. You either worked hard or you didn't work for him. He was an on hands boss, he didn't expect anyone to work harder than him, and he never demanded more out of his employee's then he demanded out of himself. If they worked, he worked, and sometimes when he gave them days off, he still worked. That is not to say he didn't allow for personal days. He understood sometimes you just had to have the day off to get things done or get over being sick. He never pushed his people beyond their limits and always tried to give them breaks when he felt they needed it. He never wanted anyone of his employee's to get burned out. He knew when they needed rest and would make sure they all got it. This is one major reason why he tried to never work them on the weekends. He valued family and wanted them to have time for theirs.

He hated when his father would work long hours and then work weekends as well, and he didn't want his people to have to do that. As much as Johnnie worked and as hard as they all worked, he understood that all work and no play was not good for any of them. He wanted them to work hard for him, but he also wanted them to enjoy life as well. He understood so much about this because there was times he had missed his father and how he hated not being able to watch every baseball game with his father because of his job, as well as his time away from everyone when he was in The House. He knew what it was like to miss people and to be missed and he didn't want that for his employee's. Life was meant to be enjoyed and that is what he wanted for them all. Building a business wasn't easy and working hard was what it was going to take to get them to where he wanted them to be. Johnnie wasn't just seeking for his own success, but wanted all of them to find success as well.

As the weekend came to a close, Johnnie was getting

geared up for another week He thought he would do something different and go on a run on Monday and make a hit on the Hells Sinners instead of waiting for the middle of the week or the weekend to come. Johnnie had backed off for a bit, to let things settle down. He knew they would be waiting for him so he took a break from hitting them while he focused on his business and his relationship with his new fiancé, Tonya. Everyone hated to shut down early on Mondays as it was their long day to get as much as they could done to ensure them their early day Friday. But it was time to make this run. Johnnie hated it, having to sit there and watch while waiting for the right moment to present itself so they could make this hit without being seen. It always felt like wasted time, but that's how they had to do it.

 Johnnie sent a text to George and Steve to let them know what time they all needed to be done. The girls were able to go ahead and work late if they wanted. Tonya worked them as usual and kept the same schedule they were used to working.

 After work was done for the day and everyone was cleaned up, they all assembled themselves together back at the camp area. Once everyone was all set, the three of them had Auto send someone to pick them up at the old playground where Randy was murdered. Auto had wasted no time in sending someone immediately to go and gather them up. After they were well on their way, everyone got themselves in the right mind frame for what they were about to do. It was hard to stay hyped and in the moment after being there for a bit and just sitting while waiting for the right time to strike.

 As they were watching they had noticed a car had pulled up just a little ways down from the ones they were watching. No one ever got out of the car and they was just sitting there also. Cypher had kept a close eye on them. It wasn't long before he realized they were more of the Hells Sinners who was watching and waiting just like they were, only they were waiting for Cypher and his group to make a hit. Seeing this he made a quick call for back up.

"Hey Ricky, we have a blue bird with four eggs just a ways down from our target. They are parked just on the north side waiting. They haven't spotted us yet, but I see them. I will text you the area where we are."

"Okay Cypher, I am sending a team of hunters to clear the way and eliminate your blue bird problem. Hang tight for a moment and they will be there shortly."

"Thank you, we are ready as soon as you can clear our path."

After Cypher texted Ricky the exact position where the car was parked, they waited for them to text back when they were close enough for them to progress with their mission. Just over thirty minutes later Cypher got a text saying they were two blocks away and coming up fast.

"Let's go, here they come to clear our way. Let's get ready to hit them just after our back up fires off shots. We can use their distraction as a means for an ambush, and take them all by surprise. The three of them all got out of the car and started after them as the West Dragons car had pulled up and fired upon the ones that had been sitting there as they shot it all up, killing everyone inside. Just as they went to speed off, Cypher and the other two was on the group they had been watching and fired at them before they could retaliate against the car that was now speeding off down the street. They had no chance as they never saw Cypher coming. The Hells Sinner that was on the corner selling drugs was all hit as George and Steve shot three of them while Cypher got the other one before they even knew what was going on. The whole thing had happened so fast, none of them had a chance to respond at all before they were fired upon and laid to rest. All eight of the Hells Sinners was killed instantly. It had only taken a few minutes for the whole scene to unfold and Cypher along with the others were already gone from the scene of the crime with no witness to report anything. It was a smooth clean hit that went fast and hard. The waiting had paid off and eight of their enemies had been eliminated at one time. That had been their most successful hit to date.

    When the news got back to Ricky he was well pleased with that run and had given Cypher much credit for pulling it off. Everything went perfect. Cypher was able to use their back up against them and it actually made their hit go so much smoother and a lot easier. They had already been dropped back off and was back at the camp area before the police even arrived at the scene of the crime. It was their best hit ever and they got away clean. The three of them was still energized from the excitement that comes with doing these runs. It would take most of the night for them to calm down.

    Tonya and the rest of the group had arrived as they all sat around the fire and talked for most of the night. It was going to be a rough work day for them with little sleep, but the payoff from the run was worth it. That put them one more step closer to finishing this war. Tonya as well as Ann both hated this, but were happy the boys were getting closer to ending this feud. It had been hard on all of them, but now they could relax for a few weeks and let things calm back down before they would do it again.

    Cypher was keeping it as random as he could, to keep from getting into a routine that would allow the Hells Sinner to anticipate their moves. After a long night with very little rest it was back to the grind with a long exhausting day ahead of this already tired group. Everyone would be happy to see this work day completed and get some much needed rest. Johnnie could feel it as they were dragging a bit. There was no way any of them were going to get as much done today as they had hoped, but they continued to push as hard as they could as they pressed toward their goals that they would fall short of. Nevertheless it was still a good work day as far as accomplishments. They knew they would all have to grind it out again the next day, but they were getting closer to being caught back up, and tomorrow would allow them to finish with one more push to get where they needed to be for an early Friday.

For Tonya's painting team though, they were ahead of the game and made a strong push even though they did not need to. They worked hard just like everyone else did, and if they were all going to work long hours again the next day then they would too. Tonya wasn't going to take an easy day while the rest worked hard. They were all tired and had pushed themselves as far as they could go before calling it a night. The sun was already going down as the moon was rising in the sky before they all got home. Johnnie and Tonya was too tired to meet up and had decided on just a phone call before bed. A good night's rest was in store for them all, as another long hard day was awaiting.

   The next day Johnnie was up earlier and met Sara in the kitchen. He decided to go ahead and help her cook so they decided to cook breakfast for the entire team. Johnnie called everyone to come earlier and have breakfast with them. Sara always loved when the whole group would meet for breakfast and then spend a little time socializing before going off to work. She had missed having her home filled with the boys and loved seeing them all together like when they were younger and would stay the night back at the camp area. However, it always made her miss the two brothers Randy and Darrell.

   After breakfast Tonya, Ann and Debra stuck around for a bit to help Sara clean up while the rest left to go work. Because they was farther along than the other teams, it allowed them to stay behind and help Sara with the mess that was left behind. Sara enjoyed their company as they stayed for some girl time after the kitchen was cleaned up. After some time chit chatting, the girls were off to get their jobs done as well, leaving Sara alone to relax and enjoy the rest of her day while Johnnie was gone.

CHAPTER 11

A NEW MAN FOR SARA

    It was early in the morning and Sara had no plans for the day as of yet. Johnnie had already helped all of his crews to get going and was on his way out with Steve to get their day going as well. This had left Sara all to herself for the day with nothing to really do. All of the house work was done and it was becoming a free day for her. It was time to go out and spend the day doing other things that didn't require her to be in the house all day. Sara had given Tammy a call to see if she wanted to get together for a little shopping, but she had to go and do some food shopping already and that was not the kind of shopping Sara had in mind. She wanted to get out and spoil herself for a bit. Maybe even buy Tonya something nice to continue to celebrate her new engagement with Johnnie. Sara didn't mind going shopping on her own, but company was always nice to have when you're out and about, and having someone to talk to while sharing the experience with would have been a real treat. Sara already knew Christina and Monica were wrapped up for the morning but would be free later that afternoon. However, Sara wanted to get out and wasn't going to wait around all morning for them to get freed up.
    She was feeling anxious today for some reason and just didn't want to be cooped up in the house all morning. She needed some fresh air and some time to herself anyways as

she hurried and got herself together and left to go get some breakfast at this small diner that was on the way. It was a nice place that she rarely visited because it was a bit cramped and sometimes the service was slow, but she had time and the food was good. As soon as she walked in a server came and seated her right away and then brought her some coffee that she had asked for while being seated. It was a very noisy background and she could hear the dishes clanging as the busboy was clearing off a table that was not too far from her. He was steadily busy and took no time to be more discreet as he had to move fast to keep tables open for the new customers that were accumulating at the door. She was thankful she had come when she did and was able to get seated right away. The bus boy had stacked as much as he could in his receptacle and quickly disappeared into the back area. This little diner was known for having some of the best waffles and pancakes. They was made fresh to order and not microwaved as some small diners had started doing.

Such a busy scene. She watched everyone eating and talking while the waitresses were constantly moving about, as they was taking orders from customers, refilling coffee cups for the customers who had ordered it with their breakfast. Some were even wiping down tables too and replacing the ketchup along with the salt and pepper that had been being used. It was several minutes before the waitress had returned to take Sara's order. By the time she returned Sara had almost finished her first cup of coffee and was in need of a refill. Sara wanted a Blueberry muffin they had made fresh every morning, but they was already out of them and it would of taken over thirty minutes before she would have been able to bring it to her. Sara loved their blueberry muffins that was stuffed with tons of blueberries and the muffin itself was of nice size. One muffin would have been all she needed to get on with her morning, but instead decided to go ahead and order their blueberry pancakes with sausage on the side which would only take several minutes. She was hungry and wanted to get breakfast done so she could move on with the next phase of her morning.

    She hadn't been out shopping for herself in a very long time and had saved up some money to really be able to enjoy spoiling herself. As she sat and watched the other customers interact with each other the waitress finally came and refilled her coffee she had been waiting for. Sara made no fuss about it as she saw how busy everyone was and just needed to be a little patient while watching them run around trying to keep everyone happy and take more orders. *The kitchen must be a mess right now. No wonder they are out of blueberry muffins. I would have waited for them, but I do want to get on with my day.*

    They did have other muffins but Sara had a craving for blueberries and didn't want anything else. The waitress brought her food while she was sipping on her coffee

    "Thank you," she said to the waitress who had been bustling about.

    "You're welcome, and I am sorry for the wait on things. We are swamped this morning."

    "Oh yes, I see that. I have been watching everyone work so fast and hard."

    "Yes we are short a cook and this rush just seems to keep on coming this morning."

    "Well you are all doing a wonderful job," Sara responded as she was trying to encourage the tired waitress who looked as if she was desperately in need of a break.

    Sara was understanding of the situation and made no fuss as it wouldn't have helped matters at all. *Perhaps a kind word in a hectic situation would make a bit of a difference.* She took a bite of her pancake.

    "This was worth the wait," Sara said.

    "Yes they are." One of the ladies responded to her comment who was sitting at the next table across from her. Sara smiled at her and thought it was nice of her to respond.

    "Do you come here often?" Sara inquired of her as they began to talk to each other.

"Yes we meet here almost every morning for coffee. They have the best pancakes and waffles, and nobody makes muffins like they do."

"Oh yes I agree, I was hoping for a blueberry muffin this morning but they were already out of them and hadn't had time to make any more as of yet."

"Yes it's a very busy morning here, actually it's busy every morning. They really need to move into a bigger building."

"Yes I suppose they do. The food here is excellent."

As Sara finished her meal she took her time to enjoy her coffee while waiting for the bill to come. The service she felt could have been better, but under the circumstances, she understood. She was sitting there still trying to figure out the tip she was going to leave. The waitress was nice considering how overworked she was right now. Perhaps a nice tip will brighten her day. Sara's coffee was gone before the waitress had returned to refill it.

"That is not necessary. I am ready for my bill if you don't mind."

"Yes of course, I have it right here. I can take it up for you if you would like."

"No, that is fine, I can do it on my way out."

"Okay, well thank you for coming and have a wonderful day."

"Thank you. You as well."

After Sara paid her bill she was well on her way to get some much needed shopping done. She was going to pamper herself for the entire day. Perhaps even stopping off to get her nails done. With Johnnie's business growing like it had, he had been able to pay all the bills while giving her a weekly check as well. She was proud of how responsible he was in making sure everything was well taken care of. He always made sure Sara had more then she needed.

Sara headed towards the Grand Mall that was in Southbend. It was the only mall they had, but it was huge and displayed every kind of store imaginable. It was the best shopping place in reasonable distance without going to the park Johnnie had taken Tonya to. She would spend the rest of the morning there and then a possible stop off at the food court for lunch. It depended on what time it was when she finished shopping. There was a nice cafe close by she liked. Johnnie also liked it. They had nice thick shakes and the burgers were delicious with nice golden fries that were cooked to perfection.

I'm feeling like a complete new outfit with matching shoes and a purse. Maybe something sleek and sexy. She had been alone for so long and now that Johnnie and Tonya was engaged, she was really starting to think about maybe dating again. She knew at some point Johnnie was going to leave and get his own home with Tonya. She didn't want to be alone again in that big house like she was when Johnnie had been gone for those three long years while he was in The House as they called it. She was still beautiful and didn't want to waste any more time being alone.

The truth was she had been scared to date after what Mike had done to her. But she knew not all men were like him. Mark certainly wasn't and she had hoped at some point she could meet someone like him again and be happy. She wanted to live again and not spend the rest of her life all alone. Sara had stayed in great shape and knew she could get plenty of men to notice her without even trying, but she wanted a good man and she wasn't about to settle for just anyone. She deserved a good man and this time they would have to really prove themselves to her. And they would have to past the Johnnie test. Sara knew how protective Johnnie was of her and he would make sure that whoever she picked would be good for her or he would put an end to their relationship.

Johnnie had become such a dangerous man. He had become used to killing to the point he could do it without hesitation. So whoever was going to date his mother better make sure he never hits her or he would for sure end up like Mike. No one was ever going to hurt her again. While shopping she received a text from Tammy about meeting for breakfast the next day, but Sara always liked to help

Johnnie in the mornings to get the crew going, plus it was the only time she got to really see them anymore. As she texted Tammy back a message she asked her if they could do lunch instead. She replied back that would be fine.

   She was going to miss Johnnie when he moved out and that wasn't something she was really looking forward to. She was going to offer Tonya to move in with them until they could save up enough to get the kind of house they both wanted. This would at least give her time to find a nice man to date and with Johnnie still there, she felt a lot more comfortable about trying to date again. As Sara was thinking about all of these things she walked into a nice clothing store to look around and see about that new outfit she wanted to buy. While she was browsing around, a worker approached to ask if she needed any assistance. "No. I am fine. But thank you anyways. I am kind of just looking to see if there is a nice outfit I might want to purchase. Not that I need it, just feeling like something new would be nice is all," she responded to the helper.
"Okay. If you have any questions I will be right over there," she said as she pointed over to a counter where she had been working.

   Sara continued to look around the store as she rummaged through the many dresses she thought would have looked nice on her. Actually anything she picked would have looked nice on her. But Sara was looking for something different, something that would jump out at her and so far nothing had. In fact she was just about to walk out when she had turned and saw a beautiful short red dress she fell in love with as soon as she saw it. *That's it. That's the one I want.* She walked over and took it off the rack. The price wasn't bad either. It was well within her budget. As she held it up against her and was looking in the mirror, the worker came from around the counter to show Sara some nice shoes that went with that particular dress.

   "Oh yes, they are perfect. I will take them both," Sara said as she walked with the worker to the counter to check out.

She was so excited and now was even more ready to have a date just so she could wear the new dress. There was still plenty of time before lunch so Sara decided to go ahead and get a manicure. It had been a while since she had her nails done and thought since she didn't spend as much on the dress and shoes as she had planned, she would get her toe nails done as well. This is just what she needed. A nice morning out by herself to just pamper herself and treat herself to some nice things.

She was planning on getting Tonya a gift while she was out and decided to check on the price for a day at the spa. Tonya had been working so hard and could use a nice day out to relax while being pampered as well. Once Sara had made it to the spa, she knew exactly what she wanted when she walked in. She took time to look at how much a day pass was that included everything in the package. The price was steep, but this was a special occasion. She bought two passes so she could do it with Tonya. Afterwards she went back with the lady who was going to be taking care of her and relaxed as she got her nails done.

Sara had nice feet and decided to get both her finger nails and toe nails done red to match the dress. She wanted to wear it out to lunch with Tammy the next day. After getting her nails done she decided to also get her hair done as well and had them add it to her bill. Sara was spending a ton of money in there today so the salon threw in some free highlights for her tips while getting her hair done. As they were working on her she couldn't help but feel how good it was going to be to spend the day here with Tonya.

After Sara was done at the spa, she decided to stop off at a Mexican Restaurant that was on the way home. She really wanted to go for a nice hamburger and fries at the diner but didn't want to go there twice in one day. It just seemed too awkward for her to come back so soon. Perhaps another day she would bring Tonya for a nice lunch there and maybe some shopping afterwards. Sara loved tacos and this place had exceptional food. She knew she would enjoy it even though she really wanted a hamburger. It was nice spending the day out by herself, but she did hate eating alone. Food always seemed to taste better with company. Sara always felt she ate too fast when she ate alone. Talking was a good way to make her meal last longer and more enjoyable.

The place smelled so good when she walked in and waited to be seated. Her stomach began to growl at the wonderful aroma as she stood by the sign that read: *Please Wait to Be Seated*. She was happy she chose this place and happier when the waitress finally came to seat her. By now she was so hungry and was more than ready to eat. The waitress asked her what she wanted to drink and Sara told her. She also told her she was ready to order and what she wanted, one soda and four tacos. When the waitress returned with her drink, she also brought some chips and salsa that came free with every meal. Sara wasted no time in digging in as she enjoyed the chips and salsa while she waited.

Once her food arrived, Sara took her time eating while thinking about Johnnie and Tonya. She felt so good he proposed to Tonya. It made Sara sad that Mark wasn't here for this. He would have been so proud of him. It would have meant so much to him to have his father here for the wedding. There had been so many special moments in Johnnie's life that would have been even more special had his father still been alive. After all of these years Sara was still missing Mark.

After finishing her tacos, Sara headed home for the rest of the day. She thought after spending that much money she should probably end her shopping spree. She needed and enjoyed it, but now it was time to get back home. Days like this didn't come too often but every woman needed to have them. Johnnie had been so good in taking care of everything and it was nice to have extra money to splurge once in a while. The house was paid off and he didn't let Sara pay for any of the bills. The money he was giving her, she had been saving as well. Every week he gave her a paycheck for the work she was doing for the company. He was making such great money that he was able to take care of everyone.

It wasn't long after Sara got back home Tammy called again. She had just talked to Tonya and found out her and Johnnie were now engaged. Tammy was just as excited as Sara when she first heard the news. She loved Johnnie and always hoped at some point he would ask Tonya to marry him and now he had.

"Sara, what wonderful news about Johnnie and Tonya! I am so excited for them!"

"Oh yes, it's so wonderful. They are finally moving forward with their relationship. I couldn't be happier for them both. I always felt they belonged together."

"Yes me too. Johnnie has always been so good to her and I know she loves him so deeply. He is going to be such a great husband. I am proud he will be our son-in-law. I have always liked him and he has become such a great young man, especially after all he has been through. To go through all of that and still accomplish all that he has, you must be so proud of him."

Sara was all smiles as she was very proud of her son who had become a very good business man and was becoming more successful every day.

"Oh yes, Tammy. He has worked so hard at building this business, and its growing all the time. I love he hired Steve and Tonya to work for him and they are all making good money together. Steve has been such a great help to Johnnie, as well as Tonya. But I knew she would. I don't think she will ever let Johnnie down."

"She has been so excited about what Johnnie has been doing, being able to help him and working with him has been a huge thrill for her. She loves being a part of everything that he does. She talks about it all the time and is proud to be a part of his life in more ways than just one."

"Are we still getting together for lunch tomorrow Sara?"

"Yes we are. It will be so much fun now that we get to talk about the wedding and everything."

Sara was so thankful after all Johnnie had been through

and after what had happened to Tonya that Tammy and Tony had still embraced Johnnie as their own. They still loved him and was happy to have him as a part of their family. That meant a lot to Sara. She knew some parents would have been different towards him, but they loved Johnnie and wanted this marriage to happen just as much as Sara did.

 Sara spent the rest of the day relaxing after a fun morning out. It wasn't long after being home she fell asleep on the couch while watching television. She slept so hard she never heard the phone ring and didn't know anyone had called until she had woke up. She went to go into the kitchen to get a drink and noticed the red light flashing on the answering machine. Sara paused for a minute to see who had called. Christina was trying to contact her after hearing the news from Tammy about Johnnie and Tonya being engaged. She wanted to put a small party together to celebrate the good news. Sara thought it was a bit too early for that since the two hadn't even set a date for the wedding yet. *I will call her back later.* She went to get a drink to quench her thirst. She sat down at the table with a nice cold glass of water as she thought about what Christina had said on the answering machine. *Maybe I will let Johnnie hear it and he can decide for himself. After all it's their engagement.* After Sara grabbed another cold glass of water she went back into the living room to watch more television until it was time to make dinner. While Sara was relaxing in front of the television Christina called back.

 "Hey girl what are you up to? You must be so excited. I know Tammy is."

 "Oh yes we are very excited for them. They make such a great couple."

 "Yes they do."

 "Have you had a chance to listen to my message about the party?"

 "Yes I did, but I was waiting for Johnnie to get home so we could talk about it before we made any decision. I suppose it's really up to him and Tonya. You know Johnnie though, any time to get everyone together always sounds like a good idea to him."

"Yes, that is true. How is the business going?"

"Busy as always. He is taking on more and more customers all the time. He has his father's work ethic."

"We do need to get together Christina for some girl talk time."

"Yes, I would love that and it's much needed."

"How is Thomas doing?" Sara asked.

"He has his good days and bad days, much like me I suppose. It's been so hard after the funeral. Some days I just sit and cry when I am here all alone," Christina said.

"It was real scary for you two there for a while. Thomas really took this so very hard. We were afraid that you two wasn't going to make it through this."

"I started to have my doubts as well. I've never seen Thomas like that before, but he loved his boys so much. It was so hard for us and still is to be honest."

"I have to meet up with Tammy tomorrow for lunch, but after that I am free if you want to make plans and spend the rest of the day together."

"Okay, that sounds good. I would love that. Do you want to go out or just sit and talk?"

"We can do both. I would like to talk for a bit but afterwards we can go out and maybe get a bite to eat?" Christina asked.

"Sounds like a plan. Call me later and we will work out the details," Sara said.

After Sara hung up, she made a quick call to Johnnie to see if he was going to be home for dinner. Johnnie had made plans with Tonya and wouldn't be home till late. Sara didn't want to cook just for herself so she decided to just make a sandwich to eat while she popped in a movie to watch. Everyone was talking about the engagement and wanted to know when the wedding was. Sara had no idea when they was going to get married, but she was hoping it would be soon. There was so much that needed to be planned and it was going to be interesting to see what

Tammy's ideas were going to be. Sara was looking forward to working with Tammy and Tonya while planning the wedding. After making a sandwich Sara settled in for the night and watched her movie until Johnnie finally got home from spending time with Tonya.

"Johnnie, there is a message from Christina. She wants to know if she can throw you and Tonya a party?"

"A party? We just got engaged."

"Yes I know but everyone is so excited for the both of you. It feels like it's all of our wedding. We have waited for this day to come and everyone wants to celebrate with you two."

"I should have expected that. Well you two work it all out and let us know when and we will be there. Did you talk to her at all?"

"Yes I did. She called back after I listened to the message."

"How is she and Thomas doing? I have been meaning to get in touch with him."

"Well she said they are doing much better, but they both still have their bad days, you know."

"Yeah, I am sure they do. We all miss them so very much. Things just aren't the same without them."

"Johnnie, are you doing anything about this? I know there are times when you get off of work early and then leave without saying anything."

"You don't want to know. In fact, the less you know the better it is."

"They have cost you a lot of pain. I knew you wasn't going to let it go."

"Sometimes you just have to take things in your own hands when it just won't stop."

"You are being careful though right?" Sara asked concerned.

"Yes Mom I am. I am always careful. Stop worrying. Nothing is going to happen to me. I just need to make things right is all," Johnnie said trying to reassure her.

"I can't help but worry. I lost your father and I don't want to lose you again."

"You're not going to lose me again. I just have to handle this is all. Everything will be okay. I promise," Johnnie said trying to convience his mother so she would stop worrying.

"I am going to hold you to that."

"I'm going to get some sleep, see you in the morning," Johnnie said to avoid the rest of that conversation.

"Good night Johnnie." Sara stayed up for a bit and watched some more television before finally turning in for the night herself.

The next morning as Sara was getting ready for her day, Johnnie was already up and in the kitchen. The coffee was going and the toast was just about ready to pop out of the toaster. He was also making scrambled eggs for the three of them. Tonya was already there and was outside getting things she was going to need for the day.

"Good morning Johnnie. Everything smells so good."

"Thank you Mom and good morning to you as well. Do you mind yelling outside for Tonya to come in, breakfast is ready."

"Sure thing."

Sara went outside to let Tonya know everything was ready rather than just yell out the window as Johnnie had suggested.

"Hey Tonya breakfast is ready."

"Oh okay. Thank you, Mom."

Sara smiled as Tonya called her mom. That made her day and it was still early. Sara and Tonya sat down at the table with Johnnie who had already fixed their plates. Sara was happy to have breakfast with just the two of them and Johnnie was such a great cook.

"The food is wonderful Honey," Tonya said as she took another bite.

"Yes it really is Johnnie. You're a wonderful cook indeed."

"Well thank you very much. I am happy both of you are enjoying it."

"Another busy day for you both?"

"Got to keep hustling Mom."

"Yes we have two houses lined up for today."

"That seems like a lot of work," Sara responded while eating her eggs and toast.

"Yes it is, but we have a pretty good system that allows us to get more done in less time and both houses are small. So we should be able to get it all done."

"Normally I would have only given them one, but with Debra helping them out now they have been kicking some serious butt," Johnnie explained.

"That's good that she is working out."

"She is a very good worker. She and Steve have really been hitting it off as well."

"That is so wonderful. I always wondered why Steve never dated. I am happy to hear that he has finally found someone. I hope they really become a couple and settle down together. There is nothing like being in love."

Sara always loved to hear when people where together. She was a real hopeless romantic and wanted everyone to be with someone. She never felt it was good for anyone to be alone and believed every person should have someone to share their lives with. Which is what had made it so hard for her to be alone for all of these years since Johnnie had killed Mike. She had been feeling lonelier as of late especially now that Johnnie and Tonya were engaged. Sara really started to feel it was time for her to try and date again. She knew Johnnie was going to be overly protective of her but she was going to have to just deal with it. She was tired of being alone. It was definitely time though. Sara didn't want to be left by herself in this house again. It just made her feel so alone to live in such a big house and she didn't want to go through that again. It was too hard on her and only made her miss Mark even more. She wanted to find a nice loving man who would treat her good like Mark had. Whoever she found would have to win Johnnie over and if they could do that, then they were the right one for her. Because winning him over wasn't going to be easy at all. They were really going to have to prove themselves to him if they we're going to date his mother and she knew that.

"Well Babe, I need to go pick up the girls and get this day started."

"Okay Honey, be safe and call me if you need anything."

"I will Baby. Talk later."

"I love you Honey."

"I love you too Baby," Tonya said as she kissed Johnnie goodbye.

"See you later Tonya, I love you."

"I love you too Mom."

After Tonya left, Johnnie got the lawn crew going and then picked up Steve. He was gone for the rest of the day. Sara cleaned up the kitchen and then did some vacuuming before getting started on laundry. She spent the whole morning cleaning before taking a shower and getting ready for her lunch with Tammy.

Tammy decided to swing by and pick Sara up since they lived so close together. It didn't make sense for the both of them to drive when they were going to the same place. Tammy was excited to spend time with Sara. They had always got along and she just loved Sara. There was so much to talk about with the wedding and Tammy just loved spending time with Sara anyways.

When Tammy arrived Sara invited her to come in for a cup of coffee before they left to go eat. Tammy loved coffee, especially when it was with a good friend. It was something about having coffee while talking that just seemed to make the time better. She could talk over coffee all day if Tony would let her.

Everyone just loved Sara and felt what Johnnie did was the right thing to do. Tony had wanted to kill Mike also, after he found out what happened. He felt bad for Johnnie and wished he killed Mike instead, rather than watch Johnnie go to prison for three years. No one liked Mike. They all knew what was going on and they respected Johnnie for doing what he had done. Tammy and Tony loved Johnnie was the kind of person who would defend his mother like that. It really showed them Tonya would be safe with him.

They also suspected the boys were involved in something they wasn't telling anyone. They all knew Randy and Darrell's death didn't just happen. No one asked anything except for Thomas, but Johnnie danced around it as much as he could. While they were talking Tammy had asked about it, but Sara really didn't know and she knew Johnnie wasn't going to tell her everything anyways.

"This is very good coffee Sara."

"Thank you. It's nice to just sit and talk for a bit. Where do you want to go for dinner?"

"You know I was thinking some Italian food was sounding good today."

"Oooh, Italian food does sound good." Sara agreed as she got up and put her shoes on.

"Let's go, I am starving."

"I am too. It's been a busy morning I wasn't expecting and I have worked up an appetite."

"Yes me too. This morning has been very busy and I am ready to eat some good food."

Sara was happy Tammy had come down to get her and they were able to talk for a bit before going to lunch. It was a little drive as Tammy turned on the radio for some background noise. She knew Sara didn't like to talk when she was in a car, whether she was driving or just riding, she was always quiet while focusing on her surroundings. Once they arrived, they were seated right away and both ordered something to drink immediately. Sara had enough coffee for the day and wanted a nice cold soda while Tammy also ordered a soda.

"This place smells so good."

"I know right. I love it here and the bread is always so fresh."

"I am so hungry, I can't decide on what I want. Everything looks so good."

"I think I want some lasagna with a meat sauce."

"Tammy I was looking at that also. But I think I am going

to get the manicotti."

When the waitress came back with their drinks and some fresh bread, she went ahead and took their order since they were both ready.

"I will bring you both a salad," the waitress said which she brought them after she had put in their order.

"So this wedding, what are your thoughts on it?" Tammy asked.

"I would like to see them get married in a Church. I was going to talk to Christina about it when I see her next time."

"She seems to want to be involved as well. But I think everyone does. Everyone feels like this is the wedding of the year. I have never seen so many people so excited over two people getting married before. But I do have to admit I am excited about it as well."

"I am too. It was meant to happen eventually and I am very happy that now it's going to happen."

"Everyone is. It's going to be so wonderful. Tonya couldn't have found a better man then Johnnie, we just love him."

"Thank you. I just love Tonya as well. She has always been there for Johnnie and I know there is no one else for him. He just loves her so much and she is perfect for him. It's so romantic for him to be marrying his childhood sweetheart. I am so happy for them both."

"I think the whole community is going to want to come. Johnnie has really impacted a lot of people's lives. I am out a lot and it always seems like someone is mentioning his name. He is so well respected by everyone. Tonya is truly blessed to have him."

"Tonya is a real blessing to Johnnie as well. I don't know what he would do without her. He really needs her. I see it all the time when they are together. He is so in love with her."

While they were talking the waitress returned with their food and took away the plates.

"Sara your food looks so good."

"So does your lasagna. I am going to feel so fat after eating all of this. I will probably go home and take a nap," Sara said laughing.

"I will to too be honest. This is so much food and it's so good," Tammy laughed as well.

They had such a great time together the time just flew by.

"You know Sara I was thinking the other day, maybe you should come to Church with us."

"I didn't know that you had started going?"

"Yes me and Tony both are going now. After we saw how much it had helped Tonya, we decided to go and try it for ourselves. I would have never thought Tony would ever go to Church but to be honest he just loves it."

"It really has helped her out a lot and you know I just love Christina and Thomas. They are just the nicest people."

"Also, there is a nice single man there who is some kind of a lawyer. He is handsome too Sara."

"A lawyer huh? Well maybe I will come and check it out."

"I think you will love it Sara. The people there are very nice and so supportive. They really make you feel like family. I have never felt so loved and made to feel like I belonged somewhere like they make us feel."

"Okay. I will come for sure. You know maybe this is meant to be. I have been thinking about dating again."

"Come check it out and I will introduce you two."

Sara sat smiling as she ate her food. She felt this was something she was supposed to do.

"I wonder if Johnnie will come?" Sara asked.

"I don't know. I do know Tonya has asked him a few times but for some reason, right now, he won't come. That's all I know. Tonya wouldn't go into any details about it," Tammy explained.

"I can ask him and see what he says."

"That would be great if we all went together."

"I think it would too. We could all sit together."

After they had both finished their lunch they sat for a bit

longer while finishing their sodas. Sara enjoyed the nice talk with Tammy as they discussed so many things. Tammy was very happy Sara was considering coming to Church with them. Although she had doubts about Johnnie's coming, he just didn't seem ready yet. So much was going on with his life. He really could use God's help to put things in the right perspective but there was things going on that Tammy didn't know about.

Steve never really went either, but he thought about it. There were many talks at their house of God and Church now that Tony and Tammy had started going also. However, for Steve, he was feeling kind of the same way Johnnie was about fighting this war while going to Church. It just didn't seem right to either of them. Perhaps when all of this was over maybe then the two would reconsider. Neither of them were hypocrites and didn't want to become one either. This was where they were in their lives until it was done and so they would keep on fighting. There was unfinished business that still needed to be settled as far as these two was concerned.

George had his own problems outside of work and the war. His drinking and getting high was becoming worse as they days went by. Ann was really starting to be concerned about what George was doing. She had been trying to get him to slow down but it was getting worse all the time. It was changing him and Ann didn't like it. Johnnie and Steve had been so busy with the repair part of the business they hadn't noticed George was high most of the time. He had done pretty good at hiding it from Nate and Timothy, but they were starting to catch on. George would disappear for a few minutes every so often to get high real fast, and that was something he never done before. So when it started becoming more consistent then it also was more noticeable. George was still a good worker but he wasn't setting a good example in front of Timothy and Nate as their leader. His attitude at times wasn't very good as well. Their definitely was something different about him. Nate and Timothy began to question it amongst themselves. They wondered if they should talk to Johnnie about it, but wasn't sure if that would be a good idea. George was their friend and they didn't want to get him into any trouble. Not sure what to do they began talking about using one of their lunch breaks to talk to him and try to find out what was going on with him. Timothy and Nate knew when there was a sudden change with someone there was a cause for alarm and they needed to at least talk to him and find out what was going on.

Meanwhile, after Sara was back home and settled in, she called Christina to talk to her about her Church. Sara was more curious now than she had been before. She visited a few times for Christmas but never really visited on a normal Sunday. After talking with Tammy she felt it would be good for her to at least give it a try, after all she had seen the change within Tonya herself. There was no denying that something was different and Tonya had seemed so much happier now. There used to be an edge to Tonya and even more so after she had been raped, but she seemed much calmer these days. Tonya had always been a tough girl who could hold her own in any fight and rarely struggled. She had a strong reputation as someone you didn't want to get tangled up with. She had never lost a fight in her life and was feared by many of the other girls in the neighborhood. But Tonya was changing and Sara could see it.

That night Johnnie came home late, had just a snack for dinner and took a shower before going to bed as he was wore out from the day. Johnnie, Steve and George decided to lay low for a bit and let the West Dragons fight this out with the Hells Sinners while they refocused on their jobs and relationships while keeping things on the down low about their involvement in this war. It was all over the place now about this war. It had become an all-out battlefield in the city and the fights were taking place all over. The heat on the streets were very hot and Johnnie knew he had to keep them out of the spotlight or else they would get caught for sure. They agreed to lay low for a few weeks at least, and maybe even longer.

The Hells Sinners were desperate at this point. Cypher

and his group had done so much damage to them it was paying off for the West Dragons. Cypher could feel the end of the war was finally starting to come as he began to relax a bit. He felt that had allowed him and the other two to take some time and breath for a bit while they let the West Dragons carry the workload for a while. They were tired and was ready for this to end.

As the week went on everything was going smooth as far as Johnnie knew. But it was time for Timothy and Nate to confront George in hopes they wouldn't have to go talk to Johnnie about it. George was less enthused about the talk and had told the two to focus on their jobs and to not worry about what he was doing. But they knew they had to worry about what was going on with George because it was clear now there was something wrong with him. For now they would let it go, but they wasn't done talking to him about this.

The week was filled with just work while they were letting the war take care of itself for a while. Johnnie knew they needed a break and some rest. The three of them were getting burned out and needed to regroup.

As the weekend came Sara knew Johnnie would be taking Tonya out to dinner. They went out almost every Friday after work was finished. She had been thinking about what Tammy said about meeting this guy. It would be nice to meet someone from the Church, especially a lawyer. *I think I will go this Sunday.* She was trying to decide what she wanted to do for the night. Fridays were the busy day for everyone so her options where slim for the night. Sara couldn't wait to wear her knew dress and had thought about wearing it on Sunday, but felt maybe it was a little too sexy for a Sunday morning service. But if things worked out with that guy Tammy had been talking about, then she was thinking of wearing it for their first date.

Johnnie had set it up for the three of them to take their girls out on a triple date. Steve was excited to go out with Debra again. Ann was also excited to go out as a group again. It had been a while since they all went out together.

But George who had said they were going decided him and Ann was going to just stay in so he could drink and get high. Ann was getting tired of missing things because of George's drinking problem that he was trying to hide from everyone. Tonya knew something was going on and had called Ann to talk about it. At first Ann tried to play it off that George was just tired, but Tonya wasn't buying it. She knew there was more to the story than Ann was telling her. Finally Ann had told her they would talk later and she would explain what was going on. Ann knew she couldn't keep trying to cover this up for him.

When they all met up and Tonya told them that George and Ann wasn't coming Johnnie began to inquire as to why they would not be joining them. Tonya simply told them that she and Ann were going to talk later and she wasn't sure as of yet about what was going on, but something wasn't right.

While they were out, Sara decided to stay in and make some popcorn and watch a movie. She was tired of being alone while everyone else went out, but tonight it was popcorn and movie night as she put in a DVD to watch. Johnnie and Tonya stayed out late and his mom was already asleep when he got home.

Steve and Debra decided to spend some alone time together as they went to the falls that was on the other side of Southbend Heights. It was a nice, quiet, romantic place that was lit up at night and the water would change colors as the lights changed. Steve had planned to take her there as a surprise before their night had ended. As they both got out, Steve grabbed a blanket from behind the seat of the truck he had put there earlier. He took her down by the river just a little ways off of the Falls so they could lay together and watch the water. As Steve laid the blanket out, Debra stood by while being amazed at all the colors as she watched the falls.

"Come here Honey," Steve said as he called out to her. Debra laid next to Steve as he held her while they talked as they were taking in the whole scenery.

"This is so beautiful Steve, so romantic."

"I am very happy that you like this."

Steve didn't tell her Johnnie told him about this spot to take her. The rest of the night Steve held her in his arms as they laid together while talking and listening to water as it ran down into the river.

***

Saturday everyone kind of did their own thing. Johnnie was spending time with Tonya while Steve took Debra to the movies. George and Ann was off on their own as usual. Ann was becoming more and more frustrated with George's drinking. It had started taking away from the things they used to do. Now everything they did revolved around him drinking even right down to the places that they would go.

***

Sara was excited about Church when she had woke up Sunday morning. She hoped Johnnie would come with her, but he told her that he would try and make it next time. Tonya came down to have breakfast with them since Sara was going to ride with her. Johnnie was up and cooking breakfast for them as Tonya had arrived. He wanted to give Sara extra time to get ready so he made breakfast. Thomas and Christina was so happy when they heard Sara would be joining them that morning. They couldn't wait for them all to sit together. After breakfast Sara and Tonya finished getting ready and then left to go to Church while Johnnie cleaned up the kitchen.

As soon as Tonya and Sara arrived, Tammy came right over to them and whispered to Sara.

"See that guy over there? He is the one I was telling you about."

"He is handsome."

"Yes he is. I will introduce you to him."

"I would like that very much," Sara said as she was

surprised at just how handsome he was. She hadn't expected him to look that nice.

After the service while everyone was getting up to leave, Tammy purposely positioned them to bump into Chris so she could introduce him to Sara.

"Oh hi Chris. Sorry, I didn't mean to bump into you. Have you met my friend Sara? She just started coming here."

"No I haven't. It's very nice to meet you Sara," Chris said as he shook her hand.

"It's nice to meet you as well." Sara returned as she took his hand.

"Sara is single," Tammy announced to Chris.

"Tammy!" responded Sara.

"Is that right? How is such a beautiful woman such as yourself not taken?" Chris said.

"She's a widow," Tammy hurried and added before Sara could even respond.

"Yes, that's right. My husband passed away several years ago."

"Well that's too bad. However I do look forward to getting to know you. Would you like to meet for coffee some time?"

"Yes I would love to. That sounds wonderful."

"Here is my card with my phone number, call me tomorrow and we will make plans."

"Okay. I will call you tomorrow then," Sara said as they all parted and went their separate ways.

Thomas and Christina had made plans for them all to have lunch together after Church. Sara had enjoyed the service and was looking forward to getting to know Chris. Christina, Tammy and Tonya was all very happy Sara decided to keep going to Church with them. Everyone had been so happy to see Sara in Church and many had hugged her. Most of the neighborhood went to the Community Church so Sara knew a lot of the members already and fit right in. Everyone so lovingly had welcomed and embraced her as she was now working on getting settled in. She loved how supportive everyone was. She had never felt anything like this before in her life. There had been a sweet, loving spirit about the place and with the people. They immediately made her feel at home. The sermon had so deeply touched her, she was moved by the encouraging words that had been spoken by the Minister.

The rest of the day Sara had felt so peaceful and so content. Johnnie could tell she was still excited about Church when she had finally got home. He was so happy to see her feeling this way and smiling. Tonya came back with her to spend some time with Johnnie and have dinner with him and Sara.

Later on that night Jason was out on the set watching the street racers compete for money. They got together every weekend to race and Jason liked to bet on the cars. As he was watching the races, a young drug dealer approached him who was trying to make a name for himself. He told Jason he had information for the Hells Sinners so Jason inquired of his information.

"I know that guy named Cypher is involved in the war between them and the West Dragons."

"How did you come across this information?" Jason asked him.

"I saw them. They hit them while the West Dragons were shooting up the ones in the car."

"Who all knows about this?"

"Just me. I haven't told anyone yet."

"Hey Rock, hold my winnings I will be back in a bit."

"Yeah sure thing Jason."

"Let's go for a ride."

"Oh, okay."

No one knows what exactly happened that night, but Jason came back alone and no one ever saw that kid again. No one had suspected anything when Jason had returned because he had kept his demeanor the same as before he left. It wasn't until a week later that people began to wonder when he was no longer seen again.

CHAPTER 12

GOODBYE MY OLD FRIEND

Johnnie had been very concerned with what was going on with George and was intending to find some time to talk with him. Steve also was concerned and was wanting to talk with Johnnie to see how he felt about them both talking to him at the same time. Steve loved George, but there was something wrong and it needed to be dealt with. While the girls were working, Tonya decided to talk to Ann while they were alone and try to see if she could get any real information about what was really going on.

The house they were working on was empty as it was a new build that Johnnie had gotten the contract for with the company that his father used to work for. They were doing some new builds in an area that was being built up closer to town that they felt would be a prime area. Johnnie's team got the contract for the whole development which would carry them for a very long time. They were building up four new communities around the town area with fifty houses per community. They had land for further builds later as needed. Tonya's team got the whole contract to paint all two hundred houses.

As they were working, Debra was ahead of them taping off everything for them. Tonya decided now was a good time to have that talk with Ann.

"So Ann, let's talk about the other night. What's really going on?"

"You mean as to why we didn't meet up for the date night?" Ann responded.

"I am talking about everything. George has seemed to be distant from all of us and especially from Johnnie. We are all concerned about him and you as well."

"Tonya, I don't know what I should say or not say to be honest. George would probably get mad if he finds out that we are even talking about this."

"About what Ann, so far we haven't talked about anything."

"You know it's been so hard for everyone with this war and working full-time. It's taken its toll on everyone. George has been really struggling with the killings and all of the violence you know. Plus losing Darryl and Randy was so hard for him and he still struggles with losing them. He gets angry about all of this. He hates it Tonya. He hates what they did to you and what all has happened after. All he talks about is revenge and wanting to kill them all, but at the same time he struggles with his conscious and having killed people. He is hurting so bad Tonya and I don't know how to help him. It's like I can't reach him anymore. All he wants to do is get high and drink. We don't go out any more unless it's to some place where he can get drunk. It's like I am losing him Tonya and I don't know what to do about it. Oh please Tonya, please don't tell anyone what I am telling you. George would be so hurt and angry if he found out."

"Johnnie plans on talking to him, maybe he can help."

"He won't tell George I talked to you about this will he?"

"No he will come at it from a different direction. Trust me Johnnie won't get you in trouble or mention your name at all. I promise Ann. We just want to help."

"Okay Tonya. I trust you. Thank you. I do feel better knowing that someone is going to try and help him."

"We will do whatever we can Ann, we love him too."

"I know you all do, and that means so much to me. Johnnie is such a wonderful man."

"Yes he is, and he cares so much for all of us."

"Yes I know, he has taken good care of us and has looked out for all of us."

"He always will Ann. No worries okay, now let's knock this house out so we can go home at some point."

"Sounds good," Ann said as she was smiling.

She did feel relieved knowing they cared so much for George and was going to try their best to help him. As the two had finished their conversation and started working on painting the house. Once Debra was done with the taping, she would start working on the second coat. Their goal was to get a house done a day. It was a lot of work but they had a good system and was able to get a lot done in a short amount of time. All they needed to do was five houses a week and with Johnnie buying them the best equipment to work with, they would make a go of it.

There was also other work coming in for them as well and Johnnie was starting to consider hiring another worker for the girls. He was already looking into buying another truck for the painting team as it was growing pretty fast. It would be nice to send someone to work on smaller jobs every now and then. Or even just send Debra ahead of the rest to get the prep work done for another job when needed.

Johnnie was still picking up jobs from the Hardware Store Mr. Smith owned. There were times when he would have to leave to go bid jobs. He was really starting to get swamped with work. His job was becoming busier all the time. He really wanted to hire another worker to help him and Steve out as well, but right now the painting team was his main priority. He hated to keep having to leave Steve on his own though, but he had no choice if they wanted to keep jobs coming in.

He did have a line on a new truck he wanted to go look at, so he took Steve with him. It was a blue truck with four doors and a back seat for a reasonable price. Johnnie knew this would be so much easier for the lawn crew so he was going to swap out with them and give the lawn crews truck to the painting team. By the time Johnnie bought the truck, got plates and insurance on it, it was already lunch time.

"Since we didn't get anything done today, why don't we have lunch, take this truck to George and swap out with him today? At least the rest of their team will be more comfortable."

"Yeah that sounds like a good idea. What do you want to do after that?"

"We can slide by and help the girls if you want, that would give you a chance to see Debra, as well as get them a good start on this contract."

"I won't argue with that. I love seeing Debra."

"I figured as much."

After they were done eating, Johnnie called George to find out where they were working so he could meet up with them. When they pulled up in the new truck, George hadn't realized it was them so he kept on working until he saw Johnnie waving at him. Once he saw Johnnie, he drove up to him on the mower.

"Got a new truck huh?"

"Nope, you got a new truck," Johnnie responded.

"Nice. Let me take a look at it," George said as he got off the mower to check out the new truck for the lawn crew.

"Hey Johnnie this is real nice. Where did you find it?"

"I saw it posted up in the Hardware Store so we went to check it out."

"I like it."

"Good cause we are leaving it with you and taking your truck for the painting crew."

"Right on," George said as he waved for Nate and Timothy to come in.

"What's up guys," Nate said as him and Timothy joined them.

"Bought you all a new truck, so we need you to transfer your stuff from the old truck to this one so we can take this one with us."

"That's cool. This is a nice truck with more room for us," Timothy said who was smiling as they would no longer be cramped.

"What are you going to do with this truck Johnnie?" Nate asked.

"We are giving it to the painting crew so I can hire another worker for them."

"They are going to need it with the new contract you just got," George said as he began to clean out the lawn truck with Nate and Timothy.

"Are you going to have two painting crews now?"

"Well for now they will all work together for the most part. But this way I can send two of them off to get some smaller jobs done when needed. I still have other jobs that need to get done as well," Johnnie explained.

After they were done there, Johnnie and Steve were off to meet up with Tonya and her crew. Steve was excited to get to spend the rest of the day working with Debra. He followed Johnnie over to the work sight to meet up with them. Tonya was very happy to see Johnnie when he came walking in.

"Hey Baby, what are you doing here?" Tonya said.

Seeing Steve with him, she called to Debra. As Debra came into the living room where they were all standing, she gave Steve a huge smile as she went and hugged him.

"What are you guys doing here?" Debra also asked.

"Well, we have a surprise for you actually. I bought a new truck today for the lawn crew, you guys get their truck."

"So you're taking our truck and giving us this one?" Tonya had asked Johnnie.

"Nope, you're getting both trucks. I am going to be hiring another worker for your crew Honey."

"Oh nice Baby. I think Debra will probably end up with it," Tonya replied.

"I was thinking that too. Steve take Debra out to look at her new truck."

"With pleasure Boss."

As they went to look at the truck Tonya wanted to talk to Johnnie for a bit about George. He told her they would talk about it later and explained that he and Steve was going to be helping them out for the rest of the day. Tonya was very happy to have Johnnie with her for the remainder of the day. Each took a room and knocked it out as they finished up the house. With all five of them painting it only took them a few hours to finish. They moved ahead and went through the next four houses and prepped them and got them ready for the rest of the week. Johnnie was hoping to have them a new worker by the end of the week, but in one day he had helped to put them ahead of the game to make their first week on this new sight a little easier.

While they was focusing on work, the West Dragons was under a severe attack from the Hells Sinners. The Hells Sinners had not stopped hitting the West Dragons ever since they found out that it was them that had been hitting them. Although they still didn't know about Cypher, they were quite aware about the West Dragons and was hitting them every chance they got. Cypher had done a lot of damage to the Hells Sinners and they were at a weak point and fighting now out of desperation. For them it had now become more about survival then revenge.

The West Dragons stayed on them as well. With the cooperative efforts of Cypher, the Hells Sinners were starting to look at being annihilated. For so long they had been the top dogs and now everything was starting to swing towards the West Dragons at being in the top spot as the Hells Sinners was trying to stay alive. Cypher hoped that in this war Ricky would die because of what he had done to Randy. One way or another it was coming whether by the Hells Sinners or Cypher himself. There was no way Ricky was going to live to see the Promised Land after what he had done, he was getting what was coming to him.

Meanwhile the streets were riddled with blood and bullets as these two rival gangs went at each other. Johnnie had picked a good time to lay low for a bit and focus on his business. Jason had made sure that he knew when things were getting to hot for them to go out on hits. Once things cooled back off for a bit, he would go on a rampage of hits to keep the pressure on the Hells Sinners and to keep this war moving forward.

Having Jason on his side was paying off big time and was probably what had kept them alive for this long. Jason was doing everything he could to help Johnnie without anyone knowing. Jason could only do so much to protect and help him, but definitely had his hand in a lot of things behind the scenes no one knew about.

Some of the Hells Sinners deaths came from the hand of Jason who was more than happy to see them fall. Cypher's victory in this war would cover Jason's own tracks and keep him from getting caught as well as earn him more money that Pauli wasn't aware of. Jason had already turned a huge profit from this war and was going to make even more when it was over. The Hells Sinners defeat was a win for everyone. Nobody wanted them to survive this. Their downfall would mean more money for everyone and peace for Cypher and his friends. It was a war that had to be won.

The Death Clicks was watching and waiting to make sure the Hells Sinners fall happened as well. They were ready to go to war with them if they won this war. It would be the perfect time to go after them in such a weakened state. They would have preferred for the Hells Sinners to take out the West Dragons and then they would take out the Hells Sinners and get almost everything. That kind of territory to one group was unheard of and would make them almost invincible. The Death Clicks had been recruiting just in case. Either way they knew they had to get stronger especially if the West Dragons won the war. They would no doubt double in size and there would be no way they could defend themselves from them if that happened. This war meant so much to everyone and its outcome was very important.

***

As the night came to a close Tonya had finally pulled Johnnie aside and talked to him about what Ann had said about George. Johnnie knew he had to do something to help him. He had known things were bothering George but he had no idea it had become this bad.

   The next day after Johnnie got Tonya going for the day, he and Steve waited for George to come. Johnnie asked him to come by before he picked up Nate and Timothy. Once they got him all set, Johnnie began to talk to him about what was going on.

   "George your personal life is your business, but I have been a bit concerned about you. What's going on with you?"

   "What do you mean?"

   "You know it's become obvious there is something going on. I mean, you never come out with us anymore. Talk to me Bro."

   "Look man, I have my own things I am dealing with okay. It's not your problem."

   "It is my problem, you're my brother. I love you George."

   "I love you too man. It's just been a hard struggle."

   "It's been hard for all of us George, but we are all in this together and we need to be there for each other. If you need to talk, we are here for you," Steve said as he was trying to help George to feel safe about talking about what was going on with him.

   "It's just a lot of things. But I have to be honest man, these killings have messed me up. I see them when I try to sleep. I think about it during the day. I hate this. I hate that we have to kill them. This is not who I am. I hate what I am doing and what I am becoming."

   "None of us are killers George," Steve said before Johnnie began to talk.

   "I know how you feel. This is exactly what I struggled with for three years when I was in The House. It was so hard not to lose myself in there. Man, it's like living in a whole new world with all new rules. This war has taken its toll on all of us. We all hate it, but we can't let it change who we are. We can't lose ourselves in this mess. If you need to step out man we will understand completely."

   "That's just it Johnnie, I can't just walk away. Not after what happened to Randy and Darryl. I want revenge. I need revenge. It's tearing me apart at the same time. On one hand I hate this and on the other hand I have to finish this. I am being pulled into two different directions."

"It's okay George. I really understand. We will all get through this together. If you need to talk then we will talk but you can't keep going on like this by yourself. But getting high and drinking isn't the answer either."

"I just can't cope with it Johnnie."

"Trust me George I thought about that too, but trading in one problem for another isn't going to help. When this is all over, then what? You get caught up in it and then you're stuck in it. This war will end, but drinking problems and getting high still remain. You don't need that Brother."

"Johnnie's right George. You don't need that problem. We make it through this war and then you die from this, what sense does that make? This stuff takes your life Bro. It ruins your life. It ruins your relationship, your family. I am telling you Bro, get out of it now before you're a slave to it. Alcoholism and drug abuse will consume your life until there is nothing left."

"We love you Bro, there has to be another way to cope with it."

"I don't know any other way. All I know is that it numbs the pain and helps me to be able to sleep at night."

"Look we are here for you, let me think about how we can help you, okay"

"Yeah sure, do whatever you want Johnnie. In the mean time I have to do what I have to do to make it through each day."

"Alright, but for now I want Nate to start driving. At least until you get a grip on things."

"Whatever Johnnie, I can do my job."

"I am not questioning your ability to do your job, but it's a company vehicle and if anything bad happens I am responsible for it."

"That's fine, it's less that I have to do then right?"

"Come on George this isn't personal, you know we have to separate personal from business. Johnnie has to protect the company," Steve said.

"Yeah I get it Steve," George snapped back at him.

"Relax Brother. You're taking this all the wrong way." Johnnie told him as things were starting to get edgy.

"Just forget about it. I will give Nate the keys when I pick him up."

"Bro, don't let this get in the way of our friendship." George just shook his head and walked off to go pick up the rest of the crew.

"I don't think we even made a difference Johnnie."

"I don't know Steve maybe he will think about it after he calms down."

"Yeah maybe."

"Anyways let's get to work and try and get ourselves back on track."

Johnnie and Steve knew this wasn't going to be easy, but they had to keep trying. George needed them even if he didn't see it. It hurt Johnnie to see George going through all of this. He knew better than anyone what this kind of situation does to you if you let it. Mentally you have to remain strong but he could see George was losing it. Through it all, Johnnie had been able to keep himself clean from drugs and alcohol, but George started using them out of dependency which wasn't good. That always leads to addiction and he knew it. George needed help but for now there was nothing he could do.

As the day went on Johnnie couldn't help but keep thinking about George as it weighed heavily on his mind. He hated seeing his best friend go through this. He knew this war would be hard on everyone, but no one could anticipate how deep that struggle would be or the effects it would have on them.

Johnnie struggled all the time with it as well, but the things Mark had instilled in him at such an early age had kept him. Constantly remembering the things his father taught him is what helped get him through three years of juvenile prison. There talk wasn't finished but he needed to find a way to approach this with George as to not push him away.

He needed to make George feel he still embraced him as his brother. There was no way he was going to let George go through this alone. He was his brother and he would find some way to try to help him.

Steve wanted to help as well. He and George were close but not as close as Johnnie was to him. If anyone could reach George it would have to be Johnnie. But he was going to have to do it alone so George would let his guard down and talk to him about everything. He needed George to open up to him so he could see just how bad this was so that he could try to help him through it. He knew it was deep. It was deep for all three of them and Tonya also. They weren't the kind of people who were killers, they never would have been at all had Wayne not pushed them so far and the Hells Sinners did what they had done to Tonya. But they had made a pack to end this once and for all and no matter the cost, they was going to see it through.

While Johnnie was off getting jobs done Sara had been home all alone doing housework. She was hoping to get everything done so maybe she could get Chris to have lunch with her the next day. After she spent the entire morning cleaning she decided to give him a call.

"Hello this is Christopher Peters Office. Chris speaking."

"Hello Chris this is Sara."

"Sara! Hello, I was just thinking about you. I am so glad that you called."

"That is so sweet. Well I was thinking about you as well so I thought I would give you a call and see if you would be free tomorrow to meet up for lunch?"

"Yes I would love to. I have been thinking about you ever since we met and had hoped you would call me. What time do you want to meet up?"

"How does noon sound?"

"Noon sounds wonderful. I can make myself available, where would you like to meet?"

"Well what do you like?"

"Oh Sara I like all kinds of food Honey. Whatever you pick will be fine with me."

"There is a nice diner that is close by where you are. Would that be okay?"

"That would be great Sara. I so look forward to having lunch with you. So noon tomorrow."

"Yes. I will text you the information so it will make it easier for you."

"No need. I know the Diner you're talking about. I have eaten there many times. I love their food."

"Yes I do too. The food there is so amazing for being a diner."

"Yes it really is. Okay Sara, I will see you at noon tomorrow."

"Okay Chris. See you tomorrow."

"I will be there for sure."

Sara felt so relieved to have made this first call and now to have a lunch date with him already. Chris couldn't stop smiling after he hung up with Sara. He was so excited to have a lunch date with her. She had made quite an impression on him when he met her at the Church. Much like Sara, Chris had been alone for some time now since his wife passed away. He missed his wife so much but he, too, had finally come to a place where he felt it was time to move on and love again. He was a romantic and had missed having someone to share his love with. For way too long his arms felt so empty without someone to hold, and now that he finally met someone, he was going to try to date again and see where it all goes.

There was something about Sara. Something that really attracted him to her, other than how beautiful she was. Sara had always been very attractive and still was. But there was so much more to her than her looks and Chris knew that. She was different. She was special and Chris could sense that about her. He sat thinking about her the rest of the day while trying to get some work done. But the way she had smiled at him kept crossing his mind and had become a great distraction.

Sara's smile light up her whole face and there was a loving way about her. Chris knew she was going to make him fall in love with her, and he wanted it. He needed it. She was what he had been waiting for. He always said it would take a very special woman to make him want to date again and now he finally found her.

***

It was late when Johnnie got home and Sara had fallen asleep on the couch waiting for him. She hoped to talk to him about Chris but fell asleep while waiting.

"Mom wake up," Johnnie said as he lightly shook her.
"What time is it Johnnie?"
"It's past eleven. You fell asleep on the couch."
"Oh, yes. I was waiting for you. I wanted to talk to you."
"Is everything okay?"
"Yes it is. Just wanted to talk to you about something."
"We can talk in the morning. I am tired also. I went out with Tonya after work."

Johnnie went up to bed as Sara turned off all the lights and shut the house down for the night. The next morning as she woke and started getting breakfast going, Johnnie came down to get ready for work. As they set down together to eat breakfast, Johnnie inquired about the night before as to what she wanted to talk to him about.

"Before I went to bed you said there was something you wanted to talk to me about?"
"Yes Johnnie there is. I think I may have met someone."
"I see, well tell me about him."
"Well I don't know much as of yet. I just met him the other day at Church. But his name is Chris and he is a lawyer."
"That doesn't sound bad. What kind of lawyer is he?"
"I didn't ask him that, but I will now. We are going to meet for lunch today and get better acquainted."
"You know all I care about is you being happy. But he better be good to you or he will end up like Mike."
"Johnnie please don't say that. I am sure he is nothing like Mike and plus he does go to Church."

"That used to mean something," Johnnie said, "but sadly today the Church doesn't seem to be much different than anyone else."

"Johnnie that is not entirely true. This Church I go to now is wonderful. Everyone is so nice and loving. They are all very friendly people."

"Well I hope so. I haven't been turned on to Church by the way Church people act these days. Some are even rude and disrespectful."

"I know Johnnie but that isn't how all of them are. You have bad apples on every tree, you know that."

"I suppose we all have our struggles."

"Yes Johnnie we do. And no one is perfect, no one but God. And until Jesus comes back we all have to strive to do our best."

"Well the only thing I am saying is this, the Church needs to show more love to the world if they want to win people for a loving God. Especially to people who are hurting and need people to be loving and understanding."

"I do agree Johnnie, but this Church is like that. I mean look at how much they embraced Tonya and how much they have helped her."

"You're right Mom. Anyways let's talk more later after you've been out on a date with him. I would like to meet him when you're ready to bring him home."

"Okay Johnnie. Also Tonya knows him too, maybe she can tell you more about him."

"Yeah that sounds good. Does she know that you're going out on a date with him?"

"No but she was there when Tammy introduced me to him."

"Oh, so Tammy also knows him."

"Yes she does, a little."

"That does make me feel better about him. When you're ready then bring him by for dinner. So the four of us can get together."

"Okay Johnnie. That does sound good. I am so happy you're okay with this."

"Well I am okay with it just as long as he treats you good," Johnnie said. "Tonya is here. I need to get her going so that I can get out of here also. George should be on his way as well."

"Okay, Johnnie you all be safe."

"We will."

As Tonya was getting out of the truck Johnnie came out to meet her.

"Good morning Baby."

"Good morning Babe. I need to go and pick up some more paint today."

"No problem Babe, just use the card. Hey um you got a minute?" Johnnie asked.

"Yes, what's up Baby?"

"Mom was telling me about this guy named Chris that she met at the Church, do you know anything about him?"

"Very little but he seems very nice. I do know he always sits alone though. I guess he is a widow."

"Oh so he used to be married?"

"Yes, but I guess his wife died from cancer. I think that's how he ended up coming to Church. Our Pastor did the funeral and the members did the dinner for him and afterwards for several weeks they took turns checking up on him."

"That's very cool. I like that."

"Yeah it was really sweet of the Church to stay in contact with him and make sure he was alright."

"Thank you Babe. I will try to see you tonight."

"Okay Johnnie, I love you."

"I love you too Baby, be safe."

"You as well. Oh and have you had a chance to talk to George?"

"Yes I did, but it was brief and we are going to have to have more talks."

"Okay Babe, see you tonight." Johnnie kissed Tonya before she left.

He met with Nate as he came to get all of the paper work for the day. Afterwards Johnnie and Steve was gone for the day to get their work done as well. After everyone was finally out of there, Sara went upstairs to take a nice long hot bubble bath. She then spent the rest of the morning relaxing until it was time to get ready to go meet Chris for their lunch date. After her bath she decided to lay out a nice outfit to wear for her time with Chris. She knew as a lawyer Chris would no doubt be dressed in a suit and looking nice so she also wanted to wear something nice without trying to be too elegant. Just something simple but not too fancy. *Just enough to get his attention.* After all it was just a diner, but she still wanted to look nice for him. She had been itching to wear her knew dress but she knew this was not the time for that but perhaps soon if things went good for lunch.

Sara decided on a nice blue summer dress with blue heels she hadn't wore in a long time. It was a very nice dress but wasn't too out of place for a diner. After she laid her clothes out and went back downstairs to relax a bit, she decided to call Tammy to let her know she was meeting Chris for lunch. Sara knew Tammy would be excited for her. She sat down on the couch, picked up the phone and made the call.

"Hello Sara how are you?"

"I am doing so very good, and how are you Tammy?" Sara asked.

"I am doing good as well. Just doing laundry again, but that's nothing new."

"My laundry days have become very light since Johnnie started doing his own. He hates having me do things for him now."

"Tonya has become the same way, but Steve is a little slow on that. He doesn't want to do his laundry so I still do it for him. I think soon I will push him to start doing his own."

"It's hard watching them grow up."

"It is. I enjoy being a mother so I don't mind Steve hasn't started doing his own. He is talking about moving out and there are things he still needs to learn."

"Where is he thinking about moving to?"

"There is a house that just opened up and he and Tonya have talked about getting it together."

"That would be wonderful."

"So what's going on with you today Sara?" Tammy asked.

"Well, I have a lunch date today with Chris."

"Oh that is wonderful Sara. I really hope it all works out."

"Yes me too. He seems so very nice."

" I thought so too. Call me later and let me know how everything goes."

"I will for sure Tammy. I am very excited."

"I can imagine. It's been a long time since you have been out on a date. But I am sure you two will hit it off."

"I hope so. Johnnie took it pretty good I think. He felt more comfortable knowing you and Tonya also knew him."

"That's great. I was a little worried about that. I am sure he still thinks about Mike and is probably pretty cautious about who you date."

"You have no idea. He is so protective over me, even more now than he was before because of what Mike did."

"I understand that, but I think he will be okay once he meets Chris and gets to know him."

"I do too. Tammy I will call you later tonight to let you know how everything went."

"Sounds great Sara, I hope you both have a wonderful lunch together. Talk soon."

As Sara hung up the phone. She laid back on the couch for a bit in her robe and watched a little television. She finally went to get dressed as the morning began to slip away from her. She hadn't noticed time had flown by. Sara took her time getting ready as she wanted to look her best for Chris. Once Sara was all set she left.

Chris was already on his way to the Diner to wait for her. He wanted to make sure that he was there early so Sara wasn't waiting for him when he got there. By the time Sara arrived Chris had already got a table for them and was drinking some coffee. Sara smiled at him as walked to the table where he was sitting. When she got to the table Chris stood up and greeted her. He pulled out her seat.

"Well thank you Chris."

"You're very welcome Sara. My you look so lovely. What a beautiful dress. You truly look amazing."

"Thank you again. You look very handsome as well in your nice suit," Sara said as she was still smiling. Chris smiled back.

"I am so happy to be having lunch with you today Sara. To be honest, I haven't been able to stop thinking about you."

"Well I feel the same way Chris. I have been looking forward to this since we got off the phone the other day."

"Me too. This is my first date in forever," Chris admitted.

"Mine as well. I am a bit nervous, but it is just lunch."

"I am a bit nervous also. Even though it is just lunch, it's our first lunch together."

"That's true. Hopefully we will have plenty more lunches together."

"I believe we will Sara."

They both sat smiling as they talked for a while. As the conversation went on they began to feel more comfortable with each other. They talked all the way through lunch. It was such an enjoyable time for the two of them as they hit if off really good and was eager to have another date. Chris asked Sara to have dinner with him the coming weekend and Sara was excited to do so. She had suggested the Italian place her and Tammy went the previous week. Chris loved Italian food and was more than happy to take her there.

Sara wanted to have a few dates with Chris before introducing him to Johnnie. She wanted to make sure things went good between them before bringing Johnnie into the mix. But if things continued on like this then a double date was soon to come.

***

After a few days Nate had picked up George for work and was on their way to pick up Timothy. On their way to get him, it was apparent George was still drunk from the night before. Nate wasn't happy about the way George was acting and the things he was saying.

"You know what Nate? I am just as good as a boss as Johnnie is. He isn't any better than me. He thinks he is better than all of us. Mr. High and Mighty. Mr. Cypher."

"What are you talking about George? Johnnie is real good to us. Man, you can't make this money anywhere else."

"Oh sure I can. I don't need him. He didn't make me. I used to protect him when we was younger. I bet he forgot that didn't he? Now that he's Cypher he thinks he is the man."

"I don't know what Cypher is, but you need to get it together George. Johnnie has been good to all of us."

"Don't you worry about it. I can run this. I can do it. I don't need anyone telling me what to do."

"George your drunk Bro. Why don't you take the rest of the day off? Timothy and I can handle this."

"You know what that's a good idea. I am the boss, I should be able to take a day off when I want to."

Nate turned the truck around and took George back home.

"Get you some rest Bro and I will see you in the morning," Nate said as he pulled up to George's house.

"I'm not going to go to sleep. I have a bottle to finish."

"Okay. I will see you in the morning."

"Yes you will Natey Nate."

Nate was shaking his head as he drove off to go pick up Timothy. While on his way he called Johnnie.

"Hey Nate what's going on?" Johnny asked when he answered the phone.

"Hey man, there is something really wrong with George."

"Yeah I know, what happened?"

"Johnnie, he was drunk and was talking a lot of crap about you."

"I see, where is he at now?"

"I took him back home."

"That was a good call. Um can you two handle it for a

few days without him?"

"Yes, we can."

"Okay good. I need to talk with him before he comes back to work."

"Yeah I think that's a good idea Johnnie. I have never seen him like this."

"I know. I need to deal with it. Just pick up Timothy for now until I tell you otherwise."

"Okay Johnnie. I am sorry man, I hated to have to call you about this."

"No, it's okay. You did the right thing. I will see you in the morning"

After Johnnie hung up, Steve asked him what was going on. Johnnie explained to him about what happened with George.

"That's not good Johnnie. Why was he saying things about you?"

"I don't know. But apparently there is an issue between me and him I wasn't aware of. But I am giving him some time off until we get this resolved."

"Yeah, I would too. You can't have your leader acting like this."

"Nope, I sure can't. His problem may be worse than we thought to be honest."

Johnnie was angry about this but wanted to calm down before he dealt with it. He honestly wasn't quite sure what he was going to do. He had always been able to trust George but right now things were real questionable with him, at least for the time being. He hated to see his best friend like this. This wasn't George at all. He was losing himself and Johnnie knew it. He was going to have to confront George but wasn't sure how he wanted to handle it. This was now spilling over into his business and he had to do something.

By the end of the day, Johnnie decided to let Steve go out on his own. He gave him a light day so that way he could take time to talk to George and try to find out exactly what was going on with him. Steve didn't mind going out on his own, but he preferred to be there. However Johnnie felt this needed to be a one on one conversation. Johnnie wanted George to be able to say whatever it was he felt he needed to say to him. Johnnie was beginning to think about shutting down the Lawn Care Business. It wasn't making nearly as much as the other departments, but it was paying the bills. But if he had to let George go, he was just going to bring Nate and Timothy over with him and Steve and shut the lawn care part down completely. No matter how this turned out, Johnnie already had worked out a backup plan. As much as it hurt Johnnie to think about it, he learned to prepare himself for anything. He was ready to make the next move if George was no longer going to be a part of the company. Nevertheless something had to change.

Johnnie spent some time with Tonya after they both finished work. Tonya was surprised about how George acted and the things he said about Johnnie. In all their years as friends, nothing like this had ever happened before and it really hurt Johnnie. As he got home and was heading off to bed, he felt as if tomorrow was going to be a bad deal. George wasn't the same and he didn't know what to expect from him. All night it had weighed heavy on his mind as he tried to sleep. He tossed and turned all night as he kept going over in his mind the endless possibilities that could transpire the next day. He was angry at George, but even more than that, he was disappointed.

It was a long night for Johnnie with very little rest as he slowly climbed out of bed to meet with his crew. He needed to get everyone going and was already getting irritated because he was tired. Tonya was asking him twenty questions about how he was going to handle things with George today. He didn't really know himself what he was going to do, and Steve was no better when he had arrived. He didn't want to deal with it and hoped that everyone would just leave it alone and let him do whatever he had to do. The truth was, it was all going to depend on George and what his attitude was.

After he got everyone out of his way he called George and asked him to come over. Johnnie wasn't really ready for this but things had been said that shouldn't have been said and he needed to know why. When George got there Johnnie greeted him in a friendly manner in hopes to resolve the issue rather than fight about it.

"Good morning George. Thank you for coming."

"Yeah, so what's this about?"

"I want to know what's going on with you."

"I told you already."

"No, you told me about why you're drinking and getting high. You didn't tell me what your problem with me is."

"You know what Johnnie? Okay. I will tell you. I am tired of always being underneath you. I am tired of you always telling me what to do."

"George you work for me."

"No Johnnie. It's not just the job. Even in this stupid war I have to answer to you. Everything we do, you're always the boss, the one in charge."

"George, listen Bro. This war, I took charge for two reasons. One, I know the West Dragons and you all didn't and two, I have more experience than you all with having to kill and do things that I don't like to do."

"Yeah you're always the man aren't you Johnnie? Always the one with the answers right? Mr. Big Shot."

"This is garbage George. All of this makes no sense to me."

"Yeah, that's right. Because you're so much smarter than me."

"Man, I didn't say that."

"You might as well have. Well guess what Johnnie? I can do whatever I want. I don't have to answer to you."

"No you don't have to answer to me, you can go work somewhere else."

"Yeah and I can go fight this war without you too," George said as he pushed Johnnie.

"Don't push me again George," Johnnie warned.

"What are you going to do Mr. Cypher?" George said as

he pushed Johnnie again.

"I am telling you George, do not push me again."

"Oh yeah and what are you going to do about it?" George said as he pushed Johnnie once more.

As Johnnie stepped back into George he laid one across his jaw. George was set back for a second before hitting Johnnie back. After that, it was an all-out fight between the two. This was not what Johnnie wanted but he was not backing down from George even though he really didn't want to hurt him. After several minutes of fighting, Johnnie caught George just above his eye and busted him open as he knocked him down.

"This isn't over Johnnie! You just wait and see!" George said as he got up and walked to Ann's car which he used to drive over.

"George, Bro, I am sorry. George wait. Come on man, I didn't mean to hit you like that," Johnnie said as George got into the car and peeled off in anger.

Johnnie felt bad about hitting George and even worse about cutting him open above his eye. He knew this had made things worse, but there was nothing he could do about it now. George pushed him too far and now things were worse. He went inside and got cleaned up.

"Johnnie, what happened?" Sara asked.

"I don't want to talk about it Mom."

"Johnnie please, tell me what happened?"

"Look Mom, I don't want to talk about it."

After a few seconds Johnnie apologized and explained he just needed time to calm down before he could talk about it.

"I'm sorry Mom. I am going to go lay down for a bit and try to relax."

"Okay Johnnie. We will talk about it later."

Johnnie went to his room to be alone while he tried to calm down and relax a bit. Things definitely didn't go the way he hoped. Nevertheless, what was done was done. He felt bad about it, but it was what George wanted.

The next day George called Ricky and told him they need to do a hit so he would send a driver for them. Ricky was surprised George had been the one who called but figured maybe Cypher was just very busy and had George call instead. So after talking to George, Ricky set it up for Auto to go pick them up that evening. When Auto got there he was surprised to see just George waiting for him.

"Where is everyone else at?"

"It's just me tonight. I'm doing a solo mission."

"I don't know if this is a good idea George."

"It's cool man I got this. We will do a quick run and be back before you even know it."

"Alright man, but I don't like this."

"Trust me Auto. I got this. When we get there I'm just going to hop out and unload on them and get out of there. They won't even know what hit them."

"In theory it sounds good," Auto said.

"Everything will be okay. I know what I am doing."

When they got to where some of the Hells Sinners was at, there was three of them standing on the corner selling dope. Auto pulled up just like George wanted him to. When George jumped out and started shooting at them, he hit two of them but they were only wounded. The third one fired back at hit George several times before he could get back in the car. The other two started shooting at the car Auto was in as he tried to speed off. Several bullets hit him as well as he was driving off. The car came to a slow rolling stop when one of the bullets hit the gas tank setting the car on fire causing the gas tank to blow up.

George was laying on the ground gasping for air as his bloody body was riddled with bullets. He had been shot five times and was lying in a puddle of blood as he was dying. One of the Hells Sinners recognized him and knew he was one of Cypher's friends.

"Hey I know him, that's one of the guys that Wayne used to fight with in school. He is one of Cypher's friends."

"Man are you serious?"

"Yes I am. He is with Cypher."

"Come on let's get out of here. We need to get you two fixed up and let Ricco know that Cypher is helping the

West Dragons.

Later that night it had got back to Ricky that George and Auto were dead. He knew that something had gone wrong when Auto never came back home. Ricky assumed the whole group was there together so he called Jason to tell him Cypher could be dead as well. Jason called Cypher immediately to find out what exactly had happened.

"Hey Jason, what's going on Bro?"

"That's what I want to know."

"What do you mean?"

"What happened tonight?" Jason asked.

"Nothing as far as I know, what did you hear?"

"Ricky called me and told me that Auto and George had both been killed tonight and thought you may have been as well."

"No man, we didn't go out tonight. But that is Ricky calling me on the other line. Let me take this and see what is going on."

"Ricky what is going on?" Cypher asked.

"You made it out of there alive I see," Ricky said.

"Made it out of where? I didn't go anywhere tonight."

"You didn't go with Auto and George?"

"I don't know anything about this, me and Steve was working."

"Well George called and asked for a ride to do a hit tonight."

"I promise you Ricky, I don't know anything about this."

"Well Auto and George are both dead. It's probably a good bet the Hells Sinners know you're involved now." There was a long pause of silence before Cypher had responded.

"George is dead?"

"Yes. He was shot down and then Auto was shot as well. The car he was driving blew up. You really didn't know?"

"No, I didn't."

"I'm sorry Cypher. I thought you knew."

"I will get back with you Ricky." Cypher said as he hung up and sat down on the edge of his bed and cried.

Several hours went by before he could pull himself together enough to call Tonya, Steve and Ann to come over. Once they were there, Johnnie told them what had happened. Ann broke down and cried along with Tonya. Johnnie didn't know how he was going to explain this to Tim and Monica Reid. George was their only son. Johnnie was also going to have to break the news to his mom as well, who considered George as one of her own. The rest of the night they sat together crying, trying to comfort each other.

In the morning when Nate and Timothy arrived Johnnie had a meeting to tell them what happened and gave them the day off. Sara was in the living room, away from everyone, crying. Johnnie told her when she first woke up.

All Johnnie kept thinking about was the fight they had and that it was the last time he saw George before he was murdered. He felt it was somehow his fault. He was thinking maybe he had somehow made George feel this way.

"Maybe if I had just tried to reason with him more," Johnnie said to the group.

"This is not your fault Bro, George was out of control," Steve said.

"Steve is right Johnnie, this wasn't your fault. George did what he did out of his own actions." Nate said to Johnnie who was a bit confused as to why George went after them. Nate and Timothy were still unaware of the war the rest of the group was in. Johnnie told them he couldn't explain it all right now, but promised to tell them when he could.

Later that morning Johnnie called Jason and told him all that happened. Jason assured him that he would find out if the Hells Sinners knew about him being involved now. Johnnie and Steve both needed to know. For now they were both going to have to lay low for a bit, until they could find out what the Hells Sinners knew.

CHAPTER 13

PRESSING FORWARD

Everyone was mourning the loss of George. It was another hard blow to the group as well as the community. Johnnie, Steve and Tonya still had a hard time believing that George had done this. He was smarter than that. Tim and Monica began to ask a lot of questions and so were the police. The heat now was being put on Johnnie. Also, Thomas and Christina began to ask more questions as it was just too obvious now the group had been involved in something.

Johnnie went on his own to meet with the Reid and Hilton families to give them the truth. Once he sat them all down at the Reid's house where they all met, Johnnie started at the very beginning. He walked them all the way through the whole story starting back when they were kids and all the fighting that went on in school. As he got to the part about Tonya it began to get harder for him to speak as it was still very emotional. Christina and Monica began to cry as well as Johnnie was telling them the story of their history with the Hells Sinners.

Johnnie told them everything except the part of Randy. He left that part of the story as it was. He never told them it was Ricky who had Randy murdered. He left it as the Hells Sinners as everyone had already thought. It was hard for Tim and Monica to hear about George's drinking problem and how he was getting high all the time. He knew he couldn't keep all of this a secret any longer so he thought it was best to just tell them everything he could. Johnnie explained to them he kept it a secret to protect him and Steve from going to jail.

Everyone sat in shock at the truth Johnnie shared. No one blamed him or Tonya like he thought they would. He had shared about taking the vote and how he had made sure this is what they all wanted to do. The Reid and Hilton families both understood their sons were old enough to make their own choices and this is what they had decided. They all knew Johnnie didn't make anyone do anything they didn't want to do. It was hard for them all to swallow but they had to face the truth and except it as it was.

Johnnie sat with them all for a few hours as he explained everything in great detail so they would understand exactly what happened and why. He didn't want any misunderstandings. Tim and Monica had known just how much George hated Wayne and his gang of friends. Thomas and Christina also were very aware of how much the Two Brothers hated them as well. There was a part of them that wanted Johnnie to finish this, but they loved him very much and began to plead with him to let this war end altogether for him and Steve. Johnnie wanted to, but he wasn't going to have any more lies between them and himself and simply said he didn't know what he was going to do at this point.

"It's too risky to keep going Johnnie. We all have lost so much because of this," Tim said as he sat holding Monica who couldn't stop crying.

"Tim is right Johnnie. We have lost three of our sons already. Sara would die if she lost you as well. And what about Tony and Tammy, if they was to lose Steve too?"

"Yes I know Thomas. We have talked about this many times, even with George. But we all felt if we had stopped then the deaths of Randy and Darryl would have been in vain and now with George gone too, what do we gain if we don't finish this?"

"You can't seriously be thinking of continuing this?" Christina asked in all sincerity.

"Steve and I haven't had a chance to talk about it. We are both still trying to figure out why George went out on his own. Give us time to process all of this as well."

"Johnnie you two have to go to the police."

"The police already know. The only thing that will do is get me and Steve in trouble as well. They are already looking at us and trying to connect us with this war and if they do, Steve and I will go to prison."

"Look Johnnie, I understand why you all did this. I probably would have to. We don't want you or Steve to go to prison," Thomas said.

"Thomas is right. We will keep this between us, but you and Steve have to get out of this war."

"You don't know how many times we have wanted too. What I can tell you is this. The war is almost over. The Hells Sinners are about to fall. We are close to it being over with anyways," Johnnie said.

Johnnie had spent the next hour answering as many questions as he could. He knew both families were going to protect him and Steve. He was still waiting to hear back from Jason on whether or not the Hells Sinners knew that he was involved. Jason was going to have a meeting with Ricco to feel it out and see if he would say anything about him. This was a very scary time for Johnnie and Steve. This war was no longer a secret which meant they had to be even more careful until this was over.

After Johnnie had finished talking to them he called Tonya to have her and Steve come meet with him so he could tell them everything. They had not yet known Johnnie went to talk to both families. Once Tonya and Steve showed up the three of them went back to the camp area. Johnnie had made a fire and sat next to Tonya.

"Well, here is where we are at. One. We don't know if the Hells Sinners are on to me but I am sure that they are. Two. I went and sat down with the Reid and the Hilton families and went through the whole story with them so they pretty much know everything."

"Man how did they take that?" Steve asked.

"Well to my surprise Steve, they were more understanding then I had expected to be honest with you. I didn't how they were going to take all of this and I figured they would be mad at us, but they weren't. So I take that as a good sign, plus they aren't going to involve us with the police either. They don't want to see us going to jail, however they did express their concerns and asked if we would leave the war altogether."

"I think you two should. It's way too risky now and you have done way more to the Hells Sinners than anyone thought you would. Besides, the West Dragons can finish this now," Tonya said.

"Tonya may be right, but I still feel like we need to finish what we started."

"I'm with Steve on that. I feel the same way. We need to see this through to the end like we said we would."

"Johnnie listen to me. You guys did great okay. I will give you that. But look what it has cost us. If you have a chance to get out of it and be able to walk away from it then you should," Tonya said.

"That's just it Tonya. I don't know if we have that chance to just walk away. It's very possible the Hells Sinners will come after us. I think its best if we stay focused and keep on until it's finished. If not we may end up fighting them on our own and right now we still have allies."

"Johnnie does make a good point. If they do come after us, I would feel much better having help from the West Dragons."

"Yeah, I suppose your right. I just hate this Johnnie. I want this to end," Tonya said.

"Baby, so do we. We want this all to be over."

"It will be okay Sis. Let us finish this with help on our side. It's almost done. I can feel it."

"I agree with Steve. This war has to be almost over with. Jason told me in one of our conversations the Hells Sinners were hurting bad."

"Yeah but the West Dragons have taken some hard blows also."

"Yes they have, but so have we. Honestly we all have. But I will say this, if they do know about us, it's better that it came at a time the Hells Sinners are at a weakened state."

"I definitely agree with that."

"I do too, better now than early on," Tonya said as she was agreeing with both Johnnie and Steve.

"So we keep going for now, and in the meantime I am waiting for Jason to call me. He was going to sit down with Ricco and try to see if he could find out if he knew we were involved in this war."

"Let me know as soon as you find out."

"I will Bro. You both will know as soon as I hear from him."

Johnnie felt much better having come clean with both families but he knew they were not okay with it even though they understood, they didn't accept it. Once the shock had worn off, both families became even less okay with it and was angry that Johnnie knew all of this and never had told them. Johnnie explained how the police never could do anything about what they were having to put up with and even reminded them there still wasn't any arrest in the murders of Randy and Darryl, plus the fact they got away with the rape of Tonya. This worked out in his favor during that conversation to show they felt they had no choice but to handle it on their own. That was the one thing that made both families understand why they did what they had done. Plus, they weren't ignorant of the things from the past and how this fight with them had been a lifelong battle.

Johnnie had a way of explaining things to get them to see it from his angle. They all felt enough was enough and that it would never stop unless they put an end to it themselves. Both parents had made many trips up to the school over this feud and knew what Johnnie was saying was true. They knew this war wasn't what the boys had wanted so for them to go after the Hells Sinners, it must have been the only thing they could have done.

The next day Johnnie called for a meeting with all of his crews. Once everyone was there, Johnnie began to explain his next plan of action concerning his business.

"I called you all here because we are making a huge change. I am going to sell the Lawn Care part of the company. We will work it until it's sold."

"What will happen to me and Timothy," Nate asked while being very concerned about his job.

"You will still be a part of this company. Steve will go back to the painting crew and Nate and Timothy will be with me. We have more than enough work to where I don't need the Lawn Care anymore. I was going to hire someone for the painting crew anyways so it helps me to be able to move Steve back there instead. Plus you both are good, hard workers and bringing you over to my crew gives me one more worker that I really needed anyways."

"Do you have a business that is interested in buying it?"

"There is a crew that is bigger than we are that works close to some of the jobs that we do. I am sure they would love to expand their territory. Once I get everything set, I will go and talk to my customers and explain the situation to them. In the meantime you two do your best and I will try to get this sold as soon as possible."

After the meeting everyone left except for Tonya. She stayed to spend some time with Johnnie but first he had to make some calls to some local Lawn Crews to try and get a buyer for his company. After a few hours of talking to different Lawn Care Companies, Johnnie went to meet with one that he thought would be good to his customers. Tonya went with Johnnie to go meet Austin who owned Skippy's Lawn Care. Skippy's was a pretty good size company that did a lot of work in the state. They had five different lawn crews and was eager to add one more if they could get Johnnie's business from him.

"You must be Austin. I am Johnnie."

"I know who you are. We are competitors. You have customers in some of the areas I work. I have been trying to get them but they really like your services."

"Yeah, we have good customers. So this is the thing that I am concerned about. I don't want to just give them to anyone. I need to make sure you will take very good care of them."

"I give you my word Johnnie. We will make sure they get the same quality care you have given to them. How soon are you wanting to sell your company?"

"Right now."

"Well how much are you asking?"

"I am asking a hundred thousand. That includes one trailer, two mowers, two weed whips and two blowers as well as all my customers."

"That's kind of steep, how much do you make a year with them."

"That's a full year's worth. A hundred thousand a year."

"Okay and how soon would you need me to take over?"

"How soon can you take it over?" Johnnie asked as he was hoping that he would say today.

"I can have a crew ready in about two weeks. How does that sound?"

"That will work, that will give me time to talk to my customers and explain everything."

"Sounds like we have ourselves a deal Johnnie."

"Cool. Once you pay me, then you can come get all the stuff. We will keep working it until you're ready to step in. I will have all the routes and everything for you."

"Perfect. I will go to the bank in the morning, give you a call and we can meet up."

"Great. I will be waiting for your call," Johnnie said as he shook Austin's hand.

Johnnie felt even more relieved to have that settled now as well. Good things were happening even though this was a real hard time for him. He was thankful some things was working out the way he had needed it to. He felt real good about Skippy's and he knew they had a very good reputation.

The rest of the day Johnnie spent with Tonya as they laid

back at the house and enjoyed some time together. Johnnie had given everyone the rest of the week off to mourn for the loss of their friend George. It only seemed right for Johnnie and Steve to volunteer to help carry the casket. No matter what happened at the end, he had been a lifelong friend and they both felt they owed it to him and to his family that had been so good to them as well. Tim and Monica had always treated Johnnie as one of their own. Steve had appreciated the way they embraced him and Tonya when they first moved into the neighborhood. Nate and Timothy had volunteered as well. George was loved and well respected by everyone. Ann was devastated and had been staying off to herself except for the times Tonya had come over to spend with her and comfort her. They were all too young to have lost this many childhood friends.

While Johnnie was home alone, he finally had gotten the phone call he had been waiting for from Jason. This would hopefully tell him what he needed to know.

"Johnnie, I just came out of a meeting with Ricco."

"So what did he say?"

"Well, they know you guys have been working with the West Dragons and to be honest, they want to make a truce with you."

"A truce? With us?"

"Johnnie they are losing this war terribly and they know that the end is near for them. No one will even join them since they started getting hit. They haven't been able to recruit any one in a long time and their numbers are dwindling fast."

"Tell them we will take it. But really we aren't going to. I just want them to think we are to take the heat off of us for the time being."

"I thought that's what you would do. Okay, I will let them know you accept their truce."

"Good deal, after we bury George I am hitting them again."

"Okay Brother. If you need anything let me know."

"I will and thank you again Jason."

"No worries. I will think of some way for you to repay me for all I do for you."

"I am sure you will," Johnnie laughed a little.

"Okay, Brother. Talk soon. I will get with Ricco and get this all clear for you."

"Good, thanks, we will talk soon."

Johnnie was feeling even more relieved. He went back to relaxing on the couch, watching television while Sara was out on another date with Chris. He was very happy to be home alone for a while to just take some time to think. Everyone was over stressed and they all needed a break, especially now after the death of George. He would take this week to talk to his lawn care customers and let them know about the company that was taking over. He knew he would have to assure them they would be well taken care of.

Johnnie couldn't wait to be done with the lawn care stuff. It had become more of a headache than anything with all the training he kept having to do from losing his leaders. With Darryl, Randy and now George, he just wasn't going to try and replace him and hire someone again. He would rather just move Nate and Timothy to help him with the repair work which was making him a lot more money anyways.

Johnnie was working on getting the Lawn Care business settled as the Reid family was preparing for the funeral of their son, George. It took a while to go through the list and contact all of the clients and explain the transition as well as assure them that everything would be the same as it was, just a different company.

Johnnie needed to keep his mind busy or else it would drive him crazy thinking about all that happened so quickly with George. Things escalated so fast he never got a grip on what all was going on with him. It was in this moment he realized just how bad things where for George. He had hidden his addictions real good until it all surfaced and before he could try to really help deal with it, George was gone.

The funeral was going to be hard for all of them, especially for Johnnie. He seriously regretted having that fight with him. He knew he couldn't go back and change any of this even though he had wished he could. He still wasn't sure having that meeting with the families was a good idea. He kept wondering how they felt about him now knowing they were all involved in this war that cost them their son's lives. He couldn't help but feel that in some ways they blamed him for what happened.

The truth was, as much as no one wanted to say it, they were happy he was going to finish this even though they all tried to talk him out of it. They all cared about him and didn't want to lose him or Steve like they had lost their sons. They knew Sara would not be able to handle it if she had lost Johnnie the same way. It was so hard for them to believe their sons where involved in killing. But at the same time they understood. With all that happened throughout the years, they could see how something like this could happen after such a long fight with the same people. Especially after what they had done to Tonya. They all knew Johnnie was a good person but everyone was quite aware he wasn't a coward and would go after anyone that hurt his family or friends.

Retribution was on the heads of the Hells Sinners from their own actions. They had caused the reckoning that was now upon them and there was no mercy. Punishment and justice was being poured out on them by the hands of their enemies as everyone was watching the fall of the biggest gang in Westbend Heights. The innocent blood they spilled and the rapes they had committed was now being repaid to them. Cypher's name now was being spread through the streets. It was now being revealed his hand was against them and it was him who had done the most damage to the Hells Sinners. Their whole organization had been shaken to its core. There was no way out but to try to make a truce with their lifelong enemy who had brought revenge and death to the most feared gang who had been greatly reduced by the bloodshed Cypher had brought against them. The Hells Sinners knew they could not continue fighting against them both and was in a desperate situation that was getting worse for them all the time. The had become afraid other gangs would start picking at them now that they were at a much weaker state and couldn't afford to keep having Cypher taking them out.

After Johnnie had finished what he had to do to complete the changeover for the lawn care, he went and picked up Tonya and took her out to dinner. While he was gone, Sara invited Chris over to watch a movie so they could sit alone. As they sat together Chris, could tell Sara wasn't herself and inquired as to what had been bothering her.

"It's my son's best friend George. He was murdered and the funeral is tomorrow," Sara explained to him as she started crying.

"I am so very sorry," Chris said as he comforted her holding her in his arms.

"He was like a son to me. They grew up together and had been best friends all their lives."

"This must be so hard for you both. Do you want me to come with you to the funeral?" Chris asked.

"Oh Chris, that would be so great if you would."

"Yes of course. I can pick you up so you don't have to drive."

"That would make it so much easier for me. Thank you so much Chris."

"Think nothing of it. I would feel better if you didn't have to drive. I know this will be so hard for you."

"I watched George grow up. He stayed here all the time. We are all so close."

"I will pick you up early so you can visit with his family before the funeral."

"I would need to be their early. His parents are good friends of mine."

"I will be here early then."

Johnnie and Tonya didn't say much at dinner as both of their minds was on what happened. The following day they saw their friend buried. It was a long hard day for them all. The Reid family was a mess as well as Tonya and the group. Sara sat crying along with Tammy.

This was the last casket that Johnnie wanted to carry. After this the only caskets would be for the Hells Sinners. It comforted Johnnie when he had turned around to scan the people to see who all was there and saw Jason sitting in the back. He knew Jason was there to honor his friendship with George. The group wouldn't meet up at the camp later on, as Johnnie just wanted to be alone after everything was finished. George was gone and Randy and Darryl was gone. He wished for Steve to get out of this war, but he knew he wouldn't. He knew Steve was in it 'til the end just like he was.

The next week came too fast for Johnnie as the crew had to get back to work to keep from falling too far behind. The lawn crew was done. The other company had already taken over and he was able to just focus on the other two parts of his business. It was going to be some long days throughout the week to make up some time they had lost. He wasn't ready for this as he was struggling with the death of George. The fight he had with him was still eating at him and he couldn't get passed it.

Ann was still struggling with the loss of her boyfriend as well. She loved George and missed him terribly. There were times she would walk off and go cry for a bit and then come back and try to refocus on her work but it just hurt so much. She was really not able to hold it all in. She hated crying on the job but she couldn't help feeling the emotions she was struggling with. Tonya was very understanding during this time and would let her take as many breaks as she needed. She knew Ann was hurting and there was little she could do to comfort her. Ann needed to go off and be alone for a few minutes and cry. Tonya left her alone to let her grieve for the loss of her love. Debra was working hard and was doing more to help cover Ann so she could have those moments to grieve that she needed. Having Steve back with them was a huge help as well.

Meanwhile it was that time of the season when the carnival came into town and everyone was very excited about it. Johnnie decided it would be best if they didn't go this year and the rest agreed. No one knew what would transpire if they were there and the Hells Sinners came through also. Johnnie knew it wouldn't be good even with the truce in place. Plus they had so much work ahead of them, they didn't really have time for it anyways. The carnival had always been a big deal to Johnnie and George. This would be the first time that he didn't go. It would be too hard for him to go without George while it was something they had done together all of their lives until now. No one wanted to miss it but they all knew that right now, it just wasn't smart to be there.

Which turned out to be a good thing for them. The Hells Sinners did show up and not only them, but the West Dragons also. The carnival was only into its second day when both gangs showed up at the same time. There was nothing security could do when the fight broke out. People were running everywhere while trying to escape the onslaught of bullets that riddled through the air. Both gangs had open fired on each other and started shooting up the carnival without thought of the innocent people who were there. This is why Cypher hated both gangs, women and children were being hit by stray bullets.

Several innocent bystanders were shot and killed while others were wounded as the carnival became a blood bath. Both gangs lost members at the carnival including Ricco who laid dead by the Ferris wheel. Viper shot him several times before he fell to the ground and died. Ricky was also shot and wounded as he took a bullet to his shoulder. The war at the carnival had been so severe they shut it down completely. What was supposed to run for two weeks was shut down after only two days.

When Johnnie and the rest of the group had heard about it, they all were glad they stayed away from it. Johnnie had felt that something like this was going to happen and knew it wasn't going to be good for them to be there. He wished both gangs would just kill each other off. He hated how they didn't value human life and was so careless when it came to shooting in crowds. Innocent people didn't need to die over their stupidity.

With Ricky being shot and Ricco now dead, both sides had taken a hard blow. Sisko had no choice but to promote Wayne even though he never really viewed him as a leader. There was others but they hadn't been in the gang as long as Wayne and everyone respected him for the time he had put in. Wayne wanted to go after Cypher and the rest of the group now that Ricco was gone but Sisko had agreed with Ricco they needed to leave him alone, at least for now. The numbers had dwindled down so much for the Hells Sinners that some of them was even thinking about going into hiding. Wayne thought about it as well until he got promoted. Which was something he couldn't turn down. He always wanted to be at the top and now he was, and that meant he had to stick it out now.

The Mob Killa's heard about the death of Ricco and took advantage of the situation. Their boss, Warlord sent Nuke and Toxic to do a drive-by on their club house that was now a main stay for bullets. The Hells Sinners club house had so many bullet holes that Sisko was looking for a new place to keep as their club house. Before he could even find a place another hit was upon them as Nuke and Toxic sprayed the house with Uzi's that killed four more members. The Mob Killa's was a smaller gang who would have never hit the Hells Sinners but they knew they had to strike while the iron was hot. When the West Dragons heard about it and knew they had got away clean, Viper felt they should also keep the pressure on them. Especially since he had no idea when or if Cypher was going to hit them again. No one had heard from him since George had been killed.

Cypher was getting ready to make a new plan and was taking his time to make sure it was how he wanted to do it. From here on out it was just going to be him and Steve and he wanted to make sure everything was good before putting the plan in motion. Jason was going to start meeting up with him to go over his plans and help him to be able to execute it as flawlessly as possible. With Jason knowing what he was doing, he could help orchestrate things from behind the scenes.

While Cypher was working on that, the West Dragons were working on their own plan of attack as well. The Death Clicks was still watching and waiting to see who was going to win this war. They still didn't want the West Dragons taking control of that much territory. But as a good showing, they would put a hit on the Hells Sinners to stay in good with the West Dragons, but only when it became very clear the Hells Sinners was too far gone to win this war. As of yet, the Death Clicks still had hope the West Dragons wouldn't win. Even though they had also heard Cypher had been involved in the war as well. They had no problems with him but rather had a great deal of respect for him that had developed when some of their top members was in The House with him. They knew he was a standup guy that didn't play around. They also knew of the bad blood between him and the Hells Sinners that spilled over into The House. Even though Cypher had never really made a name for himself on the streets until the war, he had already gained so much respect while being in The House and had built a strong reputation for himself. Everyone respected him with the exception of the Hells Sinners who hated him.

CHAPTER 14

I'M NOT A HERO

People look to me as a leader. As someone who they can follow. Where did I lead them? Where did they follow me to Death? Their graves? I should have never lead them into this war. I should have just did it on my own. I lost three brothers who didn't deserve to die. Life was just starting for them and already they are gone. Ann is a widow before she could even get married, and this war still isn't over. We didn't really count the cost. We all assumed we would walk away from this together, like we always done before. But not this time. No, this time I buried three brothers that should have never died like this. I bare their deaths in my scars. I carry with me every day the loss of my brothers. The revenge I have sought has brought them to their untimely end. My sorrow, my anger, my hatred has all become one together. It all haunts me to no end. It's in my every day, in my night. Even in my dreams it all haunts me. I am restless with an uneasy feeling of insecurity.

There is no guarantee that Steve and I will make it out of this alive. Neither one of us are willing to give it up until it's finished. We both have paid too great of a price to not give our own lives for it. We owe it to Tonya. We owe it to our brothers who have paid with their own lives the revenge we have sought, the reckoning we have brought against our enemies and the retribution we have vowed upon our enemies until justice is finally served.

I have vowed within myself Wayne will die and I will see that day come to fruition before I give up my own life to rest with my brothers. I see his death forever before me and I will have his life. The beginning of all of this starts with him and it will end with him in his own grave. By my hands he will die and by my hands I will take his life.

Suddenly the phone rang pulling Johnnie out of his deep thoughts. It was Tonya. She had been waiting for him.

"Where are you? You were supposed to pick me up."

"Yeah, sorry Baby. I was just about to leave. I had just sat down for a moment to think is all."

"Is everything okay?"

"Yes. Everything is fine. I will be there in a minute."

Johnnie and the group were going to the gravesite where George had been laid to rest. Everything had happened so fast they felt they didn't really get to say goodbye to their brother. So much had been going on they felt they didn't get the closure they needed. This would be their last goodbye to him and they wanted to do it as a group. Just them as it should be. After which Johnnie was going to take them all out for lunch. But first they needed to assemble themselves together at the site of their fallen brother.

The moment was very somber as they gathered together. Everyone bowed their heads and held each other's hands as Tonya said a prayer.

"Lord I thank You for the friendship we all had with George. He is gone now but his family remains. I ask Lord that You comfort them in their grieving. Give them strength. Our brother is gone but we remain. Be with us as we grieve the loss of our friend. Amen."

"Amen," said the entire group just before Johnnie began to say a few words.

"George was a lifelong friend. We grew up together from birth. Our parents were friends since before we were born. I have never known a time without George in my life until now. We have always been friends. I don't know what all happened at the end, I wish I did. I wish he had come to me sooner. I wish I had saw what was going on. I wish I had just gone after the Hells Sinners alone. There was no reason for George and Randy and Darryl to lose their lives at such a young age. It wasn't their time to go yet. They went out way to early." Johnnie turned and knelt down at the grave of his friend. "I will end this my Brother. I promise you this. I will avenge all of you. Your deaths will not be in vain, I give you my word." As Johnnie stood, everyone around him gathered together.

"This wasn't your fault Brother," Steve said as he had his arm on Johnnie's shoulder.

"No it wasn't. George was fighting his own demons Johnnie," Ann also said as Tonya hugged her while she cried.

Johnnie stood there and remained quiet as they all grieved together as a group for their fallen brother. Before they left, they took time to visit the graves of the Two Brothers. Being at the grave sparked a new fire within Johnnie and Steve to continue on with the war. It was time again to go on a hit as they wanted to make sure this thing kept moving forward. Everything was looking the way they wanted it to. The Hells Sinners had taken a real beating and it needed to continue on.

Wayne was starting to feel real shaky about what was happening. Things were real bad for them and he knew it. Everyday he kept thinking of bailing out and going into hiding. He had thought about skipping town and going somewhere where nobody knew him. Wayne had even considered ripping off the Hells Sinners and taking as much of their money as he could to get out of there and go somewhere where he could hide for a long time. He knew nobody would come after him for it. Winning this war now was almost getting too far out of their reach and others also had been talking amongst themselves about leaving the gang now. The ship was sinking fast and people were about to bail out.

With Ricco gone it was all Sisko could do to hold this

gang together while they were being picked off continually. Sisko knew the Mob Killa's had taken shots on them and they had to take it. There was no way they could focus on anyone but the West Dragons if they were going to have any hope whatsoever to win this war. They no longer had the man power to fight against everyone at one time. If they were going to survive, they had to put everything into fighting the West Dragons.

Wayne was thinking about how he could kill Cypher before going into hiding. He wasn't about to leave without getting his revenge on him for helping the West Dragons. If he was going to skip town, it wouldn't be before he killed him. Wayne had a lot of rivals and many gang members from other gangs wanted to see him dead. He was a marked man because of the many people he had hurt. Nobody wanted him more than Cypher though, they hated each other with no end and they both wanted to see each other dead.

Early the next morning Debra met up with Johnnie to get loaded up for work while Tonya and Steve went to pick up Ann. Debra was already on her way after getting loaded up with the supplies they needed. She had made it to the job site to start the prep work for the day before the rest had finally arrived. Johnnie called Nate and told him where to meet up with him. It had been raining all night and was still drizzling so they were going to work together painting and try to get at least two houses done.

***

It was a slow day on the books for Chris who had decided to invite Sara out for lunch again. She was so excited to be meeting up with him again already for lunch. They spent some time together over the weekend and Sara hadn't expected to see him for a few days but since it was a bit of a slow day, he wanted to take advantage of it and see her again. He was starting to develop feelings for Sara. He hadn't felt anything for another woman since his wife had passed away years earlier. It had been too hard for him to love again. The pain of losing his wife had been too much for him and he was scared to love.

But being with Sara was such a wonderful feeling he could barely resist it. She was so smart and kind. Everything about her was so wonderful. It had been a long time since he felt anything like this for a woman, but Sara had a way about her and she was so gorgeous. Chris couldn't deny what he was feeling for her. She was amazingly beautiful and had such a nice personality. She was perfect for him and he knew it.

Both being widows gave them something in common and Sara was taken by him as well. She had denied herself ever since Mike but she wasn't going to let him control her life anymore. He was gone and it was time to live and love again. Sara knew there were good men out there and she felt Chris was one of them. He made her feel special and that was something she hadn't felt since Mark. There was something in the way his eyes would sparkle when he looked at her. She felt it every time when they would look at each other. The more she was with him the more she liked him. There was a sincerity about him that was comforting to her. She could see it in his eyes and feel it in the way he would touch her. She had even began to sit with him in Church which made it even nicer since Johnnie wasn't going. Before all she had to sit with was other people's families, but now that she was seeing Chris, it made it a little better to have someone of her own to sit with.

After lunch with Chris, Sara returned home to get some work done for Johnnie. Everybody had been off for a week following the death of George but Johnnie decided to pay them anyways. Sara needed to get the payroll done for that week.

Meanwhile Jason had set up a fake meeting with the Hells Sinners' boss Sisko to feel out what he was thinking concerning the war. Jason had still been taking the money the Hells Sinners was supposed to be kicking up to Pauli and was using that as a way to get a meeting with him. Jason was itching to take care of Ricky but needed to wait for this war to end first. As he met with Sisko, he was hoping to get a good look at what shape his crew was in. But Jason didn't keep this meeting as a secret. He knew that the Hells Sinners was looking for a new club house so while he was meeting up with Sisko, he tipped off Ricky about it. Ricky had set it up to blow the club house up so they would have to move now without having a place to go.

Jason's plan was to scatter them so Cypher could continue to pick them off while the West Dragons did the same. Jason was waiting at the old warehouse where he had always conducted business. He had given Sisko strict instructions to come alone.

"Glad to see you made it."

"Things are not going so good Jason. I still don't know who is killing my delivery men or how they keep finding out where they are meeting you. I have sent thousands upon thousands of dollars to you that you keep saying you didn't received."

"Well Pauli is done with it Sisko. I wish I could help you, but this is really between you and Pauli now. This whole war has hinged on you not paying him. When the money was being delivered he had kept this war from happening but now he doesn't care and it has really hurt you."

"Tell me the truth Jason. Did you know Cypher was a part of this war?"

"Of course I did. I know everything. But I don't interfere in such matters that don't pertain to me. This war is between you all and I have nothing to do with it. You know I don't interfere in your matters or anyone else's. I just make sure things are done right and that certain people get paid. But I have to be honest, you should have known he would come after you. After what you all did to him and Tonya, you deserved this."

"We're barely hanging on now. So much had happened before we could get a grip on it."

"I understand. I know it has effected your business but

again, Pauli doesn't care about that. He wants his money regardless of what's going on."

"There is nothing you can do to help us? Can't you talk to him and get us some more time. I am willing to make a deal with him."

"What kind of deal are we talking about?"

"I mean once we get things settled and rebuild we can pay him double. I just need more time Jason." "Hmm that is if you survive this. Rumor is that you have lost seventy five percent of your gang and your numbers are dwindling down all the time."

"You could help us Jason. You have the resources to help us to survive this."

"What are you proposing?"

"An alliance with you. We will give you a portion of our earnings once this war is over with."

"You are going to give me a portion of your earnings, plus pay Pauli double?" Jason asked. He was beginning to see just how desperate the Hells Sinners were with this deal. However he knew they wouldn't survive this war to make good on that promise. But nevertheless, a fake alliance could work out to further help Cypher.

"Okay, I will see what I can do."

"All we really need is inside information. You could tip us off so we can get the upper hand on the West Dragons."

"I suppose I could do that."

"Thank you Jason. I really appreciate your help. I know you are friends with some of them but I promise you I will make it good for you in the end."

"Money is my friend. You just make sure you come through on your promises."

"I will Jason. You have my word."

"And one more thing, you never bother Cypher or any of his friends or family again."

"I give you my word Jason."

All along Jason had been pulling the strings behind the scenes and now Sisko had just made it even easier for him to control what was going on by making him an inside man into a war he had already been manipulating. Wars were always chaotic but Jason had roughly been able to direct it in the way he had wanted it to go. And now he had even more control over it. He could do almost anything he wanted.

This new control would enhance Cypher's plan and make things even easier. After the meeting Jason sent Cypher a message letting him know things had worked out better than he had hoped and now they had more control than they had expected. Cypher's plan was about to be implemented that would utterly bring an end to the Hells Sinners.

In the meantime, Sisko had called a meeting for the rest of the Hells Sinners to go over with them the meeting he had with Jason and what the next step was for them to take in trying to get this war back in their favor. Sadly for Sisko, by the time he and the rest of the Hells Sinners had shown up to meet at the club house it was no longer there. The West Dragons had already reduced it to a pile of rubble. This continued to add to their problems and now more than ever, Wayne was thinking of going into hiding. It wasn't just him, but others was thinking the same as it was becoming more and more of an impossible situation. Sisko was doing all he could to keep this gang together but this war had taken its toll on them and there wasn't nearly as many members left. Had their gang not been too large in members, they would have already been eliminated.

Cypher was trying to be patient but he couldn't subside the anxious feeling to get this war over. He had other things he wanted to focus on and this was holding him up. He was ready to move on with Tonya, get married and start their lives together as a real family. Johnnie wanted to have kids with her and build a family like he had always wanted. Time was of the essence. He knew he had to strike while the iron was hot. It was time to go and make another hit in hopes to finally cripple his lifelong enemies.

Steve was itching to get it done as well. Things with him and Debra had really began to grow. He was falling deeply in love with her and wanted to also move forward in his relationship with Debra. Seeing this war end was the key to their freedom. They were both clinging to the hope it would soon be over once and for all.

While the club house was smoldering in rubble, the police officers who were assigned to watch the Hells Sinners had been called elsewhere to investigate a crime that was supposedly being committed, but when they had arrived it was just an empty building. This wasn't the first time they had been called to a fake crime scene. The calls came from different pay phones from around the city so there was no way to find out who had kept making the phony calls. With such a violent war going on, there was no way they could watch every pay phone in the hopes of catching whoever had been making the calls.

There was so many things that had been happening with this war that made no sense until it was revealed Cypher had been involved. The Hells Sinners underestimated him once and wasn't about to do that again, especially now that survival was about all they could try to do, at least for now. They desperately needed to get a grip on this war and turn things around. They began to hit the West Dragons every time the opportunity presented itself to them.

Even though their numbers had been greatly reduced, they still had a strong band with a decent size number. With all the damage they had sustained they still had thirty five members left to fight this war. For most gangs that was about all they had anyways, but for the Hells Sinners that was enough to make them panic. Before the war had started they was well over a hundred in numbers and was thought to be invincible.

The damage Cypher had caused the Hells Sinners was being talked about all over the streets and was greatly angering Wayne to the point where all he wanted to do was get revenge. But Sisko was holding to the truce out of fear and Wayne knew it. Wayne had always been narrow sighted and was never one to see the big picture. Whereas Sisko understood the situation much better and knew they needed to keep Cypher off of them long enough to get a better handle on this war until they could turn things around and get it back in their favor. Timing was the key and Sisko knew it. He wanted to kill Cypher as well, but there was nothing they could do for now. They had to focus everything on the West Dragons if they were going to have any chance whatsoever to win. They had no idea how many soldiers Cypher had, but they suspected it had to have been a lot for the amount of damage they had inflicted.

Now with the club house gone, everyone was scattered for the time being until they could get a new meeting place. They had considered using a secluded park not too far from where they had raped Tonya, and it was right on the boarder of the West Dragons territory. However it was also a bit risky. For now, Sisko was focusing all of his attention on obtaining a place for them all to be able to meet up. The streets was so hot right now from this war that no one was willing to rent Sisko a place in fear that it too would be shot up or blown to pieces. The Hells Sinners at one point was thought to be good for business but had now become a liability.

The old club house that had been destroyed was used for drug sells and prostitution. This way they could protect the girls they had prostituted but now some of them was going to have to go back to working the streets and be less protected after being picked up. There was a sleazy motel Sisko knew he could use, but they would only give him two rooms and he knew they could only have a few girls to each room. The idea of having to spend money on the whores just so they could make money was not appealing to him, but at the moment they had no choice. It took money to win a war and they needed all that they could get right now, especially considering they were going to have to get a new club house which wasn't going to be cheap at all.

While the Hells Sinners was having their issues, Sara had decided it was finally time for Chris to come over for dinner and meet her son Johnnie. Things were now very serious between the two and she felt that it was time. Johnnie was ready to meet him also and Tonya was excited about it because she knew Johnnie would like him. Johnnie was happy his mother was with a good Christian man who everyone knew. He felt because of that, this time things would work out for her.

As Sara invited Chris over that night for dinner, he was a bit nervous about meeting Johnnie. He had no small reputation and was known by what he did to Mike. Johnnie wanted it to be known so that anyone after him who wanted to date his mother would be more cautious and would already know they had better treat her right and never hit her. Tonya wanted to make sure Johnnie would give Chris a real chance. When they were alone, she talked to him about it, in hopes he would be as friendly as possible with Chris. She asked Johnnie to pick up some lunch for the two of them so she could talk to him before they joined Sara and Chris for dinner. Johnnie was happy to do so, and Steve picked up lunch for Debra since they were together. Ann had taken the other truck and went on her own. She wanted time to sit and think. When they arrived, Tonya took Johnnie and the two of them went off to be alone while Steve sat with Debra and ate lunch with her.

"He's a good man Johnnie," Tonya said to him as they sat together holding hands.

"So I heard. I do like that he's a Christian and also a lawyer. My Mom needs a good man. Someone who understands how to take care of a lady like my father did."

"I believe Chris will. I really think that once you get to know him, you will really like him. He is a very nice man."

"Well, we will see how things go tonight."

"Just be calm tonight and let your guard down. I want you to be relaxed and just enjoy the night."

"I will Honey. I want him to get to know me as much as I want to get to know him. I need my mother to be happy again. She has been alone too long now. But she needs the right man and some of these guys who have approached her had wrong intentions. I can always tell when they come up to her what exactly they want and I will not let anyone use my mother for their own intentions. I know I have been overly protective but it's because of the kind of men that have been trying to talk to her. But if this guy is everything that you all say that he is, then I will be cool and give him a chance. But if he messes up like Mike did, he will end up like Mike."

"Johnnie he won't hurt her. I promise. He is a very good man."

After lunch they all got busy to finish the job they were on. Steve knew Johnnie and Tonya was meeting Sara and her knew man for dinner which meant they were getting out of work early. Steve had made plans with Debra as well.

It was going to be nice for Steve and Debra to have a date all by themselves for a change. Debra was very excited about it and wanted to go somewhere nice. Steve knew of a few places Johnnie had taken his sister Tonya to and thought he would surprise her with a nice romantic night out.

Johnnie was surprised he was unusually calm about this guy. Tonya seemed to have a lot of confidence that he was going to be good for Sara and Johnnie trusted Tonya's judgment. However, he still wanted to be a little skeptical so he could remain objective in examining Chris.

Johnnie was sure to make small talk with him to get a better feel about him. He could tell a lot about someone when he just talked to them. While making them feel comfortable, you're examining them without them being aware of it. *Chris was sure to know though since he was a lawyer. He probably had that happen a lot during negotiations In fact he is probably expecting me to do that. I'm sure Tonya and my mother will be watching me to make sure I behave as well. But I promised I will be good and I will. In fact that night everyone was going to be on their best behavior as Johnnie had promised.*

By the time Chris arrived, Johnnie and Tonya was already dressed up and looking presentable. Sara was just about done in the kitchen and everything was almost ready. Johnnie greeted him at the door and had welcomed him in.

"You must be Chris. Come on in. I am Johnnie and this is

my fiancé, Tonya."

"Very nice to meet you both. I have heard so much about the two of you from Sara. She loves to talk about you two. She gets so excited every time she brings your names up. She has told me so much about you that I feel like I already know you."

"Well come in and have a seat. I will let my mother know of your arrival." Johnnie went into the kitchen to make sure Sara was all set and to tell her that Chris was there.

"Everything smells so good Mom. Is there anything I can do to help you finish getting things ready?"

"No I am just waiting on the chicken to finish cooking. Just needs a few more minutes. Everything else is ready."

"Good because Chris is here and is waiting out in the living room."

"Oh dear. Please entertain him while the chicken finishes cooking."

"Sure thing Mom," Johnnie said as he walked back into the living room to talk with Chris.

"Won't be long now, just waiting on the chicken to finish baking is all."

"It smells wonderful," Chris said as he sat talking with Johnnie.

"My mother is a wonderful cook."

"Yes she is," Tonya added as she smiled at Johnnie. "You will love her cooking. She is so wonderful in the kitchen."

"Yes, my Mom is very wonderful."

"You two really sell her cooking, now I can't wait to try it. If it taste half as good as it smells then it will be delicious indeed."

There was a brief pause as they all sat quietly thinking of something else to say when finally Chris asked about their engagement.

"So you two are going to get married."

"Yes we are eventually. I just need to get a few things behind me first."

"Yes, but we are looking forward to it. Johnnie is the only man I have ever been with."

"That is really true for us both. I have never been with anyone but Tonya. She is my childhood sweetheart. We grew up together and fell in love."

"That is amazing. You don't hear about that kind of romance anymore. So the two of you have never dated anyone else?"

"Nope. I am the only man she has ever dated and she is the only woman I have ever dated."

"That's great."

As they were finishing up the conversation Sara had come in to get them as the food was now ready.

"Hello Chris," Sara said as she walked into the living room.

"Hello Sara. You look beautiful as always."

"Well thank you Hun."

"You're very welcome." Sara was wearing that dress she had bought a little bit ago.

"The food is already if you all want to come to the dining room." Sara smiled as she invited them to come with her.

"Lovely," Chris said as he got up and followed her.

Johnnie and Tonya waited for a minute and kissed each other before joining them.

"Everything looks so delicious and smells so wonderful."

"Well thank you Chris. I do hope you like it."

"I am sure I will. Johnnie and Tonya already have been talking your food up so wonderfully."

"Well they are biased."

"Your food is really good Mom."

"Yes Sara you're a wonderful cook. I just know Chris is going to enjoy it."

"Now you two stop embarrassing me and making me blush in front of our guest," Sara said as her face turned beat red.

But the truth was Sara was an amazing cook and everyone knew it. Mark used to brag about her cooking all the time to his coworkers and would invite them over every so often when they all had a Saturday off for a cookout. Everyone always complimented Sara on the food she made while Mark was grilling the meat out back. Sara would bake the moistest chocolate cake with creamy chocolate frosting, and chewy hot fresh chocolate chip cookies for the kids. She loved being a housewife and a mother. She missed having a good man to cook for. Mark always appreciated her hard work in the kitchen and often told her so.

Unlike Mike, who just complained about everything because he didn't care about anything or anybody. Mike never appreciated how wonderful Sara was. No matter the price it had cost Johnnie, he never regretted killing him. He knew how amazing his mother was and hated Mike even the more because of it. He would have shot Mike a thousand times more if he had the bullets.

Chris sat and talked with everyone at the table as he enjoyed his meal and the company. Johnnie liked the way he talked and felt pretty good about him. He watched the way Chris would look at his mother and he could tell he really did like her a lot. He would still keep a close eye on him though, and had already had Jason looking into his history and background. If there was something there, Jason would find it. He had ways of getting information that was impossible to retrieve.

After dinner the four of them all went out back to talk for a bit on the back patio. It was a nice summer night under the clear dark sky with bright shimmering stars that lit up the night. They were like a million small candles burning together with flickering flames that danced in unison. It was a quiet night and peaceful as they sat together and relaxed.

Times were changing, things were moving in a new direction. Life was always in a state of evolving motion. Nothing ever stayed the same if you wanted success. Life was always moving forward and growing in different areas. Johnnie knew he had to embrace what was happening and accept what was going on. Life was too short to let it get stale or miss opportunities and this was his mother's time to love again and he had to let it come. He had to welcome it.

She had given her life to make sure he made it and now it was her time to live again and enjoy life. The time had come for her and she needed to grab it and hold onto it with all she had.

Johnnie wanted nothing more but for them all to make it to where they needed to be, where they wanted to be. There had been enough setbacks and heartaches and with this war finally coming to an end, it was time for Johnnie to prepare for a new life. A life without death. A life without having to fight all the time. A life without killing just to be able to live.

Chris had a good time as he was able to finally talk to Johnnie. He knew that he was a young business man but Chris was still surprised at just how smart Johnnie was. It was getting late and the night was drawing to a close when Chris decided it was time to head out and go back home for the night. Everyone had to work the next day and Johnnie was getting tired as well. Chris had given Sara a good night kiss and then shook Johnnie's hand before leaving.

"Good night Honey," Chris said after he had kissed her.

"Good night Hun. I will call you tomorrow."

"That sounds good. Good night Johnnie and Tonya."

They both responded with a good night to him as Sara walked him out.

"I should probably go too Babe. Besides you're looking pretty tired."

"Yes I am. I will see you in the morning."

"Okay Babe," Tonya said as she kissed Johnnie good night.

Normally he would walk her home but he let her take the truck instead.

"Have Steve pick up Ann in the morning and I will ride with you," Johnnie said as he kissed her again before going on to bed to get some sleep.

The next day when Johnnie got up and was getting ready for work Tim Reid had called and asked if he could stop by before he left for work. Johnnie was curious as to why Tim wanted him to come down this early in the morning, but nevertheless he agreed to come over. After getting Tonya and her crew going he told her to go ahead and he would call her after he got done with his meeting with Tim.

Once he arrived Tim welcomed him in and offered him a cup of fresh coffee that he had just made.

"Thank you Tim, I would love some."

"You're welcome Johnnie."

"So what is it that you need to talk to me about?"

"I can't get closure with this Johnnie. I am having a hard time understanding all of this. Why did you have to go get revenge and drag them all into it?"

"Whoa, hold up Tim. First of all, I didn't drag anyone into anything. Second, this wasn't about revenge. I tried to tell you that the first time Tim."

"You all went to war with a gang. What were you thinking?"

"You still don't get it Tim. We'd been fighting this war with them since we were kids. The only difference now is that it's with guns instead of fists. You think this was all because of what happened to Tonya. Well you're wrong. This was about finally ending this once and for all between us and them. What happened to Tonya was just the last straw. That situation showed us that we were never going to be free from them. This didn't end when we was all done with school. It carried over and we knew if it was going to ever end we were going to have to be the ones to make it end. You think this war just started? These are the same kids we have been fighting all along. And just to clear all of this up, I gave all of them chances to get out of it, and no one would. They wanted to fight this war just as bad as I did. Randy was the only one that left it and I was relieved when he did. He died for that too. You can blame me if you want Tim, but George did what he wanted to do. I never pushed them into it or talked them into it. We all made our own choice about it. The only reason we did was because I was friends with a gang who was going to go to war with them anyways so we decided that now was the best time to do it while we had help."

"Are you telling me that you all joined a gang?"

"No Tim. I am saying we partnered with them so we could help each other eliminate a common problem."

"Johnnie listen. It's just hard for us to understand all of this. You all where such good kids and to find out that our son was killed in a gang war is very hard to wrap our heads around," Monica said as she finally spoke up.

"I understand. But you all knew of the problem we had with them all along. It just wasn't going to stop just because we were all out of school now."

"Okay. I get that Johnnie. Monica is right. It's just so hard to believe."

"I know and trust me this wasn't easy for me to tell you about either. This is not the way we wanted it to be, but it's our reality. We had to do something and this was our best option. I know it's hard for you both to accept, but that's just how it is Tim."

"Okay, Johnnie. I think we do understand a little. I am sorry if it seemed as if I was blaming you."

"I know it's all hard to swallow. You guys didn't just lose your sons. We lost brothers. We lost our best friends. We are all hurting and angry. You both know how much I loved George."

"Yes we do Johnnie," Monica said as she hugged him.

"Thanks for coming by to talk to us again. We love you Johnnie."

"I love you both as well, and any time you need to talk I will be happy to do so. But for now I need to get going. I will stay in touch and will see you both soon."

They both hugged Johnnie again before he left to go have a meeting with Jason. Once Johnnie was back home he called Jason immediately to come over and talk. As he waited for him to come, Johnnie went out back by the pool to relax. When Jason had finally arrived Johnnie was half asleep by the pool which surprised Jason who expected him to be sitting at the back patio where he usually was.

"Is it a pool party my Brother."

"I wish. Come have a seat Bro."

"What's going on?" Jason asked as he walked over and sat in the chair next to Johnnie.

"I wanted to talk to you about this war."

"Yeah, okay. What's up Johnnie?" "Where are we at with the Hells Sinners?"

"Okay. Listen. Sisko was murdered a few nights ago right after I had talked to him. The whole gang is scattered with no direction and now Wayne has been thrown into the leadership position and no meeting place, no club house and no direction. Everything will unravel now."

"We need to keep the pressure on them until they are gone."

"Yeah I agree but now you will have to hunt them down since they have no place to hold up at. Wayne came to me trying to get me to help them but I played as if I didn't know what to do."

"Wayne is going to die."

"Get this Johnnie. Four of the Hells Sinners tried to join the West Dragons the other night after they had found out Sisko had been murdered."

"What happened?"

"Well Ricky told them that they had to go through an initiation to join the club and told them to come back that night. So when they come back they had it all set up and put them in a van and drove them back into woods at the old park. Once they was all out of the van they told them to walk across the bridge. Once they go to the other side there was men waiting for them with guns and shot all four of them. It was a death sentence."

"Well that's four more that I don't have to worry about isn't it?"

"Oh yeah. I told you Bro this war is coming to an end. I suspect that the rest will run soon."

"Where do you think they will go?"

"I don't know. Some will go to another state and try to join up with another gang while some will go into hiding for a while until things settle down."

"I want Wayne dead."

"Trust me I got this. He won't get away. I am already working on something to keep him here so that you can have him."

"Good. Make sure he never leaves. I want him."

"He thinks I am trying to help him. He actually calls me constantly now. This guy has no clue what to do Johnnie. I feel that he is starting to panic. So anyways, how are you holding up?"

"Everything is crazy Bro. I feel like things are moving so fast I can't get a grip on everything. The thing with George happened so fast I didn't even get a chance to do anything. I mean, I had just found out he was having real problems with this war and was getting high and drinking all the time and I didn't even know it. By the time I found out he was deep in it and then we got into a huge fight and the next thing I know he was gone. It all happened so fast Jason. The business is blowing up but I had to sell the Lawn Care division because my leaders kept getting killed and I wasn't going to replace anyone else do to being murdered. It's just too much. Then I had to meet with George, Randy and Darrell's parents. They needed to know the truth so I had to explain from the beginning all the way up to their deaths. That was extremely hard. Then today I just came from George's parents from another meeting where they tried to put the blame on me so I had to explain it all over again. I feel like everything is in chaos and I am right in the middle of it all. Everything is just spinning like a whirlwind."

"Wow I knew things were a little difficult but I didn't know it was like that."

"I'm exhausted Bro. I need this war to end. Tonya won't marry me until it's finished."

"Well hopefully the news today set you more at ease."

"Yes it did Jason. I needed to hear this. I needed to know that it's almost done for real."

"Once I get the rabbit in the trap I will call you to come get it."

"That sounds good. It ends with him."

"The West Dragons are hunting down the rest but I will

make sure Wayne doesn't die until I set it up for you."

"Good. That one is mine. I want to be the one to take his life."

"I will see to it that's how it happens. I got a plan already set up. Just waiting for the right moment is all."

"Alright."

"Okay Johnnie. I'm out. I got to make money and keep Pauli happy."

"Okay. Thanks for coming over."

"No problem Brother, now let's get to the business of this guy you asked me about Christopher Peters."

"Yes, what did you find out about him?"

"Well he does seem to run a legit law firm. There is nothing shady in his background. In fact to my surprise he came up pretty clean. However some of his first cases came through Pauli."

"What does that mean?"

"Well, there is no cause for alarm. The cases where pretty minor and Pauli uses new lawyers from time to time on simple cases that are meaningless. It's his way of keeping this more secured. He didn't like his top lawyers knowing more than they have to. Mainly just contract stuff. No big deal."

"So he checked out then."

"Yes he did. His cases are all business deals mostly. There's no investigations going on about him or anything, no red flags or anything of any concern. The guy's legit."

"Thanks Jason. That's good news."

"We are all settled then. Let me know if there is anything else that I can do for you."

"I will Bro. Thanks."

After Jason left, Johnnie sat for a while and tried to refocus. With Sisko dead and Wayne in control, things were about to fall apart for sure. He was no leader and wouldn't know what to do if things were good. But with everything being in a mess for the Hells Sinners, Wayne was for sure going to fail and the Hells Sinners were finally about to fall. Their numbers were dwindling fast with no place to hide out. They were doing everything they could to hustle up money but was leaving themselves exposed. Every time the Hells Sinners was on a corner trying to sell dope the West Dragons would shoot them up. The West Dragons were already taking over the territory and had scouts roaming the streets looking for Hells Sinners in their new territory trying to make money.

 Jason was right they did kill the four Hells Sinners who tried to join with them but they also had killed three more earlier that day they caught standing on their corner. There was only a handful left and they were all scattered.

CHAPTER 15

AND SO COMES THE END

    As the end drew near for the Hells Sinners, they were now running for their lives. They were being hunted like prey by a hungry pack of wolves who were on the move to pick them off one by one, and no one was safe. The West Dragons showed no mercy as they hunted them down until there was only a handful left. Wayne was now in a state of panic as he had nowhere to turn to except for Jason who secretly had a plan for him.
    The police began to question members of the West Dragon about who Cypher was. The name was now being talked very heavily on the streets but not many knew who he was. Viper had been picked up for some questioning on other crimes when they began to question him during the interrogation. He acted as if he had no clue as to who they were talking about and gave them no information whatsoever about anything that they had asked him. They finally had to let him go with no real evidence to hold him on.
    He knew they would be watching him so he made a drop by where he knew Cypher was working to appear to be asking him about some work he might need done. While they were talking he made him aware of the questioning so he would be more cautious.

"This war is almost over, there is no need to get caught now."

"I appreciate that Viper. Good looking out. At least I can trust you."

"Yeah, well I better go. They are watching me to see if I contact Cypher. Hand me a business card before I go to make this conversation more legit." As Cypher handed Viper his business card he pointed at it as if talking to him about it.

"I will see you soon man."

"Okay Cypher, take care my friend." Cypher went back to work while Viper was leaving when an undercover police car pulled up and two officers got out and walked over to him.

"Excuse me, we would like to ask you a few questions."

"Well, okay. What can I do for you?"

"Do you know that man that just left?"

"No not really. Is there something wrong?"

"He is one of the gang leaders in a war that is going on. What did he want to talk to you about?"

"Well, I have been building a good reputation for doing repairs on houses and things like that, so he stopped to see me and get my business card."

"What's your name?"

"My name is Jonathon."

"Have you ever heard of someone named Cypher?"

"No, I can't say that I have. Is he also part of that gang?"

"We will ask the questions."

"Hey man there is no reason to get rude with me. You're on my job asking me question so I have the right to know why."

"You have something to hide?"

"I have work to do, that's what I have. I was willing to cooperate with you in answering whatever questions you have but if that's how you're going to talk to me then I have nothing further to say to you."

"We will be in touch with you."

"Don't waste your time." Johnnie went back to work after

the cops left. He knew they had nothing to go on as he blew off their conversation.

I don't understand why they feel like they need to be rude while they expect us to cooperate with them. If they had any common sense they would treat citizens better and maybe get more answers. Not like I was going to tell them anything anyways.

He refocused his attention on his work. He knew he was born for something greater then fighting gang wars and arguing with police who had no clue as to what was really going on. His life had meaning and purpose and this war wasn't it. He was made for greater things and he knew it. His business wasn't what it should be because of the time spent away fighting a war he was never meant to fight. Once this was all over things were going to change. He should be planning a wedding with Tonya and instead he is trying to end a war that he was stuck in.

No matter what he had been through or was going through he knew that somehow God had a greater plan for his life. He tried to ignore it and put it off until this war was finished but he felt something in him that was pushing him to a greater light in this darkness. He could feel it tugging at him, pulling at him. There was something constantly speaking to him to come up to a new level of life that he had not tasted of yet. Something more powerful, something more real. No matter how hard he tried to ignore it the louder it seemed to speak to him. He knew what Tonya had was real, he could see it, but he also could feel it, and it was reaching out to him as well. God had healed her and restored her life so she could live again. There was a newness about her. She was different, even different than before. That rough girl had been softened by Gods love. Somehow He had touched her in a way that changed her life and retransformed her into this wonderful woman that was more loving, caring and understanding. She was smarter, somehow she was a lot smarter. Whatever God had done to her, it was real. It was honest and it was pure, and Johnnie loved her more now than he ever did.

When this is all over with he wanted to pursue what she had. All of this turmoil and hatred was destroying him from the inside out. He knew he wasn't the man he used to be and desperately wanted to find himself again. He knew Tonya deserved better from him and he needed to give her the very best that he could offer her and this wasn't it. He was better than this and he knew it. His hatred and anger had driven him beyond what he had ever expected and it was time to regain himself before it was too late.

Having the police come and talk to him really made him think about some things and what was really important to him. He knew what he wanted but he wasn't about to let Wayne mess things up any more for him. He didn't care about the last few members of the Hells Sinners because he knew the West Dragons would finish them off, but he needed to be there for the death of Wayne. He needed to see this end once and for all. He was the last one as far as Johnnie was concerned. It all ended with Wayne. Once things were settled with Wayne then Johnnie could finally be done with this and get on with his life once and for all. One more killing, one more death and freedom was in his sights. It was time for some real change but this had to come first.

Tonya had longed for this moment when Johnnie would finally be free from this revenge and this hate that he pursued beyond all cost. It was time to relax for a bit and just wait for the call to come from Jason so that he could go and finish this. Everything now was focused on work and relationships. He didn't tell Tonya because he didn't want her to get her hopes up, just in case things didn't go as planned. But as soon as it was over, she would be the first to know. His marriage was hanging on the end of this war and he was tired of waiting to be Tonya's husband.

While Johnnie was waiting for Jason to deliver the goods, he was going to plan something special for him and Tonya for the weekend. He wanted to surprise her with a trip out of town. There were a few places he was going to look up online when he got home from work. To his surprise when he finally got home there was a message for him to call Chris.

"What's this about Mom?"

"Give him a call Johnnie he wants to ask you something."

"Yeah, okay."

After calling Chris, Johnnie's plans for taking Tonya out of town would have to wait for another week. Chris wanted to take Johnnie fishing and he thought he should probably go so that way he could get a better feel for Chris. They hadn't had any real time together since the dinner date and he wanted to get to know more about him and this would be the perfect opportunity to do so. He knew Chris was trying to do the same and since he was making an effort, Johnnie thought he should as well. After all the guy really did seem nice. This would give Johnnie a good chance to ask some questions or at least get a good idea of what kind of character he was. He knew right away there was something not right about Mike so Chris would be under the microscope for a bit until Johnnie could tell whether he was really what he appeared to be. Plus he knew it would make his mom happy if he went along with it.

Johnnie had been fishing many times and found it to be calming. It was always nice to be able to do something relaxing especially since how hectic his life had been. It was a good thing he hadn't mentioned anything to Tonya about going away for the weekend. With this war pretty much at the end, Johnnie would be able to relax a little more anyways and this would be a good time to just chill and refresh his battery a bit. All of this fighting and working had pushed him to his limit and he was ready for a bit of relaxing down time.

Sara was happy Johnnie had accepted the invitation from Chris. It had meant a lot to her that he was making a real effort to get to know him. Johnnie was happy to see Friday come. The weather was nice and sunny and work was almost done. Everyone was itching to get the weekend started as Johnnie cut them all lose early as usual. Normally he would take Tonya out and spend the night talking at the back patio, but he had an early morning as he was going fishing on Saturday with Chris. Johnnie had been fishing a lot but it was always at the pond that was a part of the camp. But never got up early to go like they were going to do. This was going to be a new experience for him, and he was kind of excited about getting up early and going to the lake for some morning fishing.

Sara was excited as well that he had agreed to go with Chris. This was an important morning for her and them. She needed this to be a bonding time for the two of them, and Chris wanted to have a relationship with Johnnie and was eager to pick him up in the morning. As Chris was getting everything set for them, Johnnie was taking Tonya to dinner and then was going to drop her off at home so he could go home and get his stuff ready as well.

While Johnnie was gone Sara had went out and bought him a brand new fishing pole as a surprise. She had it gift wrapped for him to make it more special. When Johnnie finally got home he found Sara sitting on the couch waiting for him.

"Hey Mom, what are you still doing up?"

"I was waiting for you."

"What's wrong?"

"Nothing, come here and sit down for a minute. I want to give you something."

"Give me something?"

"Yes I got you a gift," Sara said as she handed Johnnie his present.

"What is this?"

"Open it Johnnie and find out." Johnnie was excited as he took the gift and unwrapped it.

"Oh wow a new fishing pole! This is nice Mom, I love it. Thank you."

"You're welcome Johnnie. I wanted to give you something to show you how much I appreciate you making time to spend with Chris. Really Johnnie. Thank You."

"Awe Mom. It's okay. I really think he is a nice guy and everyone really seems to like him a lot. Plus you seem very happy with him."

"Oh Johnnie he is so good to me. I have enjoyed being with him so much. He makes me feel alive again."

"That's good Mom. I am happy for you. He seems pretty clean for being a Lawyer."

"What do you mean Johnnie?"

"I mean his record is pretty spotless as far as corruption goes."

"How do you know about his record?"

"I know people that can find out anything. So I had a friend do some digging."

"Yeah and what did you find?"

"Well that's just it. They didn't find anything. The guy is clean as soap."

"So you trust him now?"

"About as much as I trust anyone that I don't really know."

"Well, it's a start anyways. I am heading to bed Johnnie. You two be careful tomorrow."

"We will. Good night Mom. I am off to bed as well. He will be here pretty early."

Sara felt more at ease now knowing Johnnie couldn't find anything wrong with Chris as they both headed to bed to get some sleep. Johnnie also felt relieved that Chris checked out with nothing in his background that was questionable.

It was early morning and the sun hadn't fully risen as of yet when Johnnie was awakened by his alarm clock. *Why did I agree to this?* He sat up on the edge of his bed and tried to gain his focus as his eyes would barely open. Reaching over he turned off the annoying alarm clock that was still buzzing. After standing up, he had a good long stretch before grabbing his clothes, getting dressed and then went into the bathroom to freshen himself up a bit before heading downstairs to make some much needed coffee.

Johnnie was feeling a bit more with it after having splashed some cold water on his face. *People really do this.* He sat down at the table for a moment. While he was waiting for the coffee to finish brewing, Johnnie went over in his head a checklist to make sure he had everything ready. He didn't want to forget anything and was eager to make sure he was more than ready as he didn't want anything to go wrong this morning. This was a very important outing for him and Chris. He wanted everything to be perfect. He didn't quite know what to expect but he wanted to be as prepared as possible to help keep things from going wrong. Johnnie was going to go without a hat but then decided it would be best if he took one anyways, just in case. He didn't much care for wearing hats but he did have some made up with his business logo on it for the painting team that he had made for them. The girls loved them and wore them every day to keep their hair up and out of the way as they worked. That had been Tonya's idea and Johnnie thought it would also serve to promote his company as well.

   Today it was just to keep the sun out of his face as he fished. After the coffee was finally ready, Johnnie poured himself a cup and went to get his stuff together while it cooled off a bit before he sat back down to drink it. He had his new fishing pole and an old tackle box that he used. He was thinking about replacing it if this was going to become a regular thing between him and Chris. Which he was kind of hoping it would if everything went okay. He did love to fish and had never been out to the lake and was very anxious to give it a try.

   He imagined that it would be much different then fishing back at the pond that he was used to. Chris had a boat and everything for them to use which was quite different for Johnnie who had never fished from a boat before. He was almost finished with his coffee when Chris pulled into the driveway to pick him up. Taking one more, big, gulp of his coffee, Johnnie headed out with his stuff to meet Chris and load up so they could get going. Johnnie pulled out a cooler the night before so they could take some water with them so that they would have something to drink when they got thirsty.

"What's in the cooler?" Chris had asked.

"Just water. But when we stop at the gas station to fill up, I will buy some ice to keep it cold."

"That's good thinking Johnnie."

"I am looking forward to this fishing time with you Chris. I have never fished off of a lake especially from a boat," Johnnie said with a sense of excitement.

"Never?"

"No never. I have fished our pond back in the woods, which is pretty huge but never fished off of a lake and this will also be my first boating experience while fishing."

"Have you ever been on a boat before Johnnie?"

"Yes, just never fished from a boat is all."

When they finally reached the gas station Johnnie went in to pay for the gas since he had to go in and get some ice anyways. While in the gas station Johnnie decided to also pick up some snacks just in case they got a little hungry while fishing. Johnnie grabbed a few snack cakes as well as some small bags of chips. While walking past the coolers on his way to the counter, he saw some fresh sandwiches so he grabbed a couple of them as well.

After paying for everything, Johnnie filled up the cooler with the ice and food while Chris finished filling up the gas tank. While they were finishing up, Johnnie told Chris he had went ahead and got them some chips and sandwiches just in case they got hungry later. After getting the cooler filled up they went back into the gas station to get a fresh coffee and some donuts for breakfast as they ate on the way to the lake to save some time. Johnnie was always prepared no matter what he did and this was no exception. He had more than enough water and food to last them for the trip.

"This is going to be such a good time Johnnie. I have been looking forward to spending some time with just you. We need to really get to know each other and this is a great way to do it."

"Yeah, I agree. I was looking forward to it as well."

Once they arrived at the boat docks off of Sheppard's Lake where Chris had reserved a pontoon and had it waiting for them. Sheppard's Lake was a massive lake that was well known for its lake perch.

"Have you ever been out on a pontoon Johnnie?"

"Can't say that I have Chris. This is all new to me."

"You will like it. You can comfortably fish off of every side in a comfortable chair. Plus you can walk around and stretch your legs when you need to."

"That sounds good."

"I'll be right back. I just need to go check in and get the keys."

"No problem. While you're doing that I will get things loaded onto the pontoon."

"That's sounds good."

Johnnie was surprised at the size of the pontoon they were going out on. He had expected a small boat but this was nice. It had a top on it to keep the sun off of them as they fished. After Chris finished getting everything situated at the office, he joined Johnnie and was ready to go.

"This is pretty nice, Chris."

"Thanks, relax and enjoy the ride for a bit while I take us to a good spot to fish."

Johnnie loved the swiveled chairs. They were very comfortable while convenient as well.

Chris was looking forward to talking to Johnnie. Once they got out around the bend Chris began to slow down and troll for a bit.

"There is a nice fishing spot up here Johnnie, I usually do pretty good here."

"Very cool." Johnnie was getting both of their poles ready as Chris was positioning them in a good spot to catch some fish.

"This should do it Johnnie, this is my spot."

"Good deal. I have your pole all set up for you. Let's relax and catch some fish."

"Now that sounds like a plan. Work has been so busy that relaxing sounds like just what I need to be doing."

"Yeah same here. I definitely need to recharge my battery and come back a little more refreshed myself."

"So your Mother told me that you own a few businesses."

"Yes I do. I own a repair business where we go to homes and fix things inside and outside, and I also own a Painting Business as well."

"That's great. You're very young and already making it happen. Not many people your age are that focused in life to do what you're doing."

"I suppose so. So what kind of lawyer are you?" Johnnie asked as if he didn't already know.

"I am a business lawyer. I help my clients to make good deals. I go over every contract and make sure they are getting fair deals that will benefit them and also help to keep them from getting ripped off. Contracts can be very tricky, especially if the other party is shady and trying to get more then what they deserve."

"How often does that happen?"

"Way too often. American business has lost its integrity. Everyone is selfish now days and lies are way too easy to tell. When my father was a business lawyer, people where more honest. But now it seems as if everyone is shady and tries to get over on each other. Greed has destroyed American businesses. They don't care about people any more. All they care about is making more money and will screw people over fast to get it too."

"That sounds about right. I believe in treating people fair and paying good wages for the work they do for me. As well as being good to my clients and giving them honest work for honest wages, like it's supposed to be."

"Yeah that's rare these days Johnnie. It's refreshing to see someone like you so young and honest. Not many people do it right anymore. I hope you never change. We need more honest business men in this country."

"Yeah I agree. I have been blessed to have good people with me that are honest and work hard. So I make sure that I take very good care of them. I don't want to lose any of my workers, they are awesome."

"What do you think is the biggest problem with American businesses other than the obvious greed problem?"

"Well it all stems from the greed problem. That's why there is no longer any integrity in American business. It's like this Johnnie. A company used to have to tell the truth in their commercial or you could sue them. So what they did was, they came up with the marketing scheme. Now marketing has replaced integrity. Now a company can lie to you and say, well its marketing. Greed has killed integrity. Remember when the customer was always right? Now companies no longer care about the customer, they only care about the customer's money."

"Yeah, I noticed that myself. I value our customers or clients. They are what makes our business. Without them we have nothing."

"Exactly, but see these businesses say they value their customers, but do they really? Or do they just value their customer's money?"

"That's a good point. We all work for money, but you can't put money over people."

"Exactly Johnnie. But America has done just that. Families have been destroyed by big businesses taking their jobs and giving them to foreign countries. Families here have lost their homes and it ruined their marriages, just so that American businesses can make more money, even though the owners are billionaires and will never go broke. They tell you to buy American so we have American jobs, while the whole time they sold out American families. Have you ever heard of Flint, Michigan?"

"No I haven't."

"That's a good example of how big businesses valued money over people. That city at one time was booming and making good money, now it is impoverished and you can't drink the water there. Those people are lucky if they have a job now making anything over minimum wage, and the water is so toxic you can't cook with or drink it. They live everyday like a third world country while the government continues to screw them. They have to buy water to drink and cook with, even to wash themselves with. The Governor should be in jail. He knew about it and ignored it while the kids were drinking contaminated lead poisoned water and now have brain damage. That's no different than a leader of a nation using chemical warfare on its own people. We hold other countries accountable for it but don't do anything about our government officials allowing Americans to unknowingly drink poisoned water and not telling them. That's how corrupted our government and big businesses have become. They don't care about the people, it's all about the money."

"I will never become like that. People have to come first. There's no humanity in that if it's any other way. If a man values currency over human life, then his own character is perverted and is garbage. They are no different than Hitler. Kill for gain. Kill for power. Those are not real leaders at all. Real leaders seek to help other humans grow and become successful, not destroy them for their own gain or power. That is false leadership, and needs to be removed from office and replaced with men and women who will serve the people right. I see what you're saying about integrity, because these politicians are liars who never do what they say they are going to do. They lie to the people for their own gain."

"Right. America needs a real revolution, but it has to come from outside the system for it to work. Real change comes from people who are willing to do it right. Who honestly care about people and want to make a difference in the lives of others. It never comes from greedy liars who only take advantage of others. America needs to rise up and hold their officials accountable for the lies they tell and impeach them for not holding up their end of the deal. We elect them based on what they said and if they don't do it then they need to be fired and replaced with someone who will do what they promised."

"I agree. We the people have to stand up for ourselves because no one is going to do it for us. We have to take responsibility and fight for what's right. We can no longer count on anyone being our voice. We have to speak up and stand together. If someone is being wronged, we need to intervene, stand up with them and fight together against what's wrong."

"So many people count on our government when they should be trying to become successful."

"Some people will never get out of the system, and it's the system that holds them back."

"It's a trap if you're not careful. Some people get stuck and never get off of assistance."

"Yes, and it's not always their fault either. You can get stuck in situations and never climb out of it. This is why people who are on assistance need to be given opportunities."

"That's not a bad idea. Every person that goes from living off of the system to being providers for themselves makes this country stronger and more successful."

"People have potential they just lack opportunities. Not everyone wants to depend on the government. People want better lives, they just need a way out."

"I feel if we can get back to communities instead of neighborhoods then the people will help each other again and care about each other again and stop feeding off of all the negativity and become more positive. People who help others have a better chance at having an opportunity then those who don't contribute anything."

"Everything that is destructive, destroys. Like for example. Racism is a destructive attitude that only breeds hatred and does nothing positive in any way shape or form. Racism will never bring people together. It only divides the people and keeps us all from working together to help us all make it."

"Right, that makes sense. Hey I got a bite! Oh man this feels like a big one!"

"Should I grab a net and help you?"

"Yeah maybe, I am not sure just how big it is, but it's got some fight in it."

"Wait, I got a hit also. Are you going to be okay over there while I try to bring this one in?"

"Yeah I got this, just need to wear him out a little is all."

"If we catch enough fish Johnnie we can have a fish fry and invite the neighbors that you and Sara are close with. I have been looking forward to meeting everyone anyways."

"Yeah that sounds good, but first we have to get the fish in." As both was having a good time catching their fish, Johnnie was excited about them both catching one at the same time. Both had caught a couple of nice size catfish and was hoping to get some more.

"This is fun Johnnie. I haven't been out fishing like this in a while, and your pretty good company. We seem to understand each other and have some of the same ideas."

"I'm a real person you know. I don't do any of that fake crap. What you see is what you get with me. I can't stand fake people and I believe in being as honest as possible. That way people know where they stand with me."

"That's the way to be Johnnie. Too many people waste so much of their lives and time being fake that they miss so many opportunities. Always trying to be something that they aren't instead of embracing themselves and living a successful life. Funny enough, these are usually the ones who are so jealous of what other people are accomplishing and their success when they could have been working on their own success."

"Jealousy is always going to hold you back. Why spend all your time focusing on what someone else is doing when you could be doing your own thing and making your life so much better? I truly believe Chris that if everyone put all of that wasted energy into their own lives they could accomplish so much more and then they wouldn't need to be jealous of anyone else."

"You're pretty smart Johnnie for your age. You have a good mind."

"Thanks Chris, I appreciate that." The morning passed by rather quickly with all the talking they had done. They began to get hungry.

"I think I am about ready to take a break and eat some of the food that I brought. Are you hungry Chris?"

"Yes I am getting hungry as well. Let's take a break and

relax while we eat. Been a pretty good morning. We both caught a couple fish, might catch a few more before we go."

"Yeah I hope we do Chris. I liked the idea of having a fish fry and inviting everyone over. You will like the friends we have in the community, they are good people. Very solid."

"I can't wait. Sara talks so much about everyone. She has a lot of strong relationships with the people on your block."

"Well most of us are very close and all have been there for some time. We all know each other. But you have met them all I think at Church. I believe I am the only one that doesn't go as of yet, but I will be soon."

"That's great Johnnie. I have met everyone but I am still fairly new there and haven't gotten to really know any of them that well except for Sara. This will be a good opportunity for me to be able to sit and talk with them and get to know them on a personal level," Chris said as he took a bite of his sandwich.

"It was a good idea getting these sandwiches and chips. I honestly didn't expect us to be out this long, but I have to admit I am having a very good time."

They ate together while they took a break from fishing. After lunch, they fished for a few more hours until they felt they caught enough fish to have their fish fry. By the time they came back to the dock and loaded everything else back up, another hour had gone by and they were ready to get back home and get cleaned up.

Johnnie and Chris talked all the way back home. Johnnie was taking a real liking to Chris and felt very comfortable with him. He was happy his mother was happy and found a really nice guy to be with. Once they got back home, they unloaded Johnnie's gear. Chris came in to say hi to Sara before heading home to get cleaned up.

"Are you coming back over Honey?"

"I can if you want me to, but I desperately am in need of a nice long shower first."

"We can watch a movie together when you get back then."

"Okay Babe. Let me go get cleaned up then, so we can spend some time together," Chris said as he kissed Sara before heading home for a bit.

Johnnie set everything up for Sara to clean the fish and get it all prepared, after which he stocked the freezer with the fresh fish they caught for the fish fry that they were going to have the next day. Sara was excited to have a cookout again. It had been a long time since they had any real company like that.

After Johnnie got cleaned up he went out back and made sure the pool was clean for tomorrow's get together while Sara took time to call everyone to come over the next day and work out who was going to bring what. Everyone was excited Sara was having a get together and they would be able to better get to know Chris. They all liked him already but this was the first time they were going to all spend time with him outside of Church.

Once everything was all set for the next day's fish fry, Johnnie met up with Tonya and they went out to see a movie and then dinner together. Sara spent the rest of the evening with Chris as they watched a movie also and had a nice quiet dinner as well. As the night came to a close Johnnie was tired from waking up so early and was ready to call it a night.

The next day as Johnnie woke up and made some coffee. He sat and had some breakfast with his mom and talked for a bit before he went out back and started getting everything ready for the get together. When Tonya came over, they relaxed together before everyone came over.

Chris couldn't wait to have some fellowship time with his Church family. He had been looking forward to finally being able to really get to know everyone. It was mid-morning when he came over to see if Johnnie needed any help getting things together but found everything already done and ready to go.

This was different for Johnnie and Sara, they had cookouts before, but this was the first time they would be cooking fresh fish for everyone Johnnie just caught. Chris used to do it when he was married before but hadn't done it since the untimely death of his wife and was looking forward to maybe starting this with Sara as it would be new to her. Sara was always a wonderful hostess and loved entertaining guest and cooking for everyone. It had been a long time though since she had done such. It brought back great memories when she looked out the window and saw Chris and Johnnie at the grill together. She hadn't seen that since the death of Mark who used to grill while Sara was busy in the kitchen with the other ladies and Johnnie and the group was off playing until lunch time. The whole scene was a bit overwhelming for her, until she gathered herself together just before their guest started arriving. Sara was just pulling a cake out of the oven while the rest of the ladies were bringing in the side dishes they made while the rest of the men gathered together out back with Johnnie and Chris.

It was a bit of an emotional time for everyone. There hadn't been a cookout since the death of the Two Brothers and George. The men avoided talking about it while the ladies sat together crying while talking about how much they missed them. Steve was out back with Johnnie. Nate and Timothy were out of town for a few days camping for the weekend. Tony, Thomas and Tim were there hanging out with Chris, talking to him while Steve and Johnnie was talking amongst themselves.

Finally as the fish was ready to come off of the grill, the ladies all came out with the dishes they prepared and put them on the food table. Thomas gathered everyone together to say a blessing prayer over the food as well as a thanksgiving prayer for the food and for the fellowship time. After which they all made their plates. They sat together out on the back patio and talked while enjoy all of the good food that was there. Everyone had a great time and they all stayed until late evening talking and having fun.

While they were talking, Johnnie was pulled away with a phone call. After everyone left, he pulled Steve aside to discuss the phone call.

"I have good news for you. The Hells Sinners have fallen and Wayne is being held by Jason. Tomorrow I am going to go and finish this war. Keep this between us. I don't want Tonya to know until it is finally over."

"No problem Johnnie. I am just glad that this mess is finally done. Let's celebrate when this is finished."

"Sounds good to me Bro. We can take the girls out and celebrate this victory," Johnnie said as he hugged Steve.

After a wonderful evening, Johnnie and Steve spent time with the girls out back while Sara and Chris relaxed together on the couch. Tonya and Debra couldn't help but notice there was something unusually different about Johnnie and Steve as they both seemed more hyped and full of excitement. They wouldn't tell them the good news because Johnnie didn't want them to get their hopes up and then something go wrong. He wanted to wait until it was final. The rest of the night they relaxed as Johnnie was holding Tonya while Steve was holding Debra.

"This is how it's supposed to be Brother," Johnnie said to Steve.

"That it is my Brother. That it is." Tonya snuggled into Johnnie as he held her in his arms all night while Debra was enjoying having Steve's arms around her as well.

The next day Johnnie was still tired from a long day and an even longer night as he got himself together and called Jason to let him know he was on his way to take care of Wayne once and for all. Wayne had nowhere to go and had asked Jason for his help who had sheltered him at the old warehouse, where he normally did the collections for Pauli also. The tribute from the gangs he collected so they could sell drugs and prostitute women on Pauli's streets.

Wayne had no idea Jason was really just holding him there for Cypher. Jason made sure that he had arrived before Cypher did. He was inside with Wayne talking while waiting for Cypher to finally arrive. He also had another surprise for Cypher as well. When Cypher finally showed up, Jason told Wayne to wait there where they were sitting as he went to see who was at the door pretending not to know.

"Hey come on in. I have your package for you, follow me."

By the sound of the way Jason was talking, Wayne had assumed it was a business deal going on until he saw Jason turn the corner with Cypher.

"What's going on? What is this?" Wayne said excitedly as he stood up.

"You didn't really think after everything you had done to my brother that I was going to actually help you out did you?"

"It's time to pay the piper Wayne. I've been waiting a long time for this moment," Cypher said as he walked over to Wayne.

Cypher took out his gun and placed it on the table before hitting Wayne as the two began to fight while Jason stood back watching. Johnnie was beating Wayne severely when Wayne pulled out a knife and was about to stick Cypher with it before Jason pointed his gun at him.

"I don't think so Wayne, drop the knife or I will shoot you myself."

Wayne dropped the knife, knowing Jason would kill him if he hadn't. As the knife hit the floor Cypher grabbed Wayne and continued beating him until he was bleeding profusely. He let him go when he knew Wayne was in no shape to try to run. He walked over and picked up his gun off of the table and stood over Wayne pointing the gun down at him.

"Any last words before you die?"

"Johnnie, please, please don't kill me. You won okay? You can let me go and you will never have any more trouble from me again."

"I won't have any more trouble from you again either way. You're like a plague Wayne. You know how they eliminate plagues? They have to completely wipe it out. I have waited years for the day I would be rid of you once and for all. You can beg for your life though if you want. I will give you time to beg for your life, like Tonya begged for you all to stop."

"Johnnie I am sorry. I promise if you let me live, you will never see me again. I promise man, come on."

"See Wayne you're not offering me anything that I won't have already when you're dead. Say goodbye you worthless piece of garbage."

Wayne laid there begging for his life as Cypher unloaded his clip into him until Wayne was no longer breathing.

"Now it's finished," Cypher said as he dropped the gun and turned to Jason.

"It's not over yet Johnnie. We have one more thing we need to settle. Follow me," Jason said as he turned and lead Cypher outside where Ricky and Viper was waiting for them.

"We heard shots fired," Ricky inquired.

"That's of no concern to you Ricky. But I do have a bone to pick with you about the death of Randy and Darrell," Jason said to him.

"What do you mean? You know it was the Hells Sinners."

"Is that true Viper? What do you have to say about it trigger man," Cypher said as he stared at Viper who he had considered his friend.

"No it isn't true. I told Ricky that this wasn't right, but he ordered the hit on Randy anyways. I knew this wasn't right Cypher and I am sorry for it. I had no choice. It was Ricky's order and I had to follow it out."

"Shut up Viper. You snitch, you rotten snitch. Listen Cypher he is lying, I didn't do it," Ricky said.
Cypher stood shaking his head at Ricky while Jason began to speak again.

"We have known for a while that you did this Ricky. You're second in command Viper?"

"Yes Jason I am."

"Now you're in charge," Jason said as he shot Ricky several times as they all watched him fall down to the ground.

"What do you want me to do with Viper?" Jason asked

Cypher.

"I think there has been enough killing for one morning. You looked out for me Viper, now I return the favor. But I don't want to see you ever again."

"I understand Cypher. I really am sorry."

"We are done here Jason?"

"Yeah, we're good Brother. You can go while I have a talk with Viper about the deal I had with Ricky that will now carry over to him."

"Sounds good. Now I'm going to go home to start a new chapter in my life."

"Sounds good Brother. I will talk to you soon."

Cypher didn't go right home. Instead he went to see Tonya.

When Johnnie pulled up, Tonya was already outside and was just about to get in the truck to come see him as she was ready to get the work day started.

"Johnnie? I was just coming down to get a few things."

"Don't worry about that right now. We need to talk."

"Is everything okay Johnnie?"

"Everything is perfect. Tonya, Wayne is dead and the war is finally over. The Hells Sinners no longer exist."

"Oh Johnnie are you serious? It's finally over?"

"Yes it is Honey," Johnnie responded as he got down on one knee and pulled out a diamond ring that he been saving for this moment that he had previously tried to give her but she made him wait until this war was over. He had put it in his pocket before going to meet up with Jason.

"Tonya My Love, now will you marry me?"

"Yes! Yes, Johnnie! I will marry you."

Johnnie leaped up and grabbed Tonya. He hugged her as he held her so tight in his arms while tears ran down her face.

"I have waited for this moment Johnnie."

"I have too, Baby."

"Wait before we go any further, does this mean you will come to Church now?"

"Yes Baby I will. I am ready now."

Tonya took Johnnie's hand and led him in the house to share the good news with everyone. Steve was so excited Johnnie was going to officially be his brother-in-law.

Tony and Tammy couldn't believe this was finally happening after such a long wait. After they had hugged and talked for a bit, Johnnie and Tonya went to show his mom the ring he had bought for Tonya.

Sara was beside herself with great joy that it was finally official and these two were now going to get married. Tonya was so happy to share with Sara that not only were they going to finally be getting married, but also that Johnnie was going to be coming to Church now as well. Sara was so pleased with her son and now things were going to finally be going in the right direction.

The war was over and Wayne was dead. For the first time in Johnnie's life, there was no one left to fight.

ABOUT THE AUTHOR

Robert Thomas is an established Author who enjoys Art and various forms of entertainment. His background in leadership has helped to shape his writing to give his readers something they can actually live by. At age forty-four, he has released his second completed work.

You can follow Robert Thomas on Facebook under Robert Thomas Authors Page for all updates, new releases as well as encouraging post and helpful videos for new Authors. You can also follow him on twitter @camarothomas.

If you are a writer and need a little help getting started or even just finishing a project, there is help. Cynthia L. Hatcher is a Book Writing coach that can help you get your writing back on track. You can reach her at cynthia@cynthialhatcher.com.
Cynthia L. Hatcher, among other things, operates HATCHBACK Publishing if you're looking to get your book released.

www.ingramcontent.com/pod-product-compliance
Lightning Source LLC
Chambersburg PA
CBHW051034160426
43193CB00010B/942